The Gospel and the Zodiac

The Gospel and the Zodiac

The Secret Truth About Jesus

Bill Darlison

Duckworth Overlook
London · New York · Woodstock

First published in 2007 by
Duckworth Overlook

LONDON
90-93 Cowcross Street, London EC1M 6BF
Tel: 020 7490 7300
Fax: 020 7490 0080
info@duckworth-publishers.co.uk
www.ducknet.co.uk

NEW YORK
141 Wooster Street, New York, NY 10012

WOODSTOCK
One Overlook Drive, Woodstock, NY 12498
www.overlookpress.com
[for individual orders and bulk sales in the United States,
please contact our Woodstock office]

Scripture taken from the Holy Bible, NEW INTERNATIONAL VERSION®
© 1973, 1978, 1984 International Bible Society. All rights reserved
throughout the world. Used by permission of International Bible Society.
NEW INTERNATIONAL VERSION ® and NIV® are registered
trademarks of International Bible Society.
Use of either trademark for the offering of goods or services requires the prior
written consent of the International Bible Society.

Original Illustrations of the Zodiac symbols © 2007 by Dan Hodgkin
Original map (p.107) © 2007 by Stuart Morton

A catalogue record for this book is available
from the British Library

ISBN 978-0-7156-3691-6 (UK)
ISBN 978-1-59020-037-7 (US)

Printed and bound in Great Britain by
Cromwell Press Ltd, Trowbridge, Wiltshire

Contents

List of Illustrations

Acknowledgements

Numerous people over many years have helped me develop my ideas on the zodiacal structure of Mark's Gospel, but I am indebted especially to the following.

To Dan Hodgkin, whose splendid drawings of the constellation patterns have added immeasurably to the book's appeal and intelligibility.

To Paddy and Kate Symons, Michael Edwards, Eileen Harrington, Michael Barker-Caven, Rev. Cathal Courtney, Rev. Art Lester, and the late Michael Young, with all of whom, over cups of coffee, pints of Guinness, or glasses of wine, I have been encouraged to clarify and defend my theories. Marlena Thompson, who has been cajoling me for years to put these ideas into book form, deserves special mention.

To members of the Dublin Unitarian congregation who have listened to me express my maverick opinions over the past eleven years, with special thanks to Beta, (Rev.) Bridget, Chris, David, Dennis, Dorene, Patrick, Pamela, Kevin, Leila, Michael, Ruth, and Titania, on whom I tested the zodiacal theory in detail during the winter of 2006-7, and from whom came many useful suggestions about style and content.

To Nick Webb and Caroline McArthur of Duckworth who have made their own significant and valued contribution to the book's final shape.

To my wife, Morag, whose unfailing support, patience, and understanding have enabled me to see this project through to a conclusion.

Appearance in the above list in no way implies responsibility for the opinions expressed in this book, or even endorsement of them. Any solecisms, anachronisms, or weird flights of fancy found in these pages are entirely my responsibility.

Finally, I must stress that, although I am a minister in the Unitarian Church, I am not expressing specifically Unitarian opinions: this theory of the origin and structure of one of Christianity's primary documents will probably be as unsettling to Unitarians as it will certainly be to members of more orthodox churches.

Rev. Bill Darlison
Dublin, 13th July, 2007

For Morag
Uxor amicaque

Introduction

'God against man. Man against God. Man against nature. Nature against man. Nature against God. God against nature – very funny religion.' Such, according to Joseph Campbell, was the verdict of the Buddhist sage, Dr. D. T. Suzuki, on the religions of the West, Christianity in particular. The same point has been made more recently by the American comedian Emo Phillips, in what has been voted the best religious joke of all time.

Once I saw this guy on a bridge about to jump. I said, 'Don't do it!'
He said, 'Nobody loves me.'
I said, 'God loves you. Do you believe in God?'
'Yes.'
I said, 'Are you a Christian or a Jew?'
'A Christian.'
I said, 'Me too! Protestant or Catholic?'
'Protestant.'
I said, 'Me too! What franchise?'
'Baptist.'
I said, 'Me too! Northern Baptist or Southern Baptist?'
'Northern Baptist.'
I said, 'Me too! Northern Conservative Baptist or Northern Liberal Baptist?'
'Northern Conservative Baptist.'
I said, 'Me too! Northern Conservative Baptist Great Lakes Region, or Northern Conservative Baptist Eastern Region?'
'Northern Conservative Baptist Great Lakes Region.'
I said, 'Me too! Northern Conservative Baptist Great Lakes Region Council of 1879, or Northern Conservative Baptist Great Lakes Region Council of 1912?'
'Northern Conservative Baptist Great Lakes Region Council of 1912.'
I said, 'Die heretic!' and I pushed him over.

Emo's joke brilliantly captures the unfortunate irony which must strike everyone who casts even a cursory glance at the religious world: from the bloody Middle Eastern conflict between Muslim and Jew to the internecine squabbles which set one Christian group against another, religion, which is meant, etymologically at least, to bind us together, seems to be a perpetual source of division.

It would be a mistake to suggest that the origin of all this conflict is purely theological. There are sociological, historical, geographical, political, and even ethnic factors to consider, but there can be no doubt that theology plays its part by providing some intellectual weapons by means of which the battles can be conducted. Theology is about words, and words are notoriously slippery. Written documents which attempt to eliminate ambiguity – insurance policies, for example – are virtually unreadable, while narrative, which strives to engage the imagination, and which is perennially appealing, is never free from it.

Unfortunately for those who crave clarity, much of the religious literature of the world, upon which most theology is based, is presented in narrative form, and since there are no hard-and-fast rules for the interpretation of stories, disagreement goes with the territory. What is one to make of those Bible stories which contain accounts of talking snakes, the parting of sea water, the sun standing still, a talking ass, and countless other incidents which, in another context, would be considered fanciful in the extreme? The rational response would be to say that such stories must have a symbolic meaning – if they have any meaning at all – and try to investigate what the symbolism might be, but it would seem that some religious people tend to find narrative and metaphor very difficult to approach in this way. For some reason, history is deemed superior to myth, and the factual is preferred to the figurative, and as a result much of the intellectual activity of religious groups – particularly Christian groups – has been concerned with translating the oblique language of spiritual metaphor into the univocal languages of history and science. The results have been disastrous because, as Joseph Campbell says, when a religion 'gets stuck in its own metaphors, interpreting them as facts, then you are in trouble' (Campbell, 1988, page 67). Evidence of such 'trouble' is not difficult to find. Galileo found himself embroiled in it in the sixteenth century, when it was believed that Joshua's command to the sun to stand still was sufficient to refute the heliocentric theory; and since the middle of the nineteenth century, Darwin's theory of evolution has been attacked by those who hold a literal interpretation of the narratives in the early part of the Book of Genesis.

So troublesome have these religious metaphors been throughout the centuries, that many people of a more 'rationalist' disposition have suggested that it might be best to discard them altogether or, at the very least, to relegate them to the category of historical and literary curios where they can do little damage.

Jefferson's Bible

Thomas Jefferson, the third president of the United States, was of this opinion. Jefferson considered himself to be a rationalist, a child of the Enlightenment. He was a friend of the scientist and Unitarian minister, Joseph Priestley, who had taken his own brand of religious rationalism from Britain to America in the closing years of the eighteenth century, and Jefferson's intellectual heroes were the British empiricist philosophers John Locke and David Hume and the Frenchman Auguste Compte, who, in the wake of the French Revolution, had attempted to devise a 'religion of humanity', free from dogma, supernaturalism, miracle, prophecy, and revelation: a religion dedicated to reason and informed by reason.

Unlike many of his mentors, however, Jefferson claimed to be a Christian of sorts – at the time a strange claim to make in the light of his repudiation of all things supernatural. After all, wasn't the New Testament, the very foundation document of Christianity, just as full of troublesome narratives as the Old: the birth of Jesus from a virgin, for example, or the numerous miracles, or, most stupendous and incredible of all, the resurrection of Jesus from physical death? But for Jefferson and for those who thought like him, such things were not essential to Christianity, nor were they particularly useful metaphors; they were accretions which had accumulated, rather parasitically, around the elevated ethical system propounded by Jesus. They were the products of ignorance and superstition, and the task of scholars now, thought Jefferson, was to separate out the wheat from the chaff, to remove the fanciful from the factual, to strip away the 'mutilated, misstated and often unintelligible' bits of the Christian scriptures, the bits that had caused so much trouble, and so reveal 'the most sublime and benevolent code of morals which has ever been offered to man'.

And since no one else seemed keen to take on the task, Jefferson decided to do it himself, and in 1820, at the age of 77, he took his Bible and a pair of scissors and snipped out a scripture for himself. The task was easy, he said. The difference (between essential and non-essential, authentic and spurious) 'is obvious to the eye and the understanding ... and I will venture to affirm that he who, as I have done, will undertake to winnow this grain from this chaff, will find it not to require a moment's consideration. The parts fall asunder of themselves, as would those of an image of metal and clay' (Jefferson, page 30).

The result was 'The Jefferson Bible'. Its title should really be 'The Jefferson Gospel' because there is nothing in it from the Hebrew Scriptures, nor from the writings attributed to the followers of Jesus such as St Paul or St Peter.

3

Jefferson would most certainly have agreed with John Lennon who was to proclaim, 150 years later, that 'Jesus was okay but his disciples were a bunch of thick buggers.'

Consequently, Jefferson's Bible is extremely thin. In its recently published form it barely amounts to 110 small pages, probably less than half the length of the four Gospels as we have them. It contains some narratives, and all the great parables, but the bulk of it is devoted to the ethical teaching of the Gospels. It begins with the birth of Jesus, but there are no wise men, no star, no angels, no virgin; and the 'Gospel' ends with the words

> Now in the place where he was crucified, there was a garden; and in the garden a new sepulchre, wherein was never man yet laid. There laid they Jesus. And rolled a great stone to the door of the sepulchre, and departed.

So, there's no account of Jesus' resurrection; in fact, not a single miracle story appears in the whole volume.

The 'Cinderella' Gospel

Jefferson took most of his material from the Gospels of Matthew and Luke, both of which, in addition to the miracles of Jesus, contain lengthy sections devoted to Jesus' ethical teaching. Very little in Jefferson's volume is taken from the Gospel of Mark, principally no doubt because Mark is almost entirely composed of the kind of narratives which Jefferson found so troubling. In neglecting Mark, Jefferson was merely continuing a centuries-old tradition.

For example, St Augustine (354-430 CE) considered Mark to be the least valuable Gospel because, he said, it was merely an abbreviated version of Matthew and Luke. In addition, its somewhat rough-and-ready style, frenetic pace, episodic quality, colloquial language, and unsophisticated syntax contributed to the indifference with which it was viewed. There is also an air of disrespect for some of the story's main protagonists which would not have endeared it to the leaders of the early church.

Given these characteristics, it is possible that the early tradition associating the Gospel with the apostle Peter was the only reason it was accepted into the Christian canon of scripture. But this 'tradition', too, is based more on apologetics than on evidence, and it developed in order to lend apostolic authority to an account written by one who was not an apostle.

Although during the eighteenth century scholars began to question Augustine's assumption that Mark was an abbreviation of Matthew and Luke, and to suggest that it was the earliest Gospel, it has never really lost its reputation as the Cinderella Gospel. It may have the virtue of brevity, and the place it occupies within the whole gospel tradition may be of interest to scholars, but in public liturgy and private devotion it is still the least valued.

This is particularly so among religious liberals who, like Jefferson before them, are uneasy about the strange and fanciful nature of Mark's narrative. Indeed, contemporary liberals have gone much further than Jefferson, and have been in the forefront of all critical research into the historical conundrums presented by the Gospels, from Albert Schweitzer's *The Quest for the Historical Jesus* at the beginning of the twentieth century, up to and including the California-based 'Jesus Seminar' which, for two decades, has been attempting to sift what it considers to be the original, authentic words of Jesus from the 'myth' and 'fiction' that have grown around them. The general liberal assumption is the same as Jefferson's: the narrative portions of the Gospels are the least reliable historically and have little, if any, spiritual value since they are expressions of a primitive, 'magical', mythical world view which has lost any relevance it may once have had.

But Mark's Gospel is anything but primitive. Although in its present form it is probably incomplete, as we shall see, it is a highly sophisticated document. It is not a rudimentary biography of Jesus, nor is it a collection of historical reminiscences exaggerated by constant retelling. It is, in fact, a series of dramatic 'parables' designed to accompany the spiritual seeker on the journey towards enlightenment or self-transformation. It has its origin in an esoteric tradition which owes as much to the mystery schools of paganism as it does to Judaism. Most astonishing of all, it uses as its primary metaphor the yearly journey of the sun through the signs of the zodiac. *Mark's Gospel is a textbook of the spiritual journey written in an astrological code which, when unravelled, completely transforms our understanding of the Gospel's original nature and purpose.* What, to Jefferson, was 'chaff' is really the purest wheat. The 'mutilated, misstated and often unintelligible' passages of the Gospel story, which have been the cause of so much debate and division, and which ended up at the sharp end of Jefferson's scissors, are, as I shall show, its most original and imaginative elements. It's time to pick the discarded pieces off the floor, dust them down, and put them back in again.

Who is the Man with a Jar of Water?

The Vision of Christ that thou dost see
Is my Vision's Greatest Enemy:
Thine has a great hook nose like thine,
Mine has a snub nose like to mine:
Thine is the friend of All Mankind
Mine speaks in parables to the Blind:
Thine loves the same world that mine hates,
Thy Heaven doors are my Hell gates.
Socrates taught what Meletus
Loath'd as a Nation's bitterest Curse,
And Caiaphas was in his own Mind
A benefactor to Mankind:
Both read the Bible day and night
But thou read'st black where I read white.
(William Blake, *The Everlasting Gospel*)

Of all the controversies with which the Fathers of the early church entertained themselves, few seem as irrelevant to the contemporary mind as that
which concerned the duration of Jesus' ministry. For about eighteen centuries the common assumption throughout Christendom has been that,
between Jesus' baptism by John and his crucifixion by Pilate, three years
elapsed. This is based on a legitimate inference from the number of Passover
festivals mentioned in the Gospel of John, and it is difficult to see how anyone could, or would even want to, challenge it. And yet it was a dispute over
which a considerable amount of ink was expended towards the end of the
second Christian century. Irenaeus, orthodoxy's first systematic apologist
(writing about 185 CE), goes to great lengths to prove that Jesus exercised his
ministry over many years in order to counter the contention of various
Gnostic groups (principally the followers of Valentinus) that Jesus taught for
one year only and, further, that 'he suffered in the twelfth month' (Irenaeus,
page 200).

An idle piece of pedantic squabbling, we might be tempted to conclude.
But we would be wrong to conclude this. The controversy was not just over
any arbitrary twelve-month period. It concerned the solar year, which

begins at the spring equinox, and Valentinus' claim is absolutely startling: the career of Jesus is connected with the sun's annual journey through the heavens, and he implies that the various stages of it correspond with the signs of the zodiac.

For Valentinus and his followers, the Gospel story is not a rudimentary biography of a single individual, pieced together from reminiscences of eye-witnesses or those who had known eye-witnesses, but an allegory, in which the sun's cycle, from its 'birth' in Aries when spring begins, to its 'death' in Pisces twelve months later, symbolically reflects the spiritual cycle of the Gnostic initiate on his journey towards spiritual liberation or enlightenment. This is why Valentinus's claim that Jesus died in the twelfth month (March, the month of Pisces) was so crucial to his case, and why Irenaeus was at such pains to refute it.

There is no reason to suppose that this and other Gnostic 'heresies', which Irenaeus condemns so roundly and, at times, parodies so shamefully in his five-volume work, were new ideas which had parasitically attached them-selves to a history-based Christianity. Gnosticism was certainly not new in Irenaeus's time. Although it flourished in the second Christian century, its roots go back much further, some scholars tracing its ancestry back to the religion of ancient Iran, others favouring an origin in Judaism. Whatever its precise origins, it was never a unified religious movement but an approach to spiritual matters which transcended conventional boundaries. It was dualistic, and generally associated the world of matter and flesh with evil. The task of the aspirant was to attain spiritual freedom by overcoming bondage to the flesh. Despite the variety of ways in which it manifested, Gnosticism was concerned with the interior life of the spirit, with 'illumina-tion' which could be attained through prayer, meditation and the perform-ance of specific rituals. God was to be experienced within the depths of the individual, rather than demonstrated rationally or objectified historically. 'Gnosis', which comes from the Greek word for knowledge, is not primarily rational knowledge, but 'insight'. 'Gnosis involves an intuitive process of knowing oneself. And to know oneself ... is to know human nature and human destiny ... Yet to know oneself, at the deepest level, is simultaneous-ly, to know God' (Pagels, page xix).

Manuscripts which have surfaced relatively recently, particularly the Nag Hammadi documents, discovered in 1945, are demonstrating that the con-ventionally held view that Gnostic works are invariably later than the canon-ical Gospels and of inferior literary quality can no longer be sustained. What is emerging is a picture of early Christianity which is, in Elaine Pagels' words, 'far more diverse than orthodox sources choose to indicate' (Pagels, page xxxiii). Out of this diversity sprang a variety of writings which were attacked (by people like Irenaeus) and, eventually, suppressed by the emerging Catholic Church. In one of them, the Gospel of Thomas, the central figure is 'the living Jesus' who has a different relationship with his followers than does the traditional Jesus of Christendom. The latter is a uniquely divine figure whose sacrifice ensures the salvation of those who believe in him. The Jesus of Thomas's Gospel, however, 'comes as a guide who opens access to spiritual understanding. But when the disciple attains enlightenment, Jesus no longer serves as his spiritual master: the two have become equal – even identical' (Pagels, page xx).

Such thinking has always been anathema to orthodoxy. What is interesting about it, from the point of view of the present study, is its antiquity. If, as Professor Helmut Koester of Harvard maintains, the Gospel of Thomas contains some traditions which belong to the 'second half of the first century' (Pagels, page xvi), then such ideas were not later perversions of the orthodox, history-based scheme, so beloved of people like Irenaeus: they were contemporary with it. Perhaps they even preceded it.

Indeed, it is no longer unthinkable for us to invert the customary view of the relationship between 'historic' and 'esoteric' Christianities. It seems increasingly likely that the former was a perversion of the latter, that the attempt to establish historical credentials for the Jesus story came some time after the story itself originated in the fertile imagination of some esoteric group, whose poetic account of the spiritual journey was transformed into history by people who had either misunderstood the story, or who were motivated by more cynically pragmatic political or ecclesiastical considerations.

The gradual 'historicization' of imaginative religious stories is by no means restricted to Christianity. In *The Perennial Philosophy*, Aldous Huxley points out that the same process has occurred in Buddhism, in which 'the Mahayana expresses the universal, whereas the Hinayana cannot set itself free from historical fact' (Huxley, page 62). He goes on to quote the orientalist, Ananda K. Coomaraswary: 'The Mahayanist believer is warned – precisely as the worshipper of Krishna is warned in the Vaishnaivite scriptures that the Krishna Lila is not history, but a process for ever unfolded in the heart of man – that matters of historical fact are without religious significance.'

Huxley laments the fact that, despite the efforts of Christian mystics – Eckhart, Tauler, Ruysbrock, Boehme and the Quakers – who are themselves inheritors of the esoteric tradition, Christianity has never been 'liberated from its servitude to historical fact' and has 'remained a religion in which the pure Perennial Philosophy has been overlaid, now more, now less, by an idolatrous preoccupation with events and things in time – events and things regarded not merely as useful means, but as ends intrinsically sacred and indeed divine'.

The suggestion that the Gospel story is not history but 'a process for ever unfolded in the heart of man' no doubt seems pretty absurd to those of us who have been raised on a flesh and blood Jesus readily locatable in time and space. But, in fact, it is no more outrageous than the historical schema proposed to us by orthodoxy. Indeed, it is much less problematic, since it frees us from having to defend the historicity of incidents which are, to say the least, unlikely. Only familiarity with such incidents and, perhaps, a sentimental attachment to them, prevent us from declaring them fanciful. Virgins do not give birth; people do not walk on water; storms cannot be calmed with a word; a few loaves and a couple of fish cannot feed thousands of people; and people, once dead, do not come back to life again. Fundamentalist Christians, disregarding David Hume's assertion that we should doubt our senses before we doubt the consistency of nature's laws, cling desperately to the miraculous element within the Gospels, forlornly echoing Tertullian's cry: *credo quia absurdum*, 'I believe because it is absurd'. And even scholars of a more liberal hue, who readily question Jesus' birth from a virgin and are prepared to interpret the other miracles symbolically or as exaggerations of natural incidents, still insist on a literal resurrection as the absolute minimum required belief for a Christian. Those for whom the historical details are of little or no consequence, who view the Jesus stories in their entirety as dramatizations of internal processes, are no more welcome within orthodoxy than were their forebears who received the rough edge of Irenaeus's quill over eighteen centuries ago.

Gospel Discrepancies

To see the Jesus story as a collection of spiritual parables frees us from the mental gymnastics involved in trying to explain factual discrepancies within the Gospels, and strange anomalies within the New Testament as a whole. For example:

- Was Jesus born in the reign of Herod the Great, as Matthew has it, or when Quirinius, the governor of Syria, ordered a census, as Luke asserts? (Herod died in 4 BCE; Quirinius's census occurred in 6 CE, some ten years later).
- Did Jesus cleanse the Temple at the *beginning* of his ministry (John), or at the end (Matthew, Mark and Luke)?

- Did he heal *two* demon-possessed men in the country of the Gerasenes (Matthew), or just one (Mark)?
- Did the crucifixion occur on the day of the Passover (Matthew, Mark and Luke), or the day *before* the Passover (John)?
- Did the crucifixion begin at nine o'clock in the morning (Mark) or at mid-day (John)?
- Is it really possible that the normally prudent Romans would risk provoking a riot by executing a popular Jewish preacher at the time of the Passover when Jerusalem would be bursting with pilgrims from around the known world?
- Is it really possible that, during the busiest liturgical season of the year, the high priests would occupy themselves plotting the execution of Jesus?
- Why is it that the apostle Paul, with the single exception of his account of the Last Supper in 1 Corinthians 11, never refers to an incident in the life of Jesus even when it would have helped his case immeasurably to do so? For example, in his account of his dispute with Peter over Gentile Christians (Galatians 2 and 3), why does he not mention Jesus' cure of the centurion's servant (Matthew 8:5-13), or the instruction at the end of Matthew's Gospel to 'go and make disciples of all nations … teaching them to obey everything I have commanded you' (Matthew 28:19-20)? Did he not know of these traditions? Could it be that the Gospels come from a source of which Paul was entirely unaware?

The Historical Jesus

But the most valuable benefit to be gained from viewing the gospel stories as spiritual parables is that it frees us from the interminable and apparently fruitless search for the historical Jesus, which has exercised the ingenuity of scholars for at least two centuries. Albert Schweitzer's reluctant conclusion, that the historical Jesus is lost to us, must be upheld by all but the most ardent apologist for orthodoxy. The Gospels themselves furnish us with precious little biographical information, and questions concerning Jesus' physical appearance, his early life, his marital status, his personal predilections and his general character have been answered more by imaginative conjecture or doctrinal expediency than by legitimate inferences from the actual text. Even his age at the time of his crucifixion, which today seems securely fixed at 33, has been a matter of some dispute. Irenaeus concludes, quite reasonably, from the passage in John's Gospel where the Jews say to Jesus: 'You are not yet fifty years old and yet you claim to have seen Abraham' (John 8:57), that such language is only fittingly applied to someone who has

Who is the Man with a Jar of Water?

passed the age of forty. Further, he claims that, since Jesus came to save all people, he must have experienced every stage of life including old age. Irenaeus confidently asserts that he learned this from 'those who were conversant in Asia with John the disciple of the Lord, affirming that John conveyed to them that information' (Irenaeus, page 201). In our collective sentimental need for a relatively youthful Jesus we have conveniently dispensed with this item of tradition.

The extra-biblical evidence for the existence of Jesus, which has been so boldly trumpeted by generations of apologists, turns out to be pretty thin when examined closely and dispassionately. The Roman authors, Pliny and Suetonius, both writing early in the second century, tell us very little more than that people calling themselves Christians – 'followers of a depraved and excessive superstition', according to Pliny (Pliny, page 405) – were proving troublesome in certain parts of the Empire. Tacitus, who was governor of Asia around 112 CE, refers in his Annals (Book 15, chapter 44) to the 'notoriously depraved Christians ... whose originator, Christ, had been executed in Tiberius's reign by the procurator of Judea, Pontius Pilate', but such a statement, made nearly eighty years after the supposed event, demonstrates only that some people were making the claim; it certainly does not substantiate it.

Nor can we glean anything of substance from Jewish sources. Philo of Alexandria, who died around 50 CE, tells us nothing of Jesus in his voluminous writings, although he does explain that the name *Joshua* – which is the Hebrew version of the Greek name *Jesus* – means 'the salvation of the Lord', and that it is 'the name of the most excellent possible character' (Philo, page 351). Here is a possible reason why the central character in the Gospel story should be given such a name.*

The celebrated passage in the works of the Jewish historian Josephus, which claims that 'about this time lived Jesus, a wise man, if one might call him a man', and which goes on to tell of his miracles, his condemnation to the cross and his restoration to life on the third day (Josephus, page 576), has been identified as a much later Christian interpolation. Few, if any, scholars now accept this passage as genuine; its presence in the text is testimony to the fact that the historicizing tendency within early Christianity was so desperate to furnish evidence for a historical Jesus that it had to invent some.

It has long been a fundamental contention of orthodox apologetics that the growth of Christianity is only explicable if its historical claims are

---

* Another possible reason is that Jesus was also an extremely common name among Jews in the first Christian century. 'Four of the twelve high priests who held office in the first century were called Jesus' (France, page 49).

11

substantially true. After all, it is maintained, people are not prepared to die for a fiction. But this argument is based on the assumption that religious ideas are subjected to rational scrutiny before taking root in the hearts and minds of devotees, and this is plainly not the case, as the events at Jonestown and Waco demonstrate. Faith precedes justification. Indeed, we might say with the ancients, *fides quaerens intellectum*: faith seeks understanding, and attempts to furnish historical or rational evidence always follow the initial faith impetus. Mithraism – which is much older than Christianity – required no historical founder in order to flourish. It was, in fact, based on mythology and stellar symbolism, but this in no way impeded its growth or prevented it from vying with Christianity for supremacy in the early centuries of the Common Era. Christianity spread for a variety of sociological reasons, principal among these being its appeal to the lower strata of society, and it eventually triumphed because it was adopted as a political expedient by the Emperor Constantine. There is no need to invoke either divine intervention or historical credibility to account for its appeal or its endurance.

Mormonism furnishes a relatively contemporary example of the same phenomenon. Despite the extraordinarily implausible nature of its historical claims – angelic visitations, golden plates, ancient civilizations – it has, in less than two hundred years, become a world-wide religious movement with its own holy books, miracles, martyrs, and persecutions. It has also created its own philosophical, theological, scientific and historical rationale; and the whole system is ably defended by scholars of no mean ability. It is probably the fastest-growing (Christian) religion on earth, with over twelve million adherents currently, but its success owes more to its aggressive proselytizing, its simple certainties, and its comforting metaphysics than it does to the credibility of the supposedly miraculous events surrounding its inception. Successive attempts to discredit Joseph Smith's character and to demonstrate the fanciful, or even mendacious, nature of his story seem to have had little impact on the spread of Mormonism, even though information and evidence are much more accessible to contemporary investigators than ever they were in the early days of Christianity. For obvious reasons, orthodox Christian apologists are unable to accept the historical claims made by the Mormons, and are perfectly willing to explain the success of Mormonism – and other religious movements – in sociological, political, or cultural terms; however, they often seem reluctant to accept that the same factors adequately account for the growth of their own system.

It is certainly not my intention to try to prove that Jesus did not exist. I am perfectly prepared to accept that someone of that name was executed for blasphemy or for treason when Pontius Pilate was governor of Judea. It may even be possible that certain aspects of this man's life or career were incorporated into the Gospel narratives. However, insisting that the Gospels be read *primarily* as history has given us a distorted view of their original meaning and has led, in no small way, to their rejection by the contemporary world. Even liberal scholars, such as members of the California-based 'Jesus Seminar', have stripped the Gospels of much of their content in what I consider to be the mistaken belief that there is a bedrock of 'authentic' sayings and incidents, which has been overlaid by mythology, exaggeration, error, or pious fancy. Literalism asks us to accept or reject the Gospels in their entirety as divinely inspired, inerrant narratives; liberal scholarship, on the other hand, has so eroded their content that we don't even need to make the effort to reject them; the scholars have done our rejecting for us.

But, as Rudolf Steiner observed ninety years ago, a 'dialectical soul-constitution', i.e. a purely intellectual, 'left brain' approach, can make nothing of the Gospels, which, in the hands of the scholars, have become 'just a well-picked carcase' (Steiner, page 97).

The carcase has been picked even cleaner by the twentieth-century scholars, and they have done so by making a number of quite arbitrary assumptions, which have been accepted almost unquestioningly as axioms in university departments. For example, Steiner alludes to Schmiedel's principle by which we could accept as authentic the incident in Mark where Jesus is considered 'beside himself' by his family, but not the Transfiguration, where Jesus is shown to be the Son of God. (The first is probably authentic, so the reasoning goes, because it presents Jesus unfavourably, the other is probably spurious because it exalts him.) Similarly, scholars realizing that the Jesus story is a little strange to be considered as literal history, have adopted a new historical category – *geschichte* – which maintains that the Gospel stories are not just a record of what happened (although, to some extent, they are this), but they are also faith proclamations, kerygmatic stories intended to bring people to belief. In effect, what they are saying is (to adapt Mr Spock's famous dictum): 'It's history, Jim, but not as we know it.'

We also learn that, since the Synoptic* Gospels (Matthew, Mark and Luke) are, in the main, composed of apparently unconnected episodes, they must be compilations of remembered incidents, modified somewhat in the telling, collected by the individual evangelists, and strung together arbitrarily like beads on a chain.

---

* The word 'synoptic' means 'seen together', 'seen through the same eyes', and refers to the Gospels of Matthew, Mark and Luke which have a common outline of the events of Jesus' life, and tell many of the same stories, often with striking similarity in wording. They differ markedly from John in content, ordering, literary style and theological presuppositions.

Despite such academic concessions to liberalism, however, there are many who still claim that the Gospel texts show evidence of historical reminiscence. Paul Barnett argues that the Gospels provide numerous examples of details which could only have come from an eyewitness. For example, alone among the evangelists, Mark tells us that Jesus was 'asleep on a cushion' (Mark 4:38) before the storm arose on the sea, and that the Gerasene Demoniac was 'crying out and bruising himself with stones' (Mark 5:5). Barnett comments on these and similar passages:

> These words of Mark leap from the page. To my mind they can only have come from the memory of someone who was struck by the drama of the scene or its colour, or sound or strangeness. Behind these words are the recollections of someone who had been present. (Barnett, page 92)

Barnett goes on to claim that details of time, place, and people, argue factual authenticity. This can hardly be sustained. Details are the stock-in-trade of all authors. We do not claim that Homer's descriptive powers show that he was present at the events he writes about, nor that the legend of Robin Hood must be true because Sherwood Forest is mentioned. I agree with Barnett that an air of verisimilitude pervades this Gospel, but this has more to do with Mark's skill as a writer than with historical veracity; and, as we shall see, some of the details in the text have a surprising provenance.

Barnett's arguments really assume a kind of naivety on the part of Mark, suggesting that the unsophisticated nature of the document he produced must point to historical reminiscence rather than literary skill. But the 'unsophisticated' text is really an illusion. Mark's Gospel is, in fact, considerably more literary than we might initially suspect: just as with Mark Twain's *Huckleberry Finn*, we must not let the narrative style mask the artifice of the content.

Consider, for example, the account of the Stilling of the Storm (Mark 4:35-41). Barnett's claim that this contains eyewitness testimony can hardly be sustained when we realize that Mark's account is a reworking of a few verses from the Psalms. The reader is invited to compare Psalm 107: 23-30, with Mark 4:35-41.

It might be argued (and sometimes is, although not by Barnett) that what happened to the apostles on the Sea of Galilee was, in fact, a 'fulfilment' of this passage in Psalms, and that here, as elsewhere, the Psalms are as much prophecies as prayers. It is generally fruitless to argue against such a point of view, but we might remind the person who upholds it of the philosophical principle called Occam's Razor, which enjoins us to explore the natural

Psalm 107: 23-30	Mark 4:35-41
Others went out on the sea in ships; they were merchants on the mighty waters. They saw the works of the Lord, his wonderful deeds in the deep. For he spoke and stirred up a tempest that lifted high the waves. They mounted up to the heavens and went down to the depths; in their peril their courage melted away. They reeled and staggered like drunken men; they were at their wits' end. They cried out to the Lord in their trouble, and he brought them out of their distress. He stilled the storm to a whisper; the waves of the sea were hushed. They were glad when it grew calm, and he guided them to their desired haven.	That day when evening came, he said to his disciples, 'Let us go over to the other side.' Leaving the crowd behind, they took him along, just as he was, in the boat. There were also other boats with him. A furious squall came up, and the waves broke over the boat, so that it was nearly swamped. Jesus was in the stern, sleeping on a cushion. The disciples woke him and said to him, 'Teacher, don't you care if we drown?' He got up, rebuked the wind and said to the waves, 'Quiet! Be still!' Then the wind died down and it was completely calm. He said to his disciples, 'Why are you so afraid? Do you still have no faith?' They were terrified and asked each other, 'Who is this? Even the wind and the waves obey him!'

explanation of a phenomenon before we have recourse to a supernatural one: it is far more likely that Mark wove his story out of Psalm 107 than that God prompted the Psalmist to write down a prophecy of an event that was to occur some ten centuries later.

Exactly the same might be said of Mark's description of John the Baptist (Mark 1:6), which owes more to the scriptural portrayal of Elijah (2 Kings 1:8) than to supposed eyewitness testimony. However, the most striking example of this tendency to couch his story in Old Testament language and images can be found in Mark's account of the crucifixion. From 14:32 to the end of chapter 15 there are numerous echoes of the Psalms, particularly Psalms 22, 31, and 41. Do these Psalms contain prophecies of Jesus' death, or did Mark write about Jesus' death using expressions found in the Psalms?

Mark and Homer

In addition to the motifs drawn from the Hebrew scriptures, however, it seems likely that Mark also uses the Homeric epics, the *Odyssey* and the *Iliad*, as models for the construction of his narrative. This theory has recently been

15

proposed by Professor Dennis R. MacDonald, who demonstrates convincingly that incidents in Mark reflect similar incidents in Homer, in both vocabulary and content. For example, Mark's story of the Stilling of the Storm, in addition to its obvious dependence upon Psalm 107, bears comparison with Homer's story of Aeolus's bag of winds in the *Odyssey* (*Odyssey* 10:1-69), and the similarities are so dense and sequential that they could not be accidental. MacDonald comments:

> Many details in the story can be found in literary gales elsewhere, but some details are exceedingly rare. Of the hundreds of voyages in ancient literature, few involve a protagonist waking during a storm and rebuking culpable companions. Furthermore, the earliest evangelist provided distinctive flags to alert his readers to the presence of his model. Like Odysseus, who told stories to Aeolus while floating on an island, Jesus told stories floating on a boat. Only in this voyage among all the gospels does Jesus sail 'with other ships', a detail that points to Odysseus's twelve ships. Mark ends his tale with the disciples asking themselves who Jesus was, 'that even the winds and the sea obey him'. He is like Aeolus, the king of winds. (MacDonald, pages 61-2)

Similarly with Mark's account of the Passion and Death of Jesus. While acknowledging Mark's debt to the Hebrew scriptures, MacDonald says that these texts alone cannot account for the Passion narrative as we have it and proposes that Mark modelled several passages in his account – anointing at Bethany, following the water-carrier, Judas's betrayal, Jesus' agony in Gethsemane – after passages in the *Odyssey*, and that the Crucifixion is modelled on the death of Hector in *Iliad* 22. MacDonald points out that 'modelling' does not mean plagiarizing. Students of rhetoric in both Greece and Rome were taught to imitate classical authors – Homer in particular – since, in the words of Quintilian, 'it is expedient to follow whatever has been invented with success' (MacDonald, page 4). But the art was to *disguise* one's reliance on a model in order to avoid charges of pedantry or plagiarism.

> These disguises included altering the vocabulary, varying the order, length and structure of sentences, improving the content, and generating a series of formal transformations. Although students usually imitated a single work, the experienced author borrowed from many ... Such eclecticism also disguised reliance on the primary target of imitation. Skilled authors were bees that took the best nectar from many blossoms to produce textual honey. According to Seneca, such apian

authors should 'blend those several flavours into one delicious compound that, even though it betrays its origin, yet it nevertheless is clearly a different thing from that whence it came'. One achieves the height of imitation, however, when 'the true copy stamps its own form upon all the features which it has drawn from what we may call the original' so that 'it is impossible for it to be seen who is being imitated'. (MacDonald, pages 5-6)

Such imitations would often strive to be 'transvaluative', i.e. to put forward values which were different from and superior to those found in the original. This was called *zêlos* in Greek, *aemulatio* in Latin, and was an attempt 'to speak better' than the model, inviting the reader to 'judge the imitation superior, whether in literary expression, philosophical acuity, or religious power' (MacDonald, page 6). MacDonald reckons that although the author of Mark's Gospel has used the careers of Hector and Odysseus as models for Jesus, he has not simply stolen from the epics, he has *transvalued* them:

Like Hector, Jesus dies at the end of the book, his corpse is rescued from his executioner, and he is mourned by three women. But unlike Hector, Jesus is raised from the dead. (MacDonald, pages 3-4).

Similarly with the Calming of the Storm. Jesus and the apostles, like Odysseus and his crew, are beset by turbulent winds; Jesus, like Odysseus, is asleep; Jesus has his head on a cushion, Odysseus covers his head with a cloak. But *unlike* Odysseus, who has himself inadvertently let the winds out of the bag, Jesus shows no carelessness and is able to calm the windstorm with a mere word.

As we shall see in the chapter on Gemini, Mark not only echoes the Psalms and the *Odyssey* in his account of the Calming of the Storm, he also incorporates elements from zodiacal mythology, so proving himself to be truly apian!*

In the light of all this, Barnett's contention that Mark's Passion narrative may have come into existence through 'the collaborative effort of Peter and

* Equally pertinent to our contention that Mark's Gospel is structured on the zodiac, is the recently proposed theory that 'the *Iliad* was created to preserve ancient knowledge of the heavens and is not only a poem about the Siege of Troy, but also a comprehensive record of the ancients' knowledge of the skies. It is a memory aid of great sophistication, using unforgettable narrative to fix astronomical data in the mind. The poet-singers or bards who learned stories by heart and passed them down through the pre-Homeric centuries were not just entertainers but the conservators of an extensive astronomical culture.' (Wood, page 2)

17

Mark back in the middle thirties' (Barnett, page 97), (i.e. that Mark is recording the memories of Peter), is, quite frankly, preposterous. Even if we assume that the Old Testament references appear in order to lend authority and weight to the account, and that following the Greek models was a contemporary convention, we cannot escape the conclusion that we are dealing with a literary creation and not a series of reminiscences. Barnett's opinion is based more on apologetic concerns than on a dispassionate assessment of the text. There may be history in Mark, but, as Northrop Frye says, 'If anything historically true is in the Bible, it is there not because it is historically true but for different reasons. The reasons presumably have something to do with spiritual profundity or significance'. (Helms, page 126)

Such, in brief, are some of the unquestioned canons of contemporary Gospel scholarship, all of them – fundamentalist and liberal – springing from a desire to substantiate the common and apparently unassailable assertion that 'Christianity is essentially a historical religion'. Meanwhile, a bewildered and sceptical public looks on uncomprehendingly, and those who seek spiritual succour look increasingly towards the Eastern religions, whose stories have not been butchered and abused quite so severely.

Non-Literalist Approaches

But there are now, and there have always been, those Christians who do not share this obsession with history.* Valentinus and other Gnostics in the very earliest years of Christianity, while not entirely rejecting the historical Jesus, did not spend their time in teasing out the details of his life or in ironing out the inconsistencies in the record. Indeed, Origen, writing in third-century Alexandria – a centre of Gnostic thought – even claims that the writers of scripture have scattered glaring historical inaccuracies throughout their texts in order to discourage the reader from taking the narrative too literally. He writes:

---

* There are many contemporary religious and quasi-religious movements which can claim a Gnostic heritage. Christian Science, which does not identify 'the Christ' exclusively with Jesus, is in the Gnostic tradition, as are Quakerism and Unitarianism, which both stress interior 'illumination' and the primacy of conscience. More avowedly Gnostic are Theosophy, Steiner's Anthroposophy, Rosicrucianism and some branches of Freemasonry. Mormonism, which appears to have derived much of its theology from Freemasonry, has many Gnostic elements. The Liberal Catholic Church, which is an offshoot of Theosophy, and the Church of Antioch, are Christian churches which offer the sacraments of traditional Catholicism in the context of a nondogmatic, Gnostic theology.

(Sometimes) impossibilities are recorded for the sake of the more skil-
ful and inquisitive, in order that they may give themselves to the toil of
investigating what is written, and thus attain to a becoming conviction
of the manner in which a meaning worthy of God must be sought out
in such subjects ... He (the Holy Spirit) did the same thing both with
the evangelists and the apostles – as even these do not contain throughout a pure history of events, which are interwoven indeed according to
the letter, *but which did not actually occur.* (Origen, page 315)

The example Origen gives is from the very first chapter of the Book of
Genesis which tells us that God created light on the first day of creation, but
that the sun, moon and stars didn't appear until later in the week. A curious
anomaly, introduced deliberately, says Origen, so that we won't be tempted
to take it literally, so that we will be forced to seek a deeper meaning to the
text than the one which immediately suggests itself. Such 'deeper meanings'
are what certain groups of Gnostic Christians sought. Historical questions
concerning Jesus of Nazareth are largely irrelevant. What matters is the
'Christ principle', the spirit of illumination, God-consciousness, which Jesus
is portrayed as embodying, but which we can discover and embody ourselves. To such people, the original Gospel message is not seen as a procla-
mation of what God has accomplished once and for all in history through the
agency of his Son. Nor is it an unreasonable and irrational 'call to faith' in a
historically elusive Jesus. It is, rather, an allegory of the interior journey
which all who hope to achieve union with God must undertake.

St Paul himself, considered a champion of orthodoxy, was not averse to
interpreting the Hebrew scriptures allegorically. In 1 Corinthians 10 (verse
4), he says, anachronistically, that the 'rock' from which the Israelites drank
during their wilderness wanderings was Christ; and in Galatians 4 he refers
to the story of Sarah and Hagar (Genesis chapter 21) as a parable to be
understood figuratively. However, the most consistent and comprehensive
exponent of the allegorical approach to scripture was Paul's contemporary,
Philo of Alexandria (whom we mentioned above in relation to the name
'Joshua'). Philo's voluminous writings – 900 pages in double columns in a
recent edition – are devoted almost entirely to a verse by verse exposition of
the 'hidden meaning' of the biblical stories.

Here, for example, is Philo's interpretation of the 'six days of creation':

And he (the author of Genesis) says that the world was made in six
days, not because the Creator stood in need of a length of time (for it is
natural that God should do everything at once, not merely by uttering

a command, but by even thinking of it); but because the things created required arrangement; and number is akin to arrangement; and, of all numbers, six is, by the laws of nature, the most productive; for of all the numbers, from the unit upwards, it is the first perfect one, being made equal to its parts, and being made complete by them; the number three being half of it, and the number two a third of it, and the unit a sixth of it, and so to say, it is formed so as to be both male and female, and is made up of the power of both natures; for in existing things the odd number is the male, and the even number is the female; accordingly, of odd numbers the first is the number three, and of even numbers the first is two, and the two numbers multiplied together make six. It was fitting therefore, that the world, being the most perfect of created things, should be made according to the perfect number, namely six ... (Philo, page 4)

Allegorical interpretations of sacred writings are not the preserve of post-Enlightenment sceptics and infidels; they are older than Christianity itself, but they have been neglected and disparaged by generations of literalists for whom 'truth' is synonymous with 'history'.

The Zodiacal Structure of Mark

What evidence is there in the Gospel text for Valentinus' contention that Mark's Gospel uses the sun's annual journey in the heavens as a metaphor of the interior journey? There is one very conspicuous clue. Towards the end of the Gospel, Jesus instructs two of his disciples to go into the city, where they will be met by *a man carrying a jar of water* (Mark 14:13). Who is this man, and why the necessity for such a strange meeting? Commentators have made a variety of suggestions, of which this, by William Barclay, is typical:

His disciples wished to know where they would eat the Passover. Jesus sent them into Jerusalem with instructions to look for a man carrying an earthen pitcher of water. That was a pre-arranged signal. To carry a water-pot was a woman's duty. It was a thing that no man ever did. A man with a water-pot on his shoulder would stand out in any crowd as much as, say, a man on a wet day with a lady's umbrella. Jesus did not leave things until the last minute. Long ago he had arranged a last meeting place for himself and his disciples, and had arranged just how it was to be found. (Barclay, *Mark*, page 331)

But such an explanation is hardly adequate. Had Jesus met the man before and set the whole thing up in advance? Barclay thinks so, but the Gospel tells us nothing about such a meeting. And what would be the point of such a signal? Barclay himself admits that it cannot have been an attempt to do things covertly: meeting a man carrying a jar of water would have been like meeting someone dressed like a harlequin – hardly a way to go unnoticed.

To anyone familiar with zodiacal symbolism, however, the man carrying the waterjar is immediately recognizable as the symbol of the sign Aquarius. But why should he appear at this point in the narrative? And why should other Aquarian images appear close by, images of social upheaval which would be announced by signs in the 'clouds of heaven' (Mark 13:26)? More intriguing still, why are these Aquarian images followed by an array of Piscean ones – betrayal, suffering, sacrifice – as the Gospel draws to a close? If these two signs, the final two of the zodiac, are so clearly evident, is it not just possible that the others are present, too? Indeed they are present. Not with the obvious pictograms of the signs (although at least one other of these is present), but with imagery and themes drawn from zodiacal mythology and psychology. In fact, the Gospel can be divided with no trouble whatsoever into sections which bear the characteristics of each of the zodiacal signs. This only applies to Mark's Gospel. Although the other two synoptics (Matthew and Luke) contain much of the same material as Mark, the stories are ordered differently. Similarly with John: there is no zodiacal order.

The 'zodiacal' sections are shown in the table below:

Gospel Section	Main incidents	Zodiacal keywords
Aries 1:1–3:35	Baptism of Jesus Beginning of ministry Theme of newness Twelve apostles as 　New Israel Sense of urgency, daring defiance	Sign of spring equinox Initiation Action Impulsiveness Assertiveness Pioneering Associated with the head
Taurus 4:1-4:4	Parables of growth Agricultural imagery Parable of light	Production Wealth Profit Accumulation Materialism Light Associated with neck/throat
Gemini 4:35-6:29	Theme of duality Man with 'legion' Double miracle – the Woman	The Twins 'Two-ness' Short journeys

21

Gospel Section	Main incidents	Zodiacal keywords
	with the Flow of Blood, and the Cure of Jairus' daughter Theme of close family Apostles sent out in twos Herod's vacillation	Sibling relationships Indecision Communication
Cancer 6:30-8:26	Theme of nurture Attack on traditions Food and stomach concerns Attack on narrow and exclusive attitudes	Sign of summer solstice Nourishment Heritage Protection The tribe Clannishness Associated with stomach and breasts
Leo 8:27-9:29	Theme of identity Transfiguration Glory	Creative self-expression Aggrandisement Kingship 'The sign of divine splendour' Associated with the heart
Virgo 9:30-9:50	Teaching on humility Little children Warning against passivity	Service Simplicity Purity Modesty Pettiness
Libra 10:1–10:31	Teaching on Marriage Story of Rich Young Man	The sign of the autumn equinox Marriage contracts Partnerships Co-operation Grace Charm Balance The sign of 'mutual reciprocity'
Scorpio 10:32- 10:52	Teaching on power 'Secret Gospel', with death/ rebirth theme Jealousy	Regeneration Death Sexual release Hidden power Transformation Associated with the genitals
Sagittarius 11:1-11:26	Jesus as 'Centaur' Teaching on faith Cleansing Temple	Religious quest Foreigners Recklessness Philosophy Associated with hips/thighs
Capricorn 11:27-12:44	Teaching on Authority Encounters with authority figures	Responsibility Management Authority The father Coldness Pretence

Gospel Section	Main incidents	Zodiacal keywords
Aquarius 13:1-14:16	Apocalyptic transformation	The Water-Bearer
		Future hopes
	Progress	Cosmopolitan ideas
	The Man Carrying a Jar of Water	Anarchy
Pisces 14:17-16:18	Betrayal	Self-sacrifice
		Hidden things
	Suffering	Dreams
	Sacrifice	Suffering
	Death	Compassion
	Resurrection	Secret enemies
		Self-undoing
		Deception

Fig. 1 Zodiacal 'sections' in Mark's Gospel

Zodiacal Divisions of Mark's Gospel

This is remarkable enough. Even more remarkable is the fact that Mark also incorporates themes from the 'decans', i.e. the constellations surrounding the zodiacal constellations (see Appendix 2 for a list of the decans). Over half of these 36 constellations are alluded to in Mark's text. In addition, we will regularly notice that, while Mark's *structure* is zodiacal, parallel stories in the other two synoptic Gospels sometimes show their zodiacal signature more evidently than Mark. This seems to imply that all three evangelists had access to an earlier, clearly zodiacal document, and that while Mark has preserved the original sequence, Matthew and Luke sometimes reflect the astrological details better than Mark.

It may be objected that the above sections are of differing lengths – from three chapters in the case of Aries, to a few verses in the case of Virgo and Scorpio. There are a number of possible reasons for this, the most plausible being that the Gospel we now possess is a truncated version of the original. The 'Secret Gospel' of Mark would lend support to this theory.

The 'Secret' Gospel of Mark

Support for the theory that Mark is in some way connected with esoteric thought and that he employs a zodiacal structure is provided by the letter of Clement of Alexandria (second century AD) to Theodore. In this letter, discovered by Professor Morton Smith in 1958 at the Monastery of Mar Saba, Clement castigates the 'unspeakable teachings of the Carpocratians' (Barnstone, page 341) who, apparently, had been saying things about Mark's Gospel which Clement considered to be undermining to orthodoxy. He writes:

Now of the things they keep saying about the divinely inspired Gospel according to Mark, some are altogether falsifications, and others, even if they do contain some true elements nevertheless are not reported truly. (Barnstone, page 341)

Clement goes on to explain that Mark, in addition to writing 'an account of the Lord's doings' for catechumens (i.e. beginners, those under instruction), also produced a 'more spiritual Gospel', and, what is more, that he knew of other teachings and traditions which he did not write down but which would 'lead initiates into the innermost sanctuary of the truth'.

Clement then gives 'word for word' the text of the 'secret' passage and its location in the canonical Gospel. It is worth quoting in full:

And they came into Bethany. And a certain woman whose brother had died was there. And, coming, she prostrated herself before Jesus and said to him, 'Son of David, have mercy on me.' But the disciples rebuked her. And Jesus, being angered, went off with her into the garden where the tomb was, and straightway a great cry was heard from the tomb. And going near Jesus rolled away the stone from the door of the tomb. And straightway, going in where the youth was, he stretched forth his hand and raised him, seizing his hand. But the youth, looking upon him, loved him and began to beseech him that he might be with him. (Barnstone, page 342)

Death and regeneration are, in astrology, Scorpionic themes and, interestingly, Clement tells us that this passage is located *at the very beginning of what we have designated the 'Scorpio section' of this Gospel*. Clement writes, 'After these words follows the text, "And James and John come to him"', i.e. after chapter 10 verse 34.

This fragment seems to support the theory that Mark's Gospel has undergone a number of revisions and that, in Barnstone's words, 'the canonical Gospel of Mark appears to be an abridgement of the Secret Gospel of Mark' (Barnstone, page 340). The fact that our present version of Mark does not have a satisfactory ending would also tend to support this view. Did the 'secret Gospel' end in a way that orthodox clerics found objectionable? If the Secret Gospel of Mark was, as its name implies, an esoteric work, then a zodiacal structure which is still preserved in the canonical version is not unthinkable. What seems to me increasingly likely is that all the canonical Gospels owe their origin to an arcane or esoteric source whose original purpose was to provide spiritual guidance for the coming 'new age', the Age of

Pisces (see next chapter). This original purpose became obscured by the historicizing wing of the Christian church, but its presence can still be detected. Matthew and Luke reflect it in their infancy narratives, and Mark preserves it in the very structure of his Gospel.

Carrington's Calendrical Theory of Mark

> *The Spirit of the Lord is on me,*
> *because he has anointed me ...*
> *to proclaim the year of the Lord's favour.*
> *(Luke 4: 18-19)*

The structure of Mark's Gospel has been a point of contention since the earliest days of Christianity. Papias, who was Bishop of Hierapolis in South Phrygia during the first thirty years of the second century, alludes to it in his work *The Exposition of the Oracles of the Lord*, which is no longer extant, but parts of which are preserved in Eusebius's *Ecclesiastical History*, written during the fourth century. Claiming one 'John the elder' as his source, Papias informs us that:

> Mark who was (or, who became) Peter's interpreter wrote down accurately *though not in order* (or, without orderliness) all that he remembered of what Christ had said or done. He did not hear the Lord, nor was he a follower of his; but at a later date, as I have said, he followed Peter, who adapted his teaching to meet the needs of his hearers, but not as if he was giving a systematic compilation of the Lord's oracles. Mark therefore made no mistake, but he wrote down some things as he remembered them, for he had one purpose in mind, not to omit anything he had heard, and not to falsify anything in it. (Barclay, 1966, page 120; emphasis added.)

Papias' denial of orderliness in Mark's Gospel continues to puzzle commentators, particularly orthodox ones, who tend to find Mark's chronological order reasonably acceptable. Could it be that Papias is denying a *zodiacal* order in Mark which certain Gnostic groups may have been claiming it to possess?

From the point of view of the present study, however, the most significant theory about the structure of Mark was put forward in 1952 by Philip Carrington, the Anglican Archbishop of Quebec, in his book *The Primitive Christian Calendar: A Study in the Making of the Marcan Gospel*. Carrington claimed that Mark's Gospel is structured around the Jewish yearly cycle, and that the individual units of the narrative have been arranged to reflect the principal festivals of the liturgical year. Carrington suggests that the starting point was the Jewish New Year in the autumn, but despite this he puts forward an enormous amount of evidence which would link Mark with the *solar* cycle beginning in March. He tells us that although the Jewish New Year began in September, the months were counted from March. Nisan 1 was the first new moon after the equinox. He also points out that the *Diatessaron*, a digest of the four Gospels into one volume compiled by Tatian about 160 C.E, was not merely a lectionary but a calendar, too: 'Its beginning falls in the spring equinox, which agrees with the date of 25 March which seems to have become fairly settled in Rome ... as a sort of ecclesiastical New Year' (Carrington, page 29). The *Clementine Homilies*, too, which were composed no later than the 170s CE, state that *Jesus' ministry began in the spring and lasted for a full year.*

More pertinent still is the association of the Gospel of Mark with Alexandria, hotbed of Gnosticism. Carrington reminds us of Eusebius's contention that Mark was the founder of Alexandrian Christianity, whose principal heresies were 'Adoptionism' – the theory that Christ descended into the man, Jesus, at his baptism; and the 'docetic' heresy that the Christ did not die on the cross but someone else, probably Simon of Cyrene, died in his place. Such ideas would only find support in a gospel like Mark's, which lacks Birth and Resurrection narratives.

The Alexandrian, Valentinus, preached such doctrines. As we noted above, he taught that Jesus' ministry lasted for twelve months and that these twelve months *correspond to the twelve signs of the zodiac* (Carrington, page 52). This year-long ministry was attacked by Irenaeus in a kind of argument, which, says Carrington, indicates that the controversy was not a new one.

Who wrote Mark's Gospel?

In much Christian preaching and in many elementary expositions of the Gospels, the author of Mark's Gospel is assumed to be John-Mark, the son of Mary (Acts 12:12) and the cousin of Barnabas (Colossians 4:10). This is the Mark who accompanied Paul and Barnabas on their first missionary journey (Acts 12:25), but who turned back and was subsequently held in disfavour by Paul (Acts 15:36-39). A certain 'Mark' is mentioned by the author of the Second Letter of Timothy (2 Tim. 4:11), and the author of I Peter refers to 'Mark, my son' (1 Pet. 5:13); these latter may be references to John-Mark, but we have no way of knowing for sure. Such uncertainty has not deterred some Christian writers from working these isolated texts into a composite picture of a young man who was close enough to those who knew Jesus to write a brief but honest and reliable account of Jesus' life and ministry. And one still reads and hears that the author of this Gospel was the young man in the linen cloth who ran away as Jesus was being crucified (Mark 14:51).

However, such an attempt to identify the author of Mark's Gospel, and to locate him so precisely in time and space, owes more to fanciful apologetics than to evidence. The plain fact is that we have no idea who the author might be. Whatever Christian piety might assume, all four gospel authors are anonymous, an uncomfortable admission which even the most die-hard conservative Christian will have to make when pressed.

Mark is usually associated with the apostle Peter, and popular piety has Mark and Peter together in Rome just before Peter's martyrdom. But, as we saw above, there is another tradition associating 'Mark' with Alexandria, and this is a far more likely place for the Gospel's composition.

Living in Alexandria around the time of Jesus were the Therapeutae, and Philo's glowing description of this group of Jewish monks and nuns should remind us that the Judaism out of which Christianity sprang was extremely diverse and certainly not composed entirely of those who held to exoteric interpretations of the scriptures. According to Philo, they read biblical stories as allegories 'since they look upon their literal expressions as symbols of some secret meaning of nature, intended to be conveyed in those figurative expressions'. They had in their possession the writings of 'ancient men … who have left behind them many memorials of the allegorical system of writing and explanation, whom they take as a kind of model, and imitate the general fashion of their sect; so that they do not occupy themselves solely in contemplation, but they likewise compose psalms and hymns to God in every kind of metre and melody imaginable.' They pray each morning 'when the sun is rising, entreating God that the happiness of the coming day may be real happiness, so that their minds may be filled with heavenly light' (Philo, page 700).

For such people, an account of the spiritual journey based on the solar cycle would not be unthinkable and, in my view, Mark's Gospel – or the document from which the Gospel was derived – is more likely to have been composed as a text for use in this or some similar esoteric school than to have been compiled as a fragmentary history or as a 'call to faith'.

The Forgotten Language of the Stars

The heavens themselves, the planets, and this centre
Observe degree, priority and place,
Insisture, course, proportion, season, form,
Office, and custom, in all line of order;
...But when the planets
In evil mixture to disorder wander,
What plagues and what portents, what mutiny,
What raging of the seas, shaking of the earth,
Commotion in the winds! Frights, changes, horrors
Divert and crack, rend and deracinate
The unity and married calm of states
Quite from their fixture ...
Take but degree away, untune that string,
And hark, what discord follows.
       (Shakespeare, *Troilus and Cressida*, Act 1, Sc. 3)

In Charles Dickens' final, uncompleted work, *The Mystery of Edwin Drood*, the lawyer, Mr Grewgious, gazes meditatively at the stars 'as if he would have read in them something that was hidden from him'. Many of us would do the same, continues Dickens, 'but none of us so much as know our letters in the stars yet – or seem likely to, in this state of existence – and few languages can be read until their alphabets are mastered'.

Dickens seems to imply that our understanding of the stellar language lies some way in the future, that the astronomical Rosetta Stone awaits the discovery of secular science; or, perhaps, that such understanding belongs to a higher realm of existence altogether and will always elude us in our mortal state.

Dickens' fanciful notion no doubt seems even more quaint to us than it did to his first readers. The idea that the stars might be trying to communicate with us in an unknown tongue belongs in the realm, not just of fantasy, but of absurdity, we think. We know all about the incomprehensible stellar distances; we know that even those stars which look close together are really billions of miles apart; we know that those tiny points of light, whose flickering seems to invite us into dialogue, are really unimaginably large balls of mute, incandescent gas, which are daily yielding their secrets, not to linguists, but to astronomers and physicists. Sean O'Casey's question 'What is the stars?' can only receive a prosaic answer from us, Mr Gradgrind's fact-obsessed children, who live amid glaring street lights, under polluted skies, with a thousand distractions to keep our eyes firmly pointed downwards, and a culturally fostered suspicion of anything which cannot be weighed, measured, probed, or dissected.

It has not always been so. In former ages, when people had time but no television, when the poetic imagination soared nightly beneath the star-strewn heavens, our ancestors devised an intricate and beautiful stellar language: *astrology*, a mixture of primitive science, sophisticated mythology, rudimentary psychology, and fatalistic prophecy, which was the *lingua franca* of the ancient world. The language of the stars does not, as Dickens fancied, belong to the future; one dialect of it, at least, has existed for thousands of years and has had considerable influence on many aspects of our culture. The word 'influence' itself derives from an astrological world view, as do *disaster, lunatic, venereal, mercurial, saturnine, jovial.* Astrology has exercised the minds of some of the human race's most celebrated philosophers, artists, and scientists,* and although, latterly, it has become associated with fatuous newspaper horoscope columns, a small but dedicated band of contemporary authors and researchers struggles to re-establish its intellectual credibility. However, for the most part, the scholarly world has chosen to forget about it.

Such forgetfulness may not be too detrimental to our contemporary scientific endeavours, but it can only give us a distorted view of the cultural products of the past. The celebrated historian of religion, Franz Cumont, for whom astrology was 'nothing but the most monstrous of all the chimeras begotten of superstition', admitted that it was 'indissolubly linked not only with astronomy and meteorology, but also with medicine, botany, ethnography, and physics. If we go back to the earliest stages of every kind of learning, as far as the Alexandrine and even the Babylonian period, we shall find almost everywhere the disturbing influence of these astral mathematics'. He goes on to tell us that 'this hallucination, the most persistent which has ever haunted the human brain', left its mark on the religious life of past generations, dominating the religion of Babylon, informing the highest phases of

* See the impressive list in *Teach Yourself Astrology* (Mayo, 1964, page 11). It includes Pythagoras, Plato, Aristotle, Dante, Goethe, Kepler, Newton, Copernicus, and Galileo. The works of Chaucer and Shakespeare are full of astrological references (over 200 in Shakespeare). In more recent times, the novelist Henry Miller, and the poets Louis MacNeice and Ted Hughes, were students of astrology. Jung wrote extensively on astrology and often used the horoscope as a diagnostic tool in his clinical work.

Fig. 2 Detail of the rose window at Lausanne Cathedral, Switzerland (c.1230), depicting the Imago Mundi (Image of the World)

ancient paganism, and 'by changing the character of ancient idolatry, it was to prepare in many respects for the coming of Christianity' (Cumont, page xvii and page xxiv).

Given the widespread influence of astrology on virtually every aspect of life in the ancient world, it is strange that most orthodox Jewish and Christian commentators, failing to find any examples of a narrowly defined system of stellar divination in its pages, seem to assume that the Bible is uniquely free of astrology's influence. This leads to the curious irony of Christian fundamentalists sporting the Piscean fish logo on their lapels and on their cars, while loudly proclaiming that astrology is a tool of Satan. Some are even surprised to learn that the dates of Christendom's principal festivals, Christmas and Easter, are determined by reference to astronomical cycles: Christmas is celebrated at the time of the winter solstice, when the sun enters Capricorn; and Easter Sunday is the first Sunday after the first full moon following the spring equinox, i.e. when the sun is in Aries. The major Jewish festivals are also based on solar and lunar cycles.

These are relatively well known, but other features of Christian – particularly

Catholic – liturgical and devotional practice have an astrological origin, of which few, if any theologians seem to be aware. For example, eating fish on Fridays did not originally mean refraining from meat in memory of the crucifixion of Jesus (as many Catholics assume). It was a deliberate act of communing with Christ; Friday was chosen for this because it was the day of Venus, the planet said by the ancients to be 'exalted' in Pisces, the sign of the Fish. The Feast of the Transfiguration of Jesus, when his face 'shone like the sun' (Matthew 17:2) is celebrated on 6 August, when the sun is in Leo, 'the sign of divine splendour', the sign which, according to the ancient astrologers, was 'ruled' by the sun. The months of May and October, set aside by Catholics as times to give special honour to the Virgin Mary, were not chosen arbitrarily: May is the month of Taurus, October the month of Libra, both signs being associated with the planet Venus, 'The Morning Star' (one of Mary's titles in the litany of the Blessed Virgin). The great feast days in honour of Mary, her 'birthday' on 8 September, and her 'Assumption into Heaven' in August, both owe their origin to astrology, as we shall see in the chapter on Virgo. November, for Catholics the month of the 'holy souls' in Purgatory, is the Scorpio month, chosen because Scorpio is associated with purgation, expiation and regeneration.

The Jewish historian Flavius Josephus, (c.37-100 CE) tells us that certain parts of the Temple in Jerusalem were decorated with celestial and zodiacal imagery. The veil separating the inner and outer courts was decorated with symbols of the zodiac signs, the seven lamps before the altar of incense signified the seven planets, and the twelve loaves that were upon the table signified the circle of the zodiac and the year (Josephus, page 107). So, before the destruction of the Temple in 70 CE, astrological symbolism could be found at the very heart of Jewish worship. And the Jewish greeting *mazzal tov*, which means '(may you have) fortunate constellations', demonstrates that contemporary Judaism still has some residual connection with constellational astrology.

The Bible itself came into being at a time when astral mythology was in constant vogue, and was written for the most part after the Jewish people had spent fifty years of exile (586–536 BCE) in astrologically oriented Babylon. Since it was produced in such a context it would be remarkable if the Bible did *not* show signs of astrological influence.

There are many who would hold that, while this is true, the Bible only mentions astrology in order to condemn it, and that there is condemnation of *divination*, astrological or otherwise, cannot be denied. The Book of Leviticus, for example, commands the death penalty for all who have 'familiar spirits', or who are wizards (Leviticus 20:27), and the prophet Jeremiah

31

cautions his readers not to be 'dismayed at the signs of heaven' (Jeremiah 10:2). A thoroughly comprehensive condemnation of astrology can be found in Isaiah:

> All the counsel you have received has only worn you out! Let your astrologers come forward, those stargazers who make predictions month by month, let them save you from what is coming upon you ... (Isaiah 47:13)

The prophetic tradition in general is opposed to any doctrine or divinatory technique that would undermine belief in the absolute power of God. For Isaiah or for Jeremiah there can be no intermediate powers exercising control in God's universe; and there can be no cosmic factors upon which human beings can heap the blame for their own shortcomings. The moral relation between man and God demands human accountability and this can only be intelligible if people have free will.

But the Bible does not exclusively reflect this prophetic tradition. Elsewhere in its pages we can find traces of astrological thinking which indicate that antipathy towards stellar 'influence' was not universal in ancient Israel. The most celebrated passage of this type occurs in the Book of Judges, where we learn that 'From the heavens the stars fought, from their courses they fought against Sisera' (Judges 5:20). This is the only occasion that the stars are credited with autonomous power, and the statement might owe as much to poetic licence as to a genuine belief in direct stellar influence. However, Rabbi Joel C. Dobin has done extensive work on the language of stellar reference in the Bible, and he concludes that there is a significant 'paranatural' usage of a word like 'heavens' which implies that 'these Heavens or their minions are called on to exhibit intelligence or awareness not in consonance with their natural place in the physical universe' (Dobin, page 92). What he means by this is that in a text such as '"Be appalled at this, O heavens, and shudder with great horror" declares the Lord' (Jeremiah 2:12), there is a real implication that the heavenly bodies possess (figuratively, of course), some measure of consciousness which transcends their objective status as lumps of rock moving around the sky. The Hebrew root *MSL* 'rule', which is often used in connection with the sun, moon, and stars ('The sun to govern the day ... the moon and stars to govern the night ... ', Psalm 136:8-9) has, says Dobin, an ethical dimension 'which implies conscious and intelligent control of both self and subjects as well as leadership by example ... (which is) precisely the type of rulership ascribed by astrology to these heavenly bodies' (Dobin, page 89).

There are passages in the Bible which certainly lead us to infer that the stars are meant to signal God's will. In the first creation story, for example, we read that on the fourth creative day God made the sun, moon, and stars 'for signs and for seasons' (Genesis 1:14). The word translated as 'signs' is the Hebrew *'owth*, which means 'something that points to something else'* and, in this context, it certainly has an astrological dimension. This statement perceives the celestial bodies as instruments of divine providence, as messengers from God to man. The star which the magi follow in order to find Jesus (Matthew 2:2) is a clear example of this concept.

A similar idea can be found in the first verse of Psalm 19: 'The heavens declare the glory of God; and the skies proclaim the work of his hands.' There is no implication, here or elsewhere, that the planets and stars are to be worshipped, but there is a definite suggestion that, in some sense, they are a sacrament of God's presence. And when the psalm goes on to tell us that there is nowhere in the earth where their voice is not heard (verse 4), we can legitimately assume that behind such expressions lay a belief in the planets and stars as universal images of divine transcendence. The rest of the psalm leaves us in no doubt that the order in the heavens reflects the moral order of the universe, and that a God who creates such harmony must demand a life of harmony from human beings.

The Zodiac in the Bible

Despite its unfortunate contemporary association with bead curtains, crystal balls and newspaper fortune-telling, there is nothing inherently magical about the zodiac. It is defined as a belt of the sky extending eight or nine degrees on either side of the ecliptic, the circle that the sun appears to trace in its yearly journey around the earth. The constellations of the zodiac are the groups of stars which provide a backdrop to this journey.

So, when we say that the sun is 'in' the constellation Aries, for example, we mean that the stars of the constellation Aries are in the background at this particular stage of the sun's annual cycle.

The Hebrews called the zodiac *mazzaroth*, a word which means 'separated', 'divided'; the singular *mazzal* denoting an individual constellation. Chapter 9 of the Book of Job mentions 'The Bear, Orion, the Pleiades, and the constellations of the south' (verse 9). The Bear, *Arish* in Hebrew, refers to the

---

* *'owth*: sign, mark, token, badge, standard, monument, memorial, warning, omen, prodigy, symbol, miracle, miraculous sign, proof. There are approximately 80 occurrences of 'owth in the O.T. Most of them have the flavour of the miraculous: "owth is an indicator or signal of something ...' *The Hebrew-Greek Study Bible* (1986), ed. Zodhiates, A.M.G. Publishers, Chattanooga, page 1577.

constellation Ursa Major; Orion is a very conspicuous non-zodiacal constellation, and the Pleiades is a beautiful group of stars in the constellation Taurus. Later in Job we read:

> Can you bind the beautiful Pleiades? Can you loose the cords of Orion? Can you bring forth the constellations (*mazzaroth*) in their seasons or lead out the Bear with its cubs? Do you know the laws of the heavens? Can you set up God's dominion over the earth? (Job 38: 31-33)

Even though the expression 'laws of the heavens' (Job 38:33) does seem to reflect a 'paranatural' use of the word 'heaven' of the type described by Dobin, we cannot assume from this passage an endorsement of astrology by the author of the Book of Job. However, we can deduce from passages like this that nowhere in the Bible is there any *censure* of the zodiac itself. Seiss writes:

> The wonder is that the Jewish prophets never once assail it [the zodiac] or speak one word against it, even when burdened with messages of the wrath and punishment of God upon heathenism and idolatry. Had this system been nothing but an outgrowth of the wild imaginations of man incorporated as it was with false religions then dominating all over the world, it is next to impossible to explain why it was not pre-minently singled out for prophetic malediction (page 178).

That the Hebrews regarded the zodiac as originating with God himself is implied in Job 26:13:

> By his breath the skies became fair;
> his hand pierced the gliding serpent.

'Became fair' is from the Hebrew *shiphrah*, which means 'beautify', and the 'gliding serpent' is either a reference to the zodiac itself, which is often depicted as a snake with its tail in its mouth, or to the constellation Hydra, The Fleeing Serpent. This verse is an example of 'parallelism', a feature of Hebrew poetic style in which the second part of a verse repeats in modified form the sense of the first part. The implication, then, is that the spirit ('breath') of God has made the heavens beautiful by shaping the constellations themselves; that God and not the disordered human imagination is the author of the zodiac. This sentiment is repeated in Psalm 147, where we read that God 'determines the number of the stars and calls them each by name' (verse 4).

The author of the apocryphal book of Enoch (composed probably in the second century BCE) is even more convinced of the divine origin of the zodiac:

> When I beheld them (the twelve constellations) I blessed; every time in which they appeared, I blessed the Lord of glory, who had made those great and splendid signs, that they might display the magnificence of his works to angels and to the souls of men; and that these might glorify all his works and operations; might see the effect of his power; might glorify the great labour of his hands; and bless him for ever. (Enoch 35:3; See Prophet, page 135)

Archaeologists have uncovered zodiacs in the floors of ancient synagogues which clearly show the traditional astrological pictograms. The central figure in the zodiac found in the Beth Alpha synagogue is of the sun in his chariot making his journey around the circle of the stars.

The annual journey of the sun through the zodiac is a natural symbol for all journeys and, in particular, for the life-journey of the human being. The word 'zodiac' comes from the primitive root *zoad*, 'a walk, way, or going by steps' (Seiss, page 17),* and is related to the Greek word *hodos*, 'road', and the Sanskrit *sodi*, 'path'. It is worth remembering in this context that the early Christians were said to be followers of The Way (Acts 24:14). The solar myth of the hero who goes out to meet a series of ordeals (usually twelve) before returning in triumph is patterned on the sun's annual cycle. Gilgamesh is such a solar hero, as are Hercules and Theseus. Related ideas are found in the Arthurian legends, in which the king sits in the centre of a round table surrounded by twelve knights.

Such solar heroes usually have an unusual birth. Hercules, for example, although held to be the son of Amphitryon, was really the son of Zeus who, in time-honoured custom, had visited Amphitryon's wife, Alcmena, while her husband was away at the wars. Perseus was also sired by Zeus, who came to Perseus's mother Danae in the form of a golden shower. The Bible has its own solar myth in the story of Samson (Judges 13-16). Like the Greek heroes, and like Isaac (Genesis 21:1) and Samuel (1 Samuel lff.), Samson's entry into the world is the result of divine intervention. His mother is barren, but is informed of the impending conception of a son by an angelic visitor (Judges 1:2-25).

Samson's name in Hebrew is Shimshon, from the root *Shemesh*, sun. His

---

* Some astrologers consider that 'zodiac' means 'circle of living things' or 'circle of animals' from the Greek root *zoê*, life. But, Libra (the Scales) is not a living thing, and Gemini (the Twins), Virgo (the Maiden) and Aquarius (the Water-Bearer) are not, strictly speaking, animals. Nor are fish (Pisces) animals. And how do we categorize the Centaur (Sagittarius)?

name means 'Sun-one' or, as Dobin has it, 'Belonging-to-the-sun' (Dobin, page 115). Today we would probably call him 'Sonny'. His concubine is the Philistine, Delilah, whose name comes from *deliy*, 'water-bucket', the same word as is used in Hebrew for the constellation Aquarius. In astrology the sun is said to 'rule' Leo, the sign of the midsummer when the sun's rays are at their fiercest. Samson's first feat of strength is the killing of the lion (Leo) in the vineyards of Timnath. In Aquarius, a winter constellation, the sun, its power at its weakest, is said to be in its 'detriment'. Delilah (Aquarius) clips Samson's mane (the sun's rays) and so brings about his downfall. He dies in the temple of the fish god, Dagon, between two pillars, echoing the sun's death in Pisces, the sign of the (two) Fish, and prefiguring the Piscean death of Jesus between two thieves.

Cosmic Harmony

In addition to being a natural symbol of the spiritual journey, the zodiac also provided the ancient poets with a symbol of regularity, order and harmony. The stars which make up the constellations of the sky appear immutably fixed in relation one to another, and although the sun, moon and planets have their own individual movements through the zodiac, their cycles can be charted, their positions predicted. Such an orderly procession must have fascinated the ancient world, contrasting sharply with the chaotic quality of earthly life, and providing a paradigm of that search for order upon which all human beings are engaged.

Apocalyptic imagery, which can be found in both the Jewish and the Christian scriptures, springs in part from this perception of order in the night sky. Apocalyptic writing is often confused with prophecy since it purports to describe what will happen when God enters history in a decisive manner to vindicate Israel. However, the stylized imagery and the impossible nature of the supposed events mark apocalyptic writing more as a literary genre than as a realistic attempt to predict the future. The cosmic nature of the imagery is readily discernible. For instance, in Joel, we read:

I will show wonders in the heavens and on the earth, blood and fire and billows of smoke. The sun will be turned to darkness and the moon to blood before the coming of the great and dreadful day of the Lord.' (Joel 2: 30-31).

And in Isaiah:

The stars of heaven and their constellations will not show their light. The rising sun will be darkened and the moon will not give its light. (Isaiah 13: 10)

Joel makes specific reference to celestial signs presaging the calamities that the day of the Lord will bring, and this echoes the verse in Genesis which declares that the stars are for 'signs and for seasons' (Genesis 1:14). In addition, however, there is the underlying assumption in all such passages that disorder on earth will be accompanied by disorder in the heavens, that there is a connection between celestial and terrestrial events. This is an expression of the ancient axiom 'as above, so below', and is fundamentally astrological.

These themes appear in a different guise in other parts of the Bible. In Ezekiel chapter 1, a passage that has long perplexed scholars, the prophet's vision of the majesty of God is expressed in a welter of images which defy our ability to translate words into pictures. In the midst of this overwhelming array of metaphors, however, we read that out of the great cloud of God's glory 'came the likeness of four living creatures' (Ezekiel 1:5). It goes on:

> Their faces looked like this: Each of the four had the face of a man, and on the right side each had the face of a lion, and on the left the face of an ox; each also had the face of an eagle.

This is an image of the immutability of God expressed in terms of the four 'Fixed' signs of the zodiac: Aquarius, the Man; Leo, the Lion; Taurus, the Ox;

Fig. 3 'Christ in Majesty' (c.1220). Design from a psalter and prayer book carrying the astrological symbols of the four Evangelists.

Scorpio, the Eagle.* Scorpio is variously represented in ancient writings as a scorpion, a snake, or, in this case, as an eagle. It is probable that the eagle's supposed ability to 'renew its youth' (see Psalm 103:5), to regenerate itself, identified it with Scorpio, the sign of regeneration.

The image of God standing 'four-square' with his people, of the divine perfection coming to dwell on earth, is further explored by Ezekiel in the latter part of his book in which he describes his vision of the New Temple which will be built to replace the one destroyed by the Babylonians (Ezekiel 40:5ff.). The detailed measurements of the structure are reminiscent of the complex and precise instructions given for the construction of the Tabernacle (Exodus 25ff.) and for Solomon's Temple (1 Kings 5ff.). All these passages describe the attempt to reflect the perfection of God in the things of time. Symmetry and harmony, which characterize the heavens, are to be expressed in wood and stone. Strachan says:

> As the structure of the temple expressed the perfect harmony of the cosmos in architectural proportions equivalent to those of pure musical intervals, so its contents expressed the same universal harmony in its earthly form of the trees, food, and fragrance of Eden. (Strachan, page 34)

In the final drama of the whole Bible we read about the New Jerusalem which will descend 'out of heaven from God' (Revelation 21ff.). Once again the all-encompassing perfections of this cubic structure are a reflection of the harmony of the heavens which, in turn, reflect the perfections of God. John's constant repetition of the zodiacal number twelve – the twelve Tribes of Israel, the twelve Apostles, the twelve gates of the city – underlines the cosmic dimension of his vision. The jewels which are to adorn the foundation of the city wall are unquestionably astrological, and are related to the jewels that symbolized the Twelve Tribes of Israel in the breastplate of the high priest (Exodus 28:17-21).

The Number 7

The sacred number 7, which occurs in nearly 600 biblical passages (Davies, J., page 116), is probably associated with the idea of cosmic harmony. We learn from Genesis that God blessed and sanctified the seventh day (Genesis 2:3), and from Leviticus (chapter 23) that the Jewish liturgical year was con-

---

* It is surely significant that the four evangelists, Matthew, Mark, Luke and John have, from the earliest times, been associated with these four creatures. Matthew, the Man; Mark, the Lion; Luke, the Ox; and John, the Eagle (see Fig. 3).

structed around septenary cycles. The seventh month, the seventh year, and the 'seven by seven' year have great significance in Judaism. There have been a good many attempts to explain why seven is so important: it is the number of planets (including the sun and moon) visible to the naked eye; it is the number of days in a lunar quarter; it is the number of visible stars in the constellation Ursa Major which, since it never leaves the northern sky, was a natural symbol of permanence and indestructibility. These all seem plausible enough, and any or all of them could be the source of the number's symbolic reference. However, Joseph Epes Brown in his *The Spiritual Legacy of the American Indian* notes that seven was also considered sacred on the American continent, and the reason he gives could well help to explain its importance in biblical symbolism:

> The concept of the vertical axis explains the sacredness of the number seven to the Indians, and it is interesting to note that their interpretation is identical to that found in other major religions. In adding the vertical dimensions of sky and earth to the four horizontal ones of space, we have six dimensions, with the seventh as the point of centre where all directions meet. (Page 36)

For the Native American shaman, Black Elk, the 'point of centre where all directions meet' was Harney Point in South Dakota but, as he went on to remark, 'anywhere is the centre of the world' (Campbell, 1986, page 34). The centre of the world is where you are, where I am; 'though the imagery is necessarily physical and thus apparently of outer space ... the inner connotation is always ... psychological and metaphysical, which is to say, of inner space' (Campbell, 1986, page 31). The individual human being is the meeting point of outer and inner space, a point of contact symbolized by the number seven, and the function of the spiritual quest is to reproduce the macrocosmic order in the individual microcosm. In biblical terms, then, the New Temple, the Holy of Holies, the New Jerusalem, become metaphors of internal transformations rather than descriptions of physical structures. The temple we are building is the temple of our own spirit: for Mark, it is to be built according to the blueprint of perfection that we find in the skies.

Astrological Ages

In addition to its apparent annual journey around the celestial vault, the sun has another, much longer, cycle with regard to the zodiac. Because the earth 'wobbles' slightly on its axis, the sun's position at the spring equinox changes from year to year with reference to the fixed stars. The movement does not amount to much – about one degree of arc in seventy-two years* – but it has given rise to the concept of the Great Year, a period of 25,920 years, the time taken for the equinoctial point to travel throughout the circle of the constellations. Astronomically this phenomenon is known as the 'precession of the equinoxes' since the equinoctial point appears to go backwards through the constellations. Every 2,160 years (25,920 divided by 12) or so, the equinox moves from one constellation to another. At present it is moving from Pisces into Aquarius; at the beginning of the Christian era it was moving from Aries into Pisces, and, at the time of Abraham, from Taurus into Aries. According to Vera Reid, the approximate dates of these 'ages' are as follows:

Age of Leo	c10800–8640 BCE
Age of Cancer	c 8640–6430 BCE
Age of Gemini	c 6430–4320 BCE
Age of Taurus	c 4320–2160 BCE
Age of Aries	c 2160 BCE–1 CE
Age of Pisces	c 1–2160 CE
Age of Aquarius	c 2160–4320 CE

Each of these 2,160 year periods constitutes an 'age' – the Age of Aries, the Age of Pisces, the Age of Aquarius, and so on – each age representing a new phase in the spiritual history of the human race. According to this theory, the religious symbols of each new age reflect the zodiacal constellation into which the equinoctial point has passed. Biblical symbolism certainly seems to accord with this. The dominant symbol of the Age of Aries, which began c. 2,160 BCE, was the Ram (see Genesis 22:13), displacing the Bull which thereafter (among the Hebrews at least) became a symbol of wickedness and debauchery. The story of Moses, from his encounter with God in the fire (Exodus 3) to his forty years of wilderness wanderings, abounds in Arien imagery. Michelangelo, who was undoubtedly familiar with esoteric traditions, depicts him wearing ram's horns.† The Passover meal at which the lamb is ritually consumed commemorates the 'passing over' of the equinoctial point from Taurus to Aries.

---

* In Luke 10:1 we learn that Jesus sent out 70 men to preach the gospel. However, the footnote in any reputable translation of the Bible will inform us that various ancient manuscripts give '72' (*hebdomêkonta duo*) and Strachan (pages 61–62) believes that 72 is the original number. Could this particular episode of missionary activity be related in some way to 'one day' in the Great Year?

† Most translations of Exodus 34:29 inform us that when Moses came down from Mount Sinaii 'he did not know that his face was radiant'. Such a translation is not faithful to the actual Hebrew, which tells us that his face was 'horned' (*karan*).

Fig. 4 'Moses' by Michelangelo (San Pietro in Vincoli, Rome)

The word 'Passover' comes from the Hebrew word *pesach* which means 'to hop, to skip over'. It may be related to a homophonous verb meaning 'to hobble', and when we remember that it is the very unsteadiness of the earth on its axis that gives rise to the phenomenon of precession in the first place, this understanding of Passover begins to make sense. Perhaps the Hebrews knew more about the mechanics of the solar system than we generally give them credit for.

The New Testament was written as the Age of Pisces was beginning, and the Gospels are full of fish references and symbols – 28 in all (Strachan, page 92). The name 'Jesus' is the Greek version of the Hebrew Joshua, and the biblical Joshua was the 'son of Nun' (Joshua 1:1); 'Nun' means *fish* in Hebrew.

41

The Greek word for fish, *ichthus*, was used as an acrostic for the first Christian creed:

IESUS	Jesus
CHRISTOS	Christ
THEOU	of God
HUIOS	Son
SOTER	Saviour

The Oxford Dictionary of the Christian Church tells us that this acrostic probably originated in Gnostic circles because it is found in the *Sibylline Oracles*, and that 'in the fourth and fifth Centuries the fish became the emblem of the Eucharist and is frequently found in the paintings of the catacombs in combination with bread and wine' (page 514). As we saw earlier, eating fish on Fridays, customary in Roman Catholicism until quite recently, was a type of spiritual communion with Christ. Friday was chosen for this because it is the day of Venus, the planet 'exalted' in the sign of Pisces. (*Fria*, from which Friday is derived, is the Norse equivalent of Venus. The Romance languages show the connection of Venus with Friday more clearly than English.)

Christian Fish Symbol

The fish symbol which adorns many a coat and many a car these days is a simple variation of the hieroglyph of Pisces (♓), and the *vesica piscis*, a feature of much Christian art, shows figures within the overlapping lines of the Pisces hieroglyph. As Strachan comments, it is impossible to explain how such a 'cold blooded, apathetic creature of the waters' could come to symbolize the noble and exalted Saviour without reference to astral symbolism. (pages 95-6).

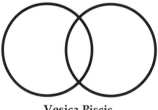

Vesica Piscis

Each age bears the characteristics of the equinoctial constellation and also of its opposite. So, the Age of Aries shows the influence of Libra, the Balance,

Fig. 5 Christ within the Vesica Piscis, from The Benedictional
of St Ethelwold (c. 908–984)

the sign of relationships, 'covenants'. Virgo, opposite Pisces in the sky, is the
sign of modesty and service, in addition to physical virginity. All these are
prominent themes within the Christian story and are characteristic of the Virgin
Mary: she and the Piscean Jesus stand as twin poles of the Virgo-Pisces axis.

The coming age is that of Aquarius, the Water-Bearer, which many hope
will be a time of brotherhood and peace, when human values predominate
and when collective responsibility for the environment and for the under-
privileged will be evident. The opposite constellation is Leo, symbolic of
individuality, and the coming age will be characterized by growing tension
between individual and group values. Astrologers say that becoming a genuine 'self' within the context of the collective will be the primary spiritual
task of the next two thousand years.

The Greek astronomer Hipparchus (second century BCE) is generally credited with the discovery of the precession of the equinoxes, but the phenomenon was *observed* long before Hipparchus provided an explanation for it. Alice Howell writes:

> There is so far no way of knowing if the Chaldeans and Egyptians knew of the Ages. There is speculation that the ancient Egyptians might have known about them since the number 25,920 appears in the measurement of the Great Pyramid. But as yet no definite proof exists beyond the indisputable fact that Egyptian symbols show each of the shifts from the Age of Gemini through the Ages of Taurus and Aries in their cosmogony, mythology and architecture. (Howell, page 133)

Joseph Campbell is completely convinced that the ancient world knew about precession before Hipparchus. His principal clue lies in what he calls the 'magic number 432' (Campbell, 1986, page 38). This number, when multiplied by 60 – the resting heart rate of a healthy man – gives 25,920, the number of years in the Great Year. He finds a link here between the rhythm of the individual human being and the rhythm of the universe: 432 is the number of that link and it can be traced in a variety of mythologies. The Kali Yuga of the Hindus is 432,000 years, and in Babylonian mythology (as reported by Berossos) the time between the rise of the first city, Kish, and the Flood is given as 432,000 years. About Icelandic mythology Campbell writes:

> I discovered that in Othin's (Wotan's) warrior hall, Valholl, there were 540 doors through each of which, on the 'Day of the Wolf' (that is to say, at the end of the present cycle of time) there would pass 800 divine warriors to engage the anti-gods in a battle of mutual annihilation. 800 x 540 = 432,000. (Campbell, 1986, page 35)

The Bible, too, contains a reference to this number in a most unlikely place. In Genesis 5 we find a list of ten antediluvian patriarchs whose ages total 1656 years. According to Julius Oppert, in 1656 years there are 86,400 seven-day weeks. 86,400 divided by 2 = 43,200. Campbell calls this a deeply hidden reference 'to the Gentile Sumero-Babylonian, mathematical cosmology of the ever-revolving cycles of impersonal time with whole universes and their populations coming into being, flowering for a season of 43,200 (432,000 or 4,320,000) years, dissolving back into the cosmic mother-sea to rest for an equal spell of years before returning, and so again, and again, and again'

(Campbell 1986, page 35). Furthermore, 432 is the number which expresses the relationship between the great pulsing cycles of the universe and the pulse of the human being, the mystic link between macrocosm and microcosm. Its veiled presence in the Bible demonstrates that 'cosmic consciousness', the perennial aim of the mystic, was not unknown to the seers of ancient Israel.

The theory of astrological ages was accepted by Jung. It is, he says, 'a Just-so story that proves itself by a thousand signs ... It was not I who invented all the fish symbols in Christianity; the fishers of men, the *pisculi Christianorum* ... To deny it would be to throw the baby out with the bathwater' (Dean, page 306). Nor, we might add, were these symbols invented by a historian or quasi-historian intent on giving us some details about the life of Jesus. The fish symbolism in the Gospels is added testimony that these documents had their origin in an esoteric tradition.

The Gospel in the Stars

In the nineteenth century, the works of J.S. Seiss enjoyed something of a vogue on both sides of the Atlantic, and his ideas are being represented by a number of modern writers. Seiss's basic thesis is that the zodiacal constellations and their 'decans',* the non-zodiacal constellations that surround them, tell the Christian story of salvation, and that God placed them in the sky at the dawn of time as a witness to, and a prefiguring of, the gospel message. He further maintains that the interpretation of these signs has been the exclusive preserve of a 'superstitious and idolatrous astrology', and that pagan mythology has picked up but perverted the stories that the constellations were originally intended by God to tell. According to Seiss, the virginal conceptions which abound in mythology are corruptions of the one genuine virginal conception in history, that of Jesus.

However, it is much more likely that the stories of heroes and ogres, gods and devils, trials and ordeals, which we find in both the Bible and pagan mythology have a *common* origin in the zodiac. The zodiac was the ancient picture book, and storybook, of the human race. The shapes perceived there are not the products of arbitrary 'dot joining', but represent universal and archetypal symbols of human spiritual awareness which have, over millennia, issued in both mythological and religious forms of

---

* The word 'decan' is used somewhat differently in modern astrology, referring to 10-degree divisions of the zodiacal signs.

expression.* So, the story of Perseus is not a 'corruption' of the story of Christ's victory over evil (as Seiss supposed), it is just another expression of the universal longing for redemption which lies behind the Christian myth, too. The zodiac inspired the myth of the Twelve Labours of Hercules, which concerns the soul's journey of liberation, and this same literary impulse, translated into Jewish categories, has given us Mark's Gospel. The Gospel provides us with abundant clues that this is the author's purpose, and I hope to be able to point these out as we proceed.

Seiss's work relies heavily on the theories of Frances Rolleston, which were published in 1863 in her book *Mazzaroth*. Rolleston investigated the meaning of the various star names – like Sirius, Rigel, Tegmine – which have come down to us from antiquity, and Seiss finds that some of these names, when translated into modern languages, can be related to the gospel story. What Seiss was not aware of is that sometimes these names reflect with astonishing accuracy the principal incidents of Mark's Gospel. For example, the Feeding of the Five Thousand and the Feeding of the Four Thousand occur in what I have called the Cancer section of the Gospel. In the constellation Cancer is a star called Ma'alaph whose name means *Assembled Thousands,* and in Ursa Major (one of the 'decans' of Cancer) we find the star Phad, which is said to mean *Numbered*. There are a good many correspondences of this type which we will point out in our analysis of the individual zodiacal sections. It could well be that Mark has chosen to weave the names of the principal stars into his text as an added testimony to its zodiacal structure.

The relevance of this approach

The strength of any theory lies only in its ability to provide answers to previously intractable questions. I hope, in the following chapters, to show how a number of problems generated by the historical or quasi-historical approach to Mark cease to be troublesome. Among these are:

• The reason why Mark does not begin his Gospel with infancy narratives;

---

* Gettings writes: 'It is suggested that the areas of sky marked out by certain star groups were first experienced as areas of spiritual influence. It is likely that such 'experience' would not be available to all men, but would be available to those initiates who had endured the disciplines and spiritual enlightenments of those teachers in the mystery schools who were the mentors of the pre-Christian culture. By more or less clairvoyant vision, such men would experience the stellar areas, and then choose names and images which would encapsulate the qualities of the stellar influences which they sensed as streaming from those areas.' (Gettings, 1987, page 102)

- Why Mark has two 'feeding' stories very close together (Mark 6:30-44; Mark 8:1-9);
- Why Jesus takes a very roundabout route to the Sea of Galilee in Mark 7:31;
- Why the account of the Transfiguration (Mark 9:1-13), which many scholars have considered a misplaced resurrection story, is, in fact, in the right place;
- Why Jesus curses the fig tree (Mark 11:13);
- Why the Last Supper is a Passover meal, in spite of the fact that no mention is made of any lamb.

This approach throws some light on the synoptic problem – i.e. the relationships between the Gospels of Matthew, Mark and Luke. As we shall see, the common assumption that Mark wrote first and that Matthew and Luke copied from him is untenable. It would seem that a more primitive document, more clearly zodiacal than any of the Gospels we now have, preceded the canonical Gospels.

However, more important than any of the above, I hope to be able to make the gospel story relevant to contemporary people. For too long the debate has centred on the historicity of the gospel accounts, and this has brought about a polarization of opinion which has tended to obscure their spiritual value. Both sides – literalist and liberal – have rejected the poetic dimension. But, as Schopenhauer reminds us, history is the 'antithesis of poetry'. History concerns only individual things; poetry concerns universal truths. By structuring his story on the zodiac, Mark has given it a cosmic dimension. His hero is an individual, like Abraham and Moses, but his message is universal. The zodiacal way is the way we all must travel in the spiritual life. Jesus may have walked the road before us but, as far as Mark is concerned, he does not walk it on our behalf. Mark tells us that we must 'take up the cross and follow' Jesus (Mark 10:21); we have to 'drink the same cup, and be baptized with the same baptism' (Mark 10:38) if we want the same reward. Using timeless metaphors drawn from the zodiacal circle, Mark has given us a textbook of the spiritual life, a life lived in harmony with the universe, a life of holiness, *wholeness*, which can only be attained with great effort and at great personal cost. There is also the possibility that, as we learn about these universal principles, we are learning about the career of one, about whom history has bequeathed us little more than a name, whose life embodied these principles, and whom we can call our brother and our exemplar.

This interpretation is not intended as a reductionist dismissal of the Jesus story as 'mere' zodiacal myth. On the contrary: I consider the Gospel of

47

Mark to be a work of profound spiritual significance. I write as a Christian minister, albeit one who has more in common with Valentinus than with Irenaeus, and I accept that there is much more to this Gospel than my own analysis can account for.* While I would want to argue for the objective presence of a zodiacal scheme in Mark, I do not think for one moment that in describing this we are exhausting all dimensions of meaning within the text. After all, a story which for two millennia has captured the imagination of untold millions must have the poetic depth to inspire manifold interpretations. What follows is one of these.

---

* I am also convinced that there is much more astrology in the text than I have been able to discover.

A Note on Sources

Throughout the chapters which follow I quote frequently and extensively from Richard Hinckley Allen's book, *Star Names: Their Lore and Meaning*, which, for over a hundred years, has been the definitive work on the mythology and astronomy of the constellations. It is a work of extraordinary scholarship, and has been the foundation upon which all subsequent attempts to describe the heavens have been based. I have used the Dover edition, first published in 1963.

I have based my astrological descriptions of the signs and constellations on the works of three ancient authors:

1. Aratos, who wrote in Greek c. 300 BCE. His *Phaenomena* is mainly descriptive of the constellation patterns. (Loeb Classical Library, Callimachus, Lycophron, Aratos, translated by A.W. Mair and G.R. Mair, 1921, Harvard University Press.)

2. Manilius, who wrote in Latin in the first century CE. I have used two versions of his *Astronomica*: the 1697 translation 'done into English verse', published by the National Astrological Library in 1953; and the Loeb Classical Library edition translated by G.P. Goold, first published in 1976. Manilius's work is the finest astrological poem ever written. I have quoted mainly from the earlier verse translation, simply because of its charm.

3. Ptolemy, who wrote in Greek in the mid-second century CE, but whose work *Tetrabiblos* faithfully transmits the astrology of antiquity. I have used the Loeb edition, translated by F.E. Robbins, first published in 1940.

The writer of the Gospel of Mark (or its predecessor) could well have been familiar with the first two of the above works.

I have felt obliged to supplement these authors with delineations from more modern astrological writers in order to emphasize particular qualities of the signs not touched upon by the ancients but which are relevant to the sections of the Gospel under discussion. Dane Rudhyar's comments on the spiritual qualities associated with each of the zodiacal signs have been included because they reflect with peculiar appositeness the various stages in Mark.

Quotations and examples from individuals born under the various signs of the zodiac (e.g. Mother Teresa is mentioned and quoted from in the chapter on Virgo, her birth sign) are given when these seem relevant. They add a little colour, but they are in no sense essential to the argument, and may safely be dismissed by those for whom astrology is anathema. Anyone who thinks I may be bending the astrological factors to fit my thesis should obtain any elementary astrological textbook (e.g. *Teach Yourself Astrology*, by Jeff Mayo) to check my statements. He or she will find that all my delineations of zodiacal characteristics are entirely in keeping with astrological tradition.

I recommend that before reading each of the following chapters, the relevant section of Mark should be read, and to enable the reader to do this without having to refer to a separate volume, Appendix 1 contains a version of Mark's Gospel, divided into what I consider to be its zodiacal sections. It is my own translation, made in order to avoid copyright problems which might arise from reproducing a complete biblical book in one of the recognized translations, but I make no claim to originality. It is simply a readable version of the text, free from distracting verse numbers. Other versions are readily available, and the interested reader might like to consult one of these. However, unless otherwise specified, biblical verses which appear in the body of the book are taken from the New International Version of the Bible, and are reproduced with permission.

No friend of mine takes his ease in my chair,
I have no chair, no church, no philosophy,
I lead no man to a dinner-table, library, exchange
But each man and each woman of you I lead upon a knoll.
My left hand hooking you round the waist,
My right hand pointing to landscapes of continents and the public road.
Not I, not any one else can travel that road for you,
You must travel it for yourself.
It is not far, it is within reach,
Perhaps you have been on it since you were born and did not know,
Perhaps it is everywhere on water and on land.

(Walt Whitman, *Song of Myself*, Section 46)

Aries (Mark 1:1-3:35)
'Take up your bed and walk!'

Whan that Aprille with his shoures sote
The droghte of Marche hath perced to the rote,
And bathed every veyne in swich licour
Of which vertu engendered is the flour;
Whan Zephirus eek with his swete breeth
Inspired hath in every holt and heeth
The tender croppes and the yonge sonne
Hath in the Ram is halfe cours yronne
And smale fowles maken melodye
That slepen at the night with open ye
(So priketh hem nature in hir corages):
Than longen folk to goon on pilgrimages.
(Chaucer: *Prologue* to *The Canterbury Tales*)

Because of the phenomenon of equinoctial precession which was explained in chapter 2, there are really two ways of dividing the zodiac. One division is based on the actual star groups as we see them in the sky, and is used today in India and by a number of western astrologers; this is called the sidereal zodiac. The other division, called the tropical or moving zodiac, uses the same names as the constellation groups but begins at the point of the spring equinox wherever this might be in relation to the fixed stars. This zodiac derives its symbolism from the year itself, from the drama of the conflict between light and darkness which has four climactic moments symbolized by the two equinoxes and the two solstices. Since the spring equinox now takes place against the background of the constellation Pisces, the two zodiacs have drifted apart and, to the confusion of everyone, a planet said to be in the *sign* Aries is, in reality, in the *constellation* Pisces. It is important for us to note, however, that at the time Mark's Gospel was written, the two zodiacs were virtually coincident: the equinox was occurring right on the cuspal division between Aries and Pisces. Consequently, Mark was able to use imagery derived from the year cycle (signs) and from the actual star groups in composing his Gospel.

The constellational zodiac has no natural beginning or ending. However, according to Cyril Fagan (page 30), it was customary in the ancient world to begin the circle with Virgo, and Seiss considers this constellation to be the natural starting point, presumably because the myths that surround it concern birth. The Gospels of Matthew and Luke are prefaced by such mythic birth stories. Mark's Gospel is not. It opens with a mature Jesus ready to embark on his public ministry, and no mention whatsoever is made of his physical birth or of his childhood. In trying to capture this theme of 'new beginning' Mark employs the symbolism of Aries, the sign of the springtime, when the cycle of growth on earth begins anew. The constellations began with Virgo, *but the signs began with Aries*. Ptolemy, who wrote only a hundred years or so after Mark, and whose work reflects the astrological traditions of antiquity, tells us that 'although there is no natural beginning of the zodiac, since it is a circle, they assume that the sign which begins with the vernal equinox, that of Aries, is the starting point of them all' (Ptolemy, pages 59-61).

It is possible that Mark knew of the virginal-conception stories since these would be part of the esoteric tradition inherited by all the evangelists. Such stories are a commonplace of mythology, and, when interpreted esoterically, relate to the birth of the spiritual life which, as the Gospel of John informs us, is not a physical birth but a 'rebirth' whose origin is not in the flesh (*sarx*) but in God (John 3). We might speculate that Mark chose not to open his Gospel with such stories, in spite of their appropriateness to his theme, because by placing them at the beginning of his narrative he would introduce Virgoan themes out of sequence. Mark is concerned with spiritual rebirth and he uses the rebirth of the year in the springtime as his primary symbol.

54

Aries (Mark 1:1-3:35)

Since the Jews did not accord the status of rabbi to anyone who was under thirty years old, the Jesus we encounter in these early chapters of Mark is (we assume) in his late twenties, and in fact, Luke's Gospel tells us that Jesus was 'about thirty years old when he began his ministry' (Luke 3:23). This is the age when youth is over and a new seriousness enters our life. It approximates to Dante's 'middle of life's journey,' and it is marked astrologically by the 'Saturn return' when, at around 29, the planet Saturn has made a complete circuit of the zodiac and has returned to the place it occupied when we were born. It signifies a change of outlook, a reappraisal of priorities; we become more conscious of our mortality, and seem better disposed than before to search for spiritual meaning to our life. Traditionally, it is the age at which the Buddha too began his search for enlightenment.

Aries and Mars

When the vernal equinox occurs around 21 March each year, and the sun enters the sign of Aries, a new optimism enters human consciousness. The bleakness of winter is past. As the daffodils bloom and new buds of life appear, nature herself seems to have found new hope. In the northern hemisphere, where systematic astrology was developed, light has begun to triumph over darkness, the day over the night, life over death. It is a time of renewed energy, of new beginnings, when, as Chaucer observed, 'folk long to go on pilgrimages'.

This struggle of new life to establish itself in the midst of death and decay characterizes the sign Aries. God's creative activity was associated with Aries in the ancient world, and some early authorities considered that the earth was created when the sun was here. Albumaser, writing in the ninth century, but no doubt reflecting a much older tradition, says that the creation took place when the seven planets – Sun, Moon, Mercury, Venus, Mars, Jupiter, and Saturn – were in conjunction in Aries, a belief reflected in Dante's *Inferno* where we learn that 'the sun was mounting with those stars that with him were, what time the Love Divine, at first in motion set those beauteous things'.

To the Egyptians the constellation was known as Arnum, *The Lord of the Head*, and to the Babylonians as Lu Hunga, *The Hired Man* (Campion, page 17). Among the Hebrews, Aries was probably associated with the tribe of Reuben, called by Jacob 'my first-born, my might, and the beginning of my strength' (Genesis 49:3). As we have seen (in 'The Forgotten Language of the Stars'), Judaism began when the equinox 'passed over' from Taurus to Aries (c 2000 BCE), and many images within the defining stories of the Jewish

55

scriptures – the ram caught in the thicket by Abraham, Moses' burning bush, the lamb of sacrifice, the wilderness wanderings, – reflect this constellation. It was when the sun was in Aries, during the month of Abib (a word meaning 'spring'), that the Exodus took place (Exodus 13:4), and thereafter this was to be 'the first month, the first month of the year' (Exodus 12:2). Later, the name of the month was changed to Nisan, and it still marks the beginning of the ecclesiastical year in Judaism, although it is the seventh month of the civil calendar.

Like all the signs which mark the equinoxes and solstices, Aries is a Cardinal sign, a sign of initiatory action, of enterprise, and of leadership. It is also a Fire sign, with all the qualities of ardour, combativeness and vigour that this connotes. The glyph of Aries (♈) depicts the horns of the ram, the aggressive, combative, leader of the flock. It is also suggestive of the springing water, the source of all life and growth, which transforms the wilderness and brings vitality and health. Manilius, a near-contemporary of Mark's, tells us that those with Aries prominent in their nature are cursed with ravenous tempers, and go where fancy takes them, ploughing new seas and making the world their own.

Astrologers have not changed much in their assessment. Isabelle Pagan, writing in 1911, has this to say about the Aries type:

> He is the Captain, the Leader, Pioneer among men; going out in sympathy to a new thought, rapidly assimilating fresh ideas, always in the van of progress in whatever kind of work – intellectual, artistic or practical – he may take up. He gets close quarters in his battles, and when highly developed, fights best with his head; that is to say, in the field of thought ... (Ariens) really enjoy facing and overcoming difficulties, and will go out of their way to challenge opposition. (Pagan, page 6)

Good contemporary examples of this Arien tendency to 'challenge opposition' are not hard to find. Ian Paisley (born 6 April 1926), is adept at presenting both his religious and his political opinions in pugnacious style. In October 1988, protesting at the Pope's visit to the European Parliament in Strasbourg, he thundered:

> This is the battle of the Ages which we are engaged in. This is no Sunday school picnic, this is a battle for truth against the lie, the battle of Heaven against hell, the battle of Christ against the Antichrist! (Cooke, page 4)

56

Secular Ariens can be equally confrontational. Daniel Dennett and Richard Dawkins, Darwin's latter-day champions, see themselves as combatants in the 'war' of science against religious obscurantism. Dennett, a neuroscientist and 'an intrepid Atlantic sailor' has, according to an article in the *Observer Review* (12 March 2006), 'called out ... some of the biggest beasts in the academic jungle ... and has never once taken a step back'. Dawkins too is always up for an intellectual fight. They were both born at the end of March (Daniel Dennett 28 March 1942; Richard Dawkins 26 March 1941).

There is something refreshingly unrefined, childlike even, about people who are strongly Arien. They seem to have a desire to strip things down to their bare essentials coupled with an inability to tolerate too much ambiguity or ambivalence; to them, things are very much black and white, with few grey areas.

The 'ruler' of Aries, the planet which is most obviously associated with it and which shares its characteristics, is Mars, the 'Red Planet', unanimously identified by the ancients as the harbinger of war and destruction. Its glyph ($\mathrm{\sigma}$), which shows the cross of matter dominating the circle of spirit, is suggestive of aggression and power, and has been adopted almost universally as the symbol of masculinity.

Ptolemy gives the following list of (positive) Martial qualities: 'noble, commanding, spirited, military, versatile, powerful, venturesome, keen, headstrong, active, easily angered, with the qualities of leadership' (Ptolemy, page 353).

The Spiritual Lessons of Aries

'Nothing will ever be attempted if all possible objections must first be overcome.'
Dr Johnson

We can legitimately extrapolate from these ancient and modern descriptions the intrinsic qualities of the sign's symbolism: beginnings, leadership, pioneering, urgency, would all, to the ancient mind, be associated with Aries.

These are all primary themes of the Gospel's first three chapters. The pace is frantic. Everything seems to happen quickly, with nobody having much time for pause or reflection. Mark's fondness for the word 'immediately' (*euthus*) is particularly apparent. Of the 40 or so times he uses the word in the Gospel, eleven occur in chapter 1 alone. Peter and Andrew, James and John all leave their nets to follow Jesus, the latter two without any evident word of goodbye to their presumably bewildered father or to the *hired men* (Mark 1:16-20).

It is remarkable how commentators down the centuries have inferred from this reference to 'hired men' that the family of James and John was quite well off. However, as we saw earlier, 'The Hired Man' is the ancient Babylonian name for the constellation Aries. This is not a biographical detail; it is an Aries 'flag'. Leaving the hired men also symbolizes leaving the age of Aries and entering the new age of Pisces.

The call of the tax collector, Levi, expresses a similar idea (Mark 2:13-17). The Levites were the priestly tribe within Judaism, the tribe to which Moses belonged. They had helped Moses punish the people for the heinous crime of building a golden calf by putting about three thousand of their fellow Israelites to the sword (Exodus 32:28). Thus they were instrumental in the symbolic change-over from the Age of Taurus (the Bull, the Calf) to the Age of Aries (the Ram, the Lamb). They were allocated no land at the time of Joshua's conquest, but were to receive tithes from other tribes instead. In Mark's Gospel, Levi is collecting taxes, not tithes, but he leaves all this behind him to follow Jesus. Just as the Levites had helped Moses in the time of the transition from Taurus to Aries, now, in the person of Levi who, along with Peter, Andrew, James, and John, was to become a 'fisher of men', they were to help Jesus in the transition from Aries to Pisces. Levi's father is appropriately called Alphaeus, a name which means *Changing*.

The speed with which these men follow Jesus has led some literalist commentators to speculate that perhaps Jesus had met them before and was only then giving the signal for them to join him permanently. It's possible, but the Gospel gives us no indication of any previous meeting, and such a prosaic explanation misses the vital meaning which these incidents have by virtue of their location in the Aries section of the Gospel. While the urgent onward movement of these early characters obviously symbolizes the passage of the equinox from the constellation Aries to the constellation Pisces, and the beginning of the new age, it also teaches a valuable spiritual lesson: that the decision to embark on a life of self-discovery is not one to agonize over in interminable internal debate. The call to discipleship demands a quick response, a willingness to go out in faith, like Abraham and Moses, without the whole battery of assurances that we normally require before prudently making our important decisions. 'Now is the acceptable time,' writes St Paul: 'now is the day of salvation' (2 Corinthians 6:2). St Teresa of Avila, born under Aries (28 March 1515), was well aware of the dangers of procrastination: 'My own temperament is such that, when I desire anything, I do so with impetuosity' (du Boulay, page 8), she wrote, and she alerted her sisters in the religious life to the fact that 'many remain at the foot of the mountain who could ascend to the top'.

All the spiritual traditions emphasize the importance of making that initial decision to live the life of the spirit, and tell us that it has to be made before we attain intellectual conviction over metaphysical propositions. We can't wait until we know for certain that God exists, or that Jesus lived, or that this or that religion is true, before we embark upon the journey of self-transformation. Such procrastination, said the Buddha, resembles the behaviour of a man who has been wounded by a poisoned arrow, but who resists the attempts of his companions to pull the arrow out until he has found out the name, the home town, the stature, the colour and the caste of the man who fired it.

The Hindu sage, Sri Ramakrishna, puts it like this:

> A wife once spoke to her husband, saying, 'My dear, I am very anxious about my brother. For the last few days he has been thinking of renouncing the world and of becoming a Sannyasin, and has begun preparations for it. He has been trying gradually to curb his desires and reduce his wants.' The husband replied, 'You need not be anxious about your brother. He will never become a Sannyasin. No one has ever renounced the world by making long preparations.' The wife asked, 'How then does one become a Sannyasin?' The husband answered, 'Do you wish to see how one renounces the world? Let me show you.' Saying this, instantly he tore his flowing dress into pieces, tied one piece round his loins, told his wife that she and all women were henceforth his mother, and left the house never to return. (Ballou, page 81)

That the early apostles should hastily follow Jesus without checking out his references and demanding a police investigation into his background makes no sense to the cautious mind of the twenty-first-century literalist, but it is perfectly in keeping with the advice given by countless spiritual mentors throughout the ages.

Baptism by John

Themes of beginning, starting again, turning one's back on the past are very much in evidence in these early chapters of Mark. The Gospel opens with the words, 'The beginning (*archê*) of the gospel of Jesus Christ' (Mark 1:1), and in his depiction of John the Baptist we can detect Mark's conviction that Jesus is qualitatively different from all his predecessors, John included. He is greater than John, and John is not even worthy to loosen the strap of his sandal (Mark 1:7). John's baptism is performed with water: Jesus will baptize

Fig. 6 The Adoration of the Lamb (Ghent Altarpiece), Jan van Eyck

'with holy spirit' (Mark 1:8). At this point, Matthew (3:11) and Luke (3:16) add 'and with fire', reflecting the Fire sign Aries even more closely than Mark, and although John's Gospel does not have an account of Jesus' baptism by John the Baptist it does describe an encounter between the two men in which the Arien symbolism is clear. The passage runs:

> The next day John saw Jesus coming towards him, and said, 'Look, the Lamb (*amnos*) of God who takes away the sin of the world'. (John 1:29)

John himself, with his functional dress, his no-frills diet, and his uncompromising, confrontational message, is the very embodiment of Aries.* He represents the old dispensation, the religion of the age of the Ram which is now coming to an end. He dresses like Elijah, and he eats like Moses: the

---

* Even the manner of John's death – *beheading* – suggests Aries. His execution is described later in the Gospel (Mark 6:16-29, in the Gemini section), but it *is told as a 'flashback'*.

swarming locusts of John's desert sojourn echo the swarming quail consumed by Moses in the Sinai wilderness; manna was not available to him,
but wild honey would at least have the same taste (Exodus 16:31).

He announces himself as one 'preparing the way', as a forerunner: legal-
istic, exoteric Judaism in the person of John was now giving way to another
religious approach in the person of Jesus; the Ram was to hand over to the
Fish. The 'head' of Aries was to defer to the 'feet' of Pisces, a process alluded
to in John's remark about the sandal strap.

The newly initiated son of God is immediately driven into the wilderness
to be tempted by the devil (Mark 1:12-13). This is reminiscent of the other
Arien figures of the Bible, Abraham and Moses, who leave the security of
home and convention to enter the unmapped country which God will show
them. The forty days of this experience echo the forty years that Moses and
the Israelites spent in the wilderness (Deuteronomy 2:7), and are symbolic of
the spiritual journey which lasts for the full length of a person's mature life
(between ages 30 and 70). Mark's brief account of this incident – Matthew's
and Luke's are much longer – should not lead us to underestimate its symbolic significance. 'The wilderness' represents all the terrors that beset the
spiritual seeker. Henry James, himself born under the sign of Aries (15 April
1843), puts it like this:

> Every man who has reached even his intellectual teens begins to suspect
> that life is no farce; that it is not genteel comedy even; that it flowers
> and fructifies on the contrary out of the profoundest tragic depths of
> the essential dearth in which its subject's roots are plunged. The natural
> inheritance of everyone who is capable of spiritual life is an unsubdued
> forest where the wolf howls and the obscene bird of night chatters.
> (Quoted in Rushdie, *The Satanic Verses*, page 397.)

It is significant that this is undertaken at the Spirit's prompting, and that
angels provide help for Jesus, just as God had ensured that the Israelites
were fed in the wilderness, and that their clothing did not wear out
(Deuteronomy 8:4). The meaning is clear: to embark on the spiritual life is to
lay oneself open to all kinds of danger ('Satan' and 'wild beasts' are there),
but this is a God-ordained journey, and God's ministers will sustain the neophyte on the way.

These themes of newness continue as the narrative unfolds. Jesus begins
his ministry when John the Baptist has been imprisoned (Mark 1:14). A new
chapter is opening. John, the last of the prophets of the Old Covenant, with
his quaint garb, his frugal diet, and his apocalyptic message, has been

removed from the scene. The old is being replaced by the new. The heavens have been split open again, the voice of God has been heard once more (Mark 1:11), and a new message is about to enter human consciousness.

The Kingdom of God

The message is a simple one: the longed-for kingdom of God is *here already* (Mark 1:15). Of course, if Jesus was promising an economic or political utopia, he was completely mistaken; if anything, things were to get worse for the Jews, and two thousand years later a just and equitable political system still eludes us. But the kingdom of God, to the mystic, is a state of being, not a social arrangement. Entry into the kingdom requires a complete change of mind, a willingness to re-orientate our perceptions. This is the meaning of the Greek word *metanoia*, which is generally translated as 'repentance', but which involves much more than regret for past actions. It implies a resolution to begin again from the beginning, *to make a fundamental alteration to the way one looks at the world*, which St Paul calls 'transformation by the renewing of the mind' (Romans 12:2). Luke's Gospel tells us that 'The kingdom of God does not come visibly, nor will people say, "Here it is," or "There it is," because the kingdom of God is within you' (Luke 17:21). From the Gnostic Gospel of Thomas we learn, 'The kingdom of the Father is already spread out on the earth, *and people aren't aware of it*' (saying 113), which means that the kingdom of God is not something that we can create with political action and economic redistribution (important though these may be), nor is it something that will be imposed upon us by divine intervention; it is instead something we can discover *by correcting our eyesight*.

The Sufis, Islam's mystics, tell the story of how Nasrudin, the 'holy fool', would take his donkey across a frontier every day, its panniers loaded with straw. The customs inspector suspected the increasingly prosperous Nasrudin of smuggling, but despite regular and extensive searches, he could never find any contraband. Years later, when both were retired, they met in the marketplace. 'I know you were smuggling something,' said the customs officer. 'What was it? You can tell me now.' 'Donkeys,' replied Nasrudin.

The story illustrates the Sufi contention – shared by Jesus – that the mystical goal, the kingdom of God, is nearer than is generally realized. In fact, it is here, 'at hand', but we are so busy looking for something else that we never find it. The mystic poet and painter William Blake, who stands in a similar esoteric tradition, writes:

And I know that this world is a world of imagination and vision. I see everything I paint in this world but everybody does not see alike. To the eyes of a miser a guinea is far more beautiful than the sun, and a bag worn with use of money has more beautiful proportions than a vine filled with grapes. The tree which moves some to tears of joy is in the eyes of others only a green thing which stands in the way. Some see nature all ridicule and deformity, and by these I shall not regulate my proportions; and some scarce see nature at all. But to the eyes of the man of imagination, nature is imagination itself. As a man is, so he sees. As the eye is formed, such are its powers ...

'When the sun rises, do you not see a round disc of fire, somewhat like a guinea?' 'O no, no, I see an innumerable company of the heavenly host crying, "Holy, holy, holy is the Lord God Almighty"' ... If the doors of perception were cleansed every thing would appear to man as it is, infinite. For man has closed himself up, till he sees all things through narrow chinks of his cavern ...

How do you know but every bird that cuts the airy way, is an immense world of delight, closed by your senses five?

For everything that lives is holy.
(Haddon, pages 12-13)

To see the world as Blake saw it is to become a citizen of the kingdom of God.

Newness

'I love to see a young girl go out and grab the world by the lapels. Life's a bitch. You've got to go out and kick ass.' (Maya Angelou, born 4 April 1928)

The radical nature of Jesus' teaching is acknowledged by the people who witness the exorcism he performs in the synagogue at Capernaum (Mark 1:21-28). It is 'new' (*kainê*), qualitatively different, not just novel or recent (*neos*). Jesus teaches with authority, not like the scribes who slavishly followed the traditions of the elders and taught by means of precedent. The calling of the Twelve Apostles (Mark 3:13-19) symbolizes the completeness of this break with the past: they are the new Sons of Israel, citizens of the kingdom which is already present to those with eyes to discern it.*

---

* Of the numerous attempts to ascribe the apostles to specific signs of the zodiac, none has been entirely successful. There are two major reasons for this. First, the Christian scriptures are not clear as to who the Twelve were; each of the four Gospels gives a different list. The second difficulty is paucity of information. We know so little about most of the apostles that we cannot

Jesus uses two images to describe the unprecedented nature of his own teaching: new cloth must not be used to patch up an old garment; and new wine must not be kept in old wineskins (Mark 1:21-22). The old garment and the old wineskins represent the religious teachings of the past; but following Jesus does not involve making adjustments and concessions to the past, it means leaving it behind.

The spiritual life is a new life which will constantly be at odds with religious convention. Matthew's parallel account further underlines these themes.

> Then a teacher of the law came to him and said, 'Teacher, I will follow you wherever you go.' Jesus replied, 'Foxes have holes and birds of the air have nests, but the Son of Man has no place to lay his head.' Another man, one of his disciples, said to him, 'Lord, let me first go and bury my father.' But Jesus told him, 'Follow me, and let the dead bury their own dead.' (Matthew 8: 19-22)

The conflict between old and new shows itself clearly in these three chapters. Jesus defies Jewish law by claiming to be able to forgive sins (Mark 2:5), by eating with tax-collectors and sinners (Mark 2:16), by not encouraging his disciples to fast (Mark 2:18), by picking ears of corn on the Sabbath day (Mark 2:23), and by healing on the Sabbath (Mark 3:2). In all these incidents Jesus displays the Arien qualities of courage, defiance, audacity. Nowhere are we further from the Sunday-school image of 'gentle Jesus meek and mild' than in this section of Mark's Gospel. He is shown freeing the people from the shackles of the past, from slavery to the religion of the past, from sickness and sin, which are the accumulated consequences of the past. And he does so with no regard for his own personal safety or reputation.

---

make any real zodiacal connection based on character or actions. The names give us some information. James and John, called 'Sons of Thunder', seem to have a martial quality and could be associated with Aries and Scorpio, the Mars-ruled signs. They are the ones who impetuously leave their father to go and follow Jesus (Mark 1:20); they wish to call down thunder upon the Samaritan villages (Luke 9:54), and they are the ones who request power in the kingdom (Mark 10:35-45), a very Scorpionic thing to do, as we shall see. Philip, whose name in Greek means 'Lover of Horses', could be associated with Sagittarius, and Thomas, called in John's Gospel *Didymus*, the Twin, may represent Gemini. Judas is probably associated with Judah, and hence with Leo, but there is a strong case to be made for a Scorpio attribution: secrecy and betrayal are not generally thought to be Leonine characteristics. The names tell us little more than this. Peter's name ('Rock') associates him with Taurus, but his impetuosity suggests Aries, and his vacillation indicates Pisces! Without recourse to legendary material – and imagination – we can go no further.

Aries (Mark 1:1-3:35)

The Aries Miracles

Your problem is you're ... too busy holding on to your unworthiness.
(Ram Dass, born 6 April 1931)

Although Jesus 'heals many people of various diseases' (Mark 1:34), there are four accounts of specific healings, each of which has an Aries signature. The Healing of the Leper (Mark 1:40-45) emphasizes the newness of life to which the spiritual aspirant is called. Physical leprosy, which was incurable until the twentieth century, was the ancient world's most feared disease, and was characterized by wasted muscles, gross disfigurement, anaesthetized limbs, progressive mental decay and certain death. Lepers had to live apart from the community and, in the Middle Ages, the priest would actually read the burial service over the living leper. As William Barclay says, 'the leper was a man who was already dead, though still alive' (Barclay, *Mark*, page 45). Physical leprosy has been overcome by modern drugs (although, to our shame, there are still lepers), but spiritual leprosy is still as prevalent as ever it was. Leprosy here is a metaphor for that deadness of spirit and disenchantment with life, which so many have to suffer in the cultural and spiritual desert of prosperous societies. It is the 'living death' which the poets have told us about, in which, with Hamlet, we view existence as 'dull, stale, flat, and unprofitable', and with Macbeth as 'a tale told by an idiot'. Leprosy is the evangelist's term for that sense of futility and alienation that we experience in T.S. Eliot's *The Waste Land*, the 'inauthentic' existence of the existentialists, from which the power of the Christ within can release us.

The Cure of the Paralytic (Mark 2:1-12), and the Cure of the Man with a Withered Hand (Mark 3:1-6), concern the most common disorder of the spiritual life – spiritual impotence. Its main symptom is that sense of powerlessness we feel in regard to the past. We tell ourselves – and we are told – that we are victims of our circumstances, our parents, our culture, our society. The claims of the past upon us are so great that we feel incapable of sloughing them off, of starting again, of taking control. We are borne along on a symbolic stretcher, carried by other people, unable to make our own decisions, tangled up in the web of other people's power and influence. 'It's too late to change, now,' we think. 'I've always done things this way.' This is spiritual torpor, and we've all got it, or had it. Jesus says two things to the paralysed man, which, as the story makes clear, are really the same thing: 'Your sins are forgiven', and 'Take up your bed and walk!' 'Your sins are

65

forgiven' is not uttered as some magical formula which will ensure a passage to heaven; it is a statement of fact. It means that the past is over, so leave it, don't allow it to cripple you, don't let it continue to blight your present or your future. And 'Take up your bed and walk!' means: 'Get up, grow up, stop being a victim, leave your comfortable but debilitating habits, and start to transform your life now'. This same idea is reinforced in the story of the man with the withered hand: what better image is there for the restoration of full control to one who is approaching life with a diminished sense of personal power?

These are undoubtedly Arien themes, but Aries appears in an apparently inconsequential element, too. The paralysed man is lowered down to Jesus *through the roof* of the house. In the 'Zodiacal Man' Aries rules the head and so, by analogy, the top of anything, including roofs. What looks like a memorable, authenticating detail is yet another zodiacal signature.

The fourth miracle, the Cure of Peter's Mother-in-law, is dealt with below.

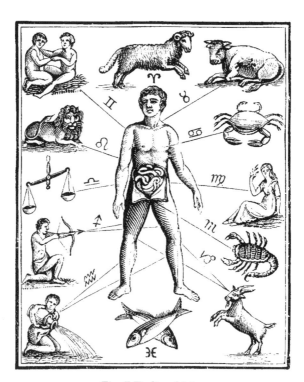

Fig. 7 Zodiacal Man

Aries (Mark 1:1-3:35)

The Decans of Aries

Cetus, Perseus and Cassiopeia, the three non-zodiacal constellations which surround Aries (its 'decans'), are quite clearly reflected in these first three chapters of Mark. Cetus, the Sea-monster, is one of the largest constellations in the sky, extending 50 degrees in length and 20 degrees in breadth. It is associated mythologically with the creature sent to devour Andromeda, but which was turned to stone by the sight of the Medusa's severed head in Perseus' hand. The combat between Perseus and Cetus mirrors the challenge to the powers of evil which Jesus makes in these early chapters of Mark. He is tempted by Satan in the wilderness (Mark 1:13); he casts out an unclean spirit (Mark 1:21-8); he declares that the kingdom of Satan is at an end (Mark 3:26), and he implies that Satan has been 'bound' (Mark 3:27), clearly reflecting the names of two stars in Cetus: Menkar, *The Chained Enemy*, and Diphda, *The Overthrown, The Thrust-down*.

The name 'Satan' (which means *Adversary*) occurs only six times in this Gospel, and four of them are in the Aries section. This is all the more noteworthy when we consider the meaning of the name Algol, one of the principal stars in Perseus. Allen writes:

Algol, the Demon, the Demon Star, and the Blinking Demon ... the Demon's Head, is said to have been thus called from its rapid and wonderful variations ... The Hebrews knew Algol as Rosh ha Satan, Satan's Head ... Astrologers of course said that it was the most unfortunate, violent and dangerous star in the heavens. (Allen, page 161)

(Algol was also associated by the ancients with beheading, another reason why the Arien John the Baptist is said to have met this particular fate.)

Aratos calls the constellation Perseus 'The Bridegroom' (i.e. the bridegroom of Andromeda), the very term that Jesus uses in explaining why his disciples do not fast (Mark 2: 18-20):

Now John's disciples and the Pharisees were fasting. Some people came and asked Jesus, 'How is it that John's disciples and the disciples of the Pharisees are fasting, but yours are not?' Jesus answered, 'How can the guests of the bridegroom fast while he is with them? They cannot, so long as they have him with them. But the time will come when the bridegroom will be taken from them, and on that day they will fast.'

Fig. 8 Cassiopeia

The Cure of Peter's Mother-in-law (Mark 1:29-31)

As soon as they left the synagogue, they went with James and John to the home of Simon and Andrew. Simon's mother-in-law was in bed with a fever, and they immediately told Jesus about her. So he went to her, took her hand and helped her up. The fever left her and she began to wait on them.

This short account of what is an unremarkable cure of an unnamed woman reads like an actual reminiscence, and many have assumed that it appears here because Peter was the source of much of Mark's information. But the matter-of-factness of the story is deceptive, since it reflects, in a rather amusing way, the constellation Cassiopeia, one of the decans of Aries.

The mythological Cassiopeia was the wife of Cepheus and the mother of Andromeda whom Perseus had married after releasing her from the rock to which she had been chained by the sea-god Poseidon. Cassiopeia was eventually translated to the sky by her enemies the sea-nymphs but, because of her vanity and arrogance, was placed so close to the pole that she appears to be lying prone. As Milton has it in *Il Penseroso*:

> ... that starr'd Ethiop queen that strove
> To set beauty's praise above
> The sea-nymphs, and their power offended.

Aratos, describing the shape of this easily identifiable constellation two and a half centuries before the Christian era, said that she no longer sits comfortably on her throne, but 'headlong plunges like a diver'. The Romans called the constellation *Mulier Sedis*, the Woman of the Chair.

Mark's text says that Jesus and his apostles went to visit *Simon's* mother-in-law, but Matthew's Gospel uses Simon's other name 'Peter', and Peter, of course, means 'rock'. The woman was 'reclining' (*katakeito* – a word used for reclining at the meal table), in the grip of a high fever. Jesus cures her with a word and a touch and she gets up and waits upon them. The mother of the one chained ('married') to the rock (Peter) is Cassiopeia (the Reclining Woman). Cassiopeia's husband is Cepheus and her daughter is Andromeda, names which are hinted at in the names Andrew and Cephas (the Aramaic version of Peter). These few lines contain a series of puns which are lost on us, but which would have brought a little smile to people who had some familiarity with the skies. The 'transvaluative' spiritual message (see page 17) is clear, too: by rising up and serving Jesus and his friends, she is shown to be released from both the ancient curse, and the arrogance which originally provoked it.

The fever from which this woman was suffering was – and still is – a common complaint in that part of the world, and is a typical ailment of the Fire sign Aries. No doubt in the belief that like cures like, the remedy was typically Arien, too. The Talmud gives detailed instructions about how it should be cured. An iron knife was to be tied by a strand of hair to a thorn bush, and on three successive days one had to repeat verses from Exodus chapter 3 (2-3, 4-5). Iron and thorns are both associated with Mars, the ruler of Aries; hair is taken from the head (Aries), and the Exodus passage is the account of Moses with the Burning Bush! Four clear indications of Aries. A fifth is in the name of the constellation Cassiopeia, which is derived from the Phoenician and means – appropriately for a feverish woman – 'The Rose-Coloured Face'! (http://www.ufrsd.net/staffwww/stefanl/myths/cassiopeia.htm)

Jesus rejects his family

The Aries section ends with the much-misunderstood passage concerning the family of Jesus. It reads:

> Then Jesus' mother and brothers arrived. Standing outside, they sent some-
> one in to call him. A crowd was sitting around him, and they told him, 'Your
> mother and brothers are outside looking for you.' 'Who are my mother and
> my brothers?' he asked. Then he looked at those seated in a circle around
> him and said, 'Here are my mother and my brothers! Whoever does God's
> will is my brother and sister and mother.' (Mark 3:31-35)

Commentators have had difficulty with this passage because no amount
of glossing can explain the callousness which Jesus seems to display. If
it is a genuine historical incident, then Jesus shows a disregard for his
family which, to the contemporary sentimental religionist, appears less than
exemplary.

But we do not need to interpret it in this way. Instead we can view it as a
symbolic rejection of all those inherited influences which subtly inhibit any
attempt we might make to discover our own unique calling. The family is
the carrier of culture and we are encouraged to obey its voice as we set the
goals for our life. Refusal to conform takes enormous courage, particularly
when one's particular family has all the trappings of apparent respectability
and success. But as Arien Erich Fromm (born 23 March 1900) tells us, individuality has a high price: 'When one has become an individual, one stands
alone and faces the world in all its perilous and overpowering aspects'
(Fromm, page 23). This is too daunting for many.

In his account of the spiritual requirements symbolized by Aries, Dane
Rudhyar, one of the foremost astrological thinkers of the twentieth century,
says that leading a spiritual life – which, whatever else it is, is a life of
genuine self-discovery, of establishing individuality – is never easy because
it 'implies an emergence from usually quite binding and possessive psychic
and social matrices: family, culture, religion, tradition, way of life' (Rudhyar,
page 64), and this will often involve strenuous confrontation.

The first three chapters of Mark dramatically describe the qualities
required to effect just such an emergence from restrictive social ties. They
are the qualities displayed by the archetypal Arien, Abraham, who found
the ram caught in the thicket, and who left the land of his birth to go to a
place that God would show him. They are the qualities of Moses as he
leaves the securities of Egypt in order to find the promised land. They are
the qualities of the Buddha as he rejects the luxuries of home in his pursuit of enlightenment, and of Huckleberry Finn as he travels down the
river in search of himself.

They are the qualities which all who seek to follow Jesus must cultivate as
they prepare to embark on the interior journey.

Taurus (Mark 4:1–4:34)
Sowing, Reaping and Shining

The best of us still have our aspirations for the supreme goals of life, which is so often mocked by prosperous people who now control the world. We still believe that the world has a deeper meaning than what is apparent, and that therein the human soul finds its ultimate harmony and peace. We still know that only in spiritual wealth does civilization attain its end, not in a prolific production of materials, and not in the competition of intemperate power with power. (Rabindranath Tagore, born 6 May 1861)

Taurus and Venus

A poll among BBC Radio 4 listeners in the summer of 2005 found that Britain's favourite philosopher was Karl Marx. The runner-up was David Hume, and in third place was Ludwig Wittgenstein. Immanuel Kant was sixth. All of these were born under the sign of Taurus. In fact, since no one knows the birthdays of Socrates, Plato, Aristotle and St Thomas Aquinas, only two of the top ten – Karl Popper (Leo), and Friedrich Nietzsche (Libra)

– were certainly *not* born under Taurus.* This is a remarkable statistic, and although it may be dismissed as 'coincidental' by mathematicians, it should come as no surprise to students of astrology. Taurus is the sign which symbolizes our relationship with the material universe, and so its sons and daughters should have a particular interest in attempting to define the nature of that relationship, which, on one level at least, is the function of philosophy.

As Aries symbolizes the sprouting seed struggling for life amidst the forces of decay, so Taurus represents the next stage of the process: establishing roots which will supply nourishment to the growing plant. After the primary impulse of the Cardinal sign comes the crystallization of Fixity. Symbolically, the raw energies of Aries are collected, shaped, and given direction in Taurus. The momentum is slowed and practical issues have to be faced. This is a natural process of development for any activity: the force of the initial impulse is often tremendous, but it lacks effectiveness until it has encountered the real world of experience.

In astrology, Taurus represents the 'real world'. In addition to being a Fixed sign, it is also an Earth sign concerned with life's tangible paraphernalia, such as houses and chattels, and also its sensual pleasures. It is the sign of the builder, and it is surely not without significance that some of the human race's grandest structures – including Stonehenge and the pyramids of Egypt – were erected during the astrological age of Taurus (c 4,000–c 2,000 BCE). Taurus is the Bull, archetypal symbol of the earth and sacrificial victim of the devotees of Mithras, and of the nature-worshippers with whom the Hebrew prophets strove tirelessly, albeit vainly, for control of the popular mind. Its hieroglyph (♉) is the bull's head and horns. The Jews called Taurus *Bayt*, a word meaning 'house', and the building of Solomon's Temple ('The House of the Lord') was begun when the sun was in Taurus (1 Kings 6:1). Among the Jewish tribes it was assigned variously to Manasseh and Ephraim (the sons of Joseph), or to Simeon and Levi.

Astrological writers have not been terribly kind to Taurus (despite its

* Karl Marx 5 May 1818; David Hume 26 April 1711; Ludwig Wittgenstein 26 April 1889; Immanuel Kant 22 April 1724. Other famous Taurean philosophers include Marcus Aurelius 26 April 121; John Stuart Mill 20 May 1806; Fichte 19 May 1762; Carnap 18 May 1891; Bertrand Russell 18 May 1872; Kierkegaard 5 May 1818; and Thomas Reid 26 April 1710. Thomas Aquinas was called 'The Dumb Ox' by his student peers, and this almost certainly indicates Taurus. May (Taurus) birthdays have been suggested for both Socrates and Plato. See David Perkins, 'Socrates, the Man, his Ideas, and his Horoscope' at Matrix Software/Articles. http://www.astrologysoftware.com/resources/articles/getarticle.asp?ID=75. Perkins says that 'Socrates' birth was recorded as being May 20, 466 BC at 12 noon in Athens, Greece.' The Ancient/Classical history site says that Plato was born around 21 May 427 BC. I don't know the source of either of these conjectures.

association with philosophy), often depicting it as gross and materialistic, and those in whom its characteristics are most evident as slow-witted, rather dull, and fitted for work of a practical nature. 'Taurus,' says Carter, 'tends to agricultural pursuits' (Carter, 1925, page 68), although he is quick to point out that this assessment is based on traditional accounts of the sign. The tradition was probably very old even when Manilius wrote the following:

> Dull honest Plowmen to manure the Field
> Strong Taurus bears, by him the Grounds are till'd,
> No gaudy things he breeds, no Prize for worth,
> But Blessed Earth, and brings her Labour forth;
> He takes the Yoke, nor doth the Plough disdain,
> And teacheth Farmers to manure the Plain:
> He's their Example, when he bears the Sun
> In his bright Horns, the noble toyl's begun;
> The useful Plowshare he retrieves from Rust,
> Nor lies at ease, and wants his strength in Dust.
> (Manilius 1697, page 124)

The Taurean philosophers don't generally plough the fields, but they tend to expound one version or another of 'no nonsense' materialism, which Britain's Radio 4 listeners seem to find congenial. Marx's 'dialectical materialism', John Stuart Mill's Utilitarianism, and David Hume's scepticism, all bear the unmistakable signature of Taurus. Thomas Reid was called 'the common sense philosopher'; Bertrand Russell was a thoroughgoing materialist, prepared even to reduce human thought to chemistry; and Wittgenstein, who, in true Taurus style, designed and built a house in Vienna for his sister, summed up the anti-metaphysical bias of Taurus when he said, 'Whereof we cannot speak, thereof we must be silent'.

The 'ruler' of Taurus is Venus, the beautiful Morning and Evening Star. Venus complements the positive, 'masculine' qualities of Mars. Its glyph (♀), which has become the universal symbol of the feminine, shows the circle of spirit above the cross of matter, symbolizing the predominance of receptivity and nurture over aggression and enterprise. Ptolemy has this to say about the astrological nature of this planet:

Venus ... causes fame, honour, happiness, abundance, happy marriage, many children ... the increase of property ... she brings about ... successes, profits, and the full rising of rivers; of useful animals and the fruits of the earth she is the pre-eminent cause of abundance, good yields, and profit. (Pages 185-7)

The association of Taurus with agriculture is very ancient and widespread. The Pleiades, a prominent and beautiful group of stars in the shoulder of the Bull, was used to mark the seasons in ancient times. Philo of Alexandria, Mark's contemporary, tells us that the rising and occultation of the Pleiades bring great benefits to human beings:

> For when they set, the furrows are ploughed up for the purpose of sowing; and when they are about to rise, they bring glad tidings of harvest; and after they have arisen, they awaken the rejoicing husbandmen to the collection of their necessary food. And they with joy store up their food for their daily use. (Philo, page 17)

The natives of the Tonga Islands used these stars to divide the year into seasons, and Hippocrates 'made much of the Pleiades, dividing the year into four seasons, all connected with their position in relation to the sun'. They are the 'hoeing-stars' of South Africa, and 'take the place of a farming-calendar to the Solomon Islanders, and their last visible rising after sunset is, or has been, celebrated with rejoicings all over the southern hemisphere as betokening the waking-up time to agricultural activity' (Allen, pages 400-401). Virgil, in his First Georgic, mentions how those farmers who don't refer to the Pleiades when planting usually pay a heavy price:

> Some that before the fall oth' Pleiades
> Began to sowe, deceaved in the increase,
> Have reapt wilde oates for wheate.

The 'sweet delights' of the Pleiades are mentioned in the Book of Job (Job 38:31). This refers principally to their beauty, but there is also a possibility that it describes the sensual concerns of Taurus, the constellation of which the Pleiades is the most beautiful and conspicuous feature.

The Spiritual Lessons of Taurus

In the light of these testimonies to the Taurus/Venus association with farming, growth, abundance and fecundity, it can be no coincidence that in this clearly defined second section of his Gospel Mark has drawn together a number of parables which, with one exception, are concerned with these

very themes. (But the 'exception' is still related to Taurus, as we shall see.)*
Mark's parable section begins with the Taurean figure of the sower going
out to sow his seed:

> 'Listen! A farmer went out to sow his seed. As he was scattering the seed, some
> fell along the path, and the birds came and ate it up. Some fell on rocky places,
> where it did not have much soil. It sprang up quickly, because the soil was shal-
> low. But when the sun came up, the plants were scorched, and they withered
> because they had no root. Other seed fell among thorns, which grew up and
> choked the plants, so that they did not bear grain. Still other seed fell on good
> soil. It came up, grew and produced a crop, some multiplying thirty, some sixty,
> some a hundred times.' Then Jesus said, 'Whoever has ears to hear, let them
> hear.' (Mark 4:3-9)

The 'explanation' of this parable which Jesus is said to have delivered privately to his apostles (Mark 4:10-20), spells out what the Taurus phase of the
spiritual life demands of us: we need to have the Taurean virtues of
endurance and stability in addition to the Arien ones of enthusiasm and
vigour. The seed that falls by the side of the road never even begins to put
down roots. This is a warning that the spiritual impulse alone is not enough.
The desire may be sown in the heart, but without adequate nurture it will
easily be destroyed. Similarly with the seed that falls on the rocky ground:
this flourishes for a while but, lacking any real foundation, it soon withers in
the face of difficult circumstances. The spiritual life requires perseverance
and tenacity, the two most striking Taurean qualities. Isabelle Pagan writes
of the Taurus type:

> The chief characteristic of the highly developed Taurean type is his
> stability of character and of purpose. He is the steadfast mind, unshaken
> in adversity, and his is the power of quiet persistence in the face of
> difficulties ... in hard circumstances his patience and perseverance are
> marvellous. (Pagan, page 23)

There is another side to Taurus, however, which is not so admirable from a
spiritual point of view, and which this parable clearly admonishes us to
avoid: conformity with the world and its values. The thorns that choke the

---

* The parallel section in Matthew (chapter 13) contains even more parables than Mark's,
each one of which employs Taurean imagery: The Wheat and the Tares (Matthew 13: 24-30);
The Hidden Treasure (Matthew 13: 44); The Pearl of Great Price (Matthew 13: 45-6); The Net
(Matthew 13: 47-50). Mark has obviously shortened the original, which he admits at chapter 4
verse 33: 'With *many similar* parables Jesus spoke the word to them.'

plant are the 'cares of the age and the deceit of wealth' (Mark 4:19), which seduce the seeker from the things of the spirit. The realm of Taurus is the realm of the flesh and its appetites, and this is in constant warfare with the things of the spirit. Chaucer's Wife of Bath puts her own lasciviousness down to Mars rising in Taurus in her horoscope:

> For certes, I am al venerien
> In feelynge, and myn herte is marcien.
> Venus me yaf my lust, my likerousnesse,
> And mars yaf me my sturdy hardynesse
> Myn ascendant was taur, and mars therinne,
> Allas! allas! that evere love was synne!
> (Wife of Bath's Prologue, lines 609-614)

In the Jewish scriptures we observe that the 'flesh-pots' of Egypt (Exodus 16:3) are a perpetual source of temptation to the newly freed Israelites. Their spiritual resolve is weakened by the 'sweet delights' of Taurus for which Egypt is the biblical symbol.* But for all that their bellies were full when they lived there, they were in bondage, the peculiarly seductive bondage of materialism which this passage in Mark warns us to break away from. As Fred Gettings reminds us, Taurus 'is always productive' (Gettings, 1972, page 39), but if this productivity is seen entirely in terms of dividends, shares, bank accounts and bull markets, then the spiritual journey will be cut short before it has really begun.

Dane Rudhyar considers that the spiritual lesson of the Taurus phase is non-possessiveness because 'Where there is possessiveness ... there can be no spiritual living'. He goes on:

> The zodiacal sign Taurus is traditionally thought to be a possessive sign, but its possessiveness arises from its concentration upon productivity. In order to produce a rich harvest, limits have to be set to the field in which natural processes have to operate efficiently. There must be a concentration of efforts, a focusing will to keep away all interfering activity ... Possession, however, need not mean binding attachment. There is a level at which the Taurean capacity to produce fruits can operate, not in an 'indefinite' but rather in a multi-defined or universally operative manner. Thus one can transcend the 'This is mine' mentality. (Rudhyar, 1979, pages 66-7)

---

* According to Philo of Alexandria, Egypt symbolizes 'the passions which excite the body' (Philo, page 147).

It is remarkable how the sentiments – and the imagery – of Rudhyar in this passage reflect those of the Markan parable under review. Both are designed to teach us that the Taurean attributes of endurance and tenacity will reap enormous benefits if they are applied to the spiritual and not to the material life, and that the 'sweet delights' of the world must never be allowed to deflect us from our spiritual purpose. The things of Taurus can be massive impediments to the life of the spirit, but they do not have to be, and cultivating a proper relationship with them is a vitally important spiritual task – probably the hardest spiritual task we are called upon to undertake.

Buddhism, with its emphasis on ascetic detachment and the eventual elimination of desire, offers one way of dealing with the material world, and is strongly connected with Taurus; both the birth and the enlightenment of the Buddha are celebrated at the time of the May full moon, when the sun is in the sign of the Bull. The Taurean Karl Marx was also acutely aware of the impediments that the lust of ownership places in the way of human spiritual and cultural development, and his celebrated dictum, 'From each according to his ability, to each according to his need', offers an economic and political solution to the perennial problems of attachment and possession.

The Jesuit geologist and mystic, Pierre Teilhard de Chardin (born 1 May 1881), expressed his Taurean commitment to the reality and importance of the physical world so clearly and so passionately that he was accused of pantheism by the heresy hunters among his fellow religionists. For Teilhard the world was holy, a sacrament of the divine, and a means by which we can all find our way to God. In *The Divine Milieu* he wrote:

> Matter, you in whom I find both seduction and strength, you in whom I find blandishment and virility, you who can enrich and destroy, I surrender myself to your mighty layers, with faith in the heavenly influences which have sweetened and purified your waters. The virtue of Christ has passed into you. Let your attractions lead me forward, let your sap be the food that nourishes me; let your resistance give me toughness; let your robberies and inroads give me freedom. And finally, let your whole being lead me towards Godhead. (Pages 110-111)

Taurus and Light

The parable of the Light under a Bushel which follows the Sower does not have the Taurean imagery of growth and productivity, except in rather an oblique sense, but it is related to Taurus nevertheless because, in addition to

77

its association with the earth and with agriculture, *Taurus was always considered by the ancients to be connected with light.* Alice Bailey writes:

> Light, illumination, and sound, as an expression of the creative force: these are the three basic ideas connected with this constellation. The 'interpreter of the divine voice' as Taurus was called in ancient Egypt, can be paraphrased into Christian terminology and called 'the Word made flesh'. It is an interesting sidelight on the power of the zodiacal influences to recall that the bull's eye lantern can be traced back to the bull's eye in Taurus, and the pontifical bull, or the papal enunciations which were regarded as interpreters of God's voice, is a term in common usage today ... The consummation of the work that is undertaken in Taurus, and the result of the Taurean influence, is the glorification of matter and subsequent illumination through its medium.' (Bailey, 1974, pages 44-5)

For the mystic, the material world is neither an idol to be worshipped, nor a distraction to be despised; it is instead the very vehicle of our enlightenment. In the words of Gerard Manley Hopkins:

> The world is charged with the grandeur of God.
> It will flame out like shining from shook foil.

Hopkins' fellow Jesuit, Teilhard de Chardin, echoes these sentiments:

> Throughout my whole life, during every moment I have lived, the world has gradually been taking on light and fire for me, until it has come to envelop me in one mass of luminosity, flowing from within ... The purple flush of matter fading imperceptibly into the gold of spirit, to be lost finally in the incandescence of a personal universe ... This is what I have learnt from my contact with the earth – the diaphany of the divine at the heart of the glowing universe, the divine radiating from the depths of matter a-flame. (Teilhard de Chardin, page 13)

The light which breaks through the material world and leads us to enlightenment provides the mystical connection between Taurus and Light, but there is a more obvious astronomical one: in and around the constellation are some of the most spectacular sights in the night sky.

In Akkadia Taurus was known as The Bull of Light, and Orion, one of the decans of Taurus, 'admired in all historic ages as the most strikingly brilliant of the stellar groups' (Allen, page 303), derives its name from the Akkadian Uru-anna, *the Light of Heaven,* and Seiss says that the name means 'He who Cometh Forth as Light, The Brilliant, The Swift' (Seiss, page 105). It is one of the most easily recognized sights in the heavens, and its clarity and brilliance were the basis of Gerard Manley Hopkins' metaphor, 'for thou art above, thou Orion of light,' in his poem *The Wreck of the Deutschland.* And Aldebaran, one of the most brilliant stars in Taurus, and principal star of the Hyades group, situated in the 'eye' of the Bull, was called by Ptolemy Lampadias, *the Torch.* Venus, the ruler of Taurus and the most brilliant sight in the evening and morning sky (after the moon), was called by the Greeks Phos, *Light,* and by the Romans Lucifer, *The Light Bearer.* To the ancient occultists, Venus was the planet of inner light, illumination.

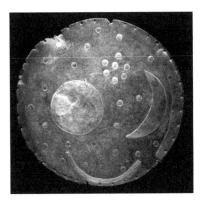

Fig. 9 The Nebra Disc (dating from c.1600 BCE).
The Pleiades are at the top right.

In the shoulder of the Bull are the Pleiades which, although not especially bright, are undoubtedly among the most observed and noted stars in the sky, inspiring astronomers, poets and myth-makers since the dawn of time. Many cultures throughout history have referred to the Pleiades as a Hen with her Chickens, another instance, says Allen, 'of the constant association of the Pleiades with flocking birds, and here especially appropriate from their compact grouping. Aben Ragel and other Hebrew writers mentioned them, sometimes with the Coop that held them ... these also appearing in Arabic folk-lore and still current among the English peasantry.' (Allen, page 399)

One is immediately reminded of the saying of Jesus reported by Matthew and Luke:

'O Jerusalem, Jerusalem, you who kill the prophets and stone those sent to you, how often I have longed to gather your children together, as a hen gathers her chicks under her wings, but you were not willing!' (Luke 13:34. A parallel passage can be found in Matthew 23:37.)

(Matthew locates the saying in his general condemnation of the Pharisees but, in Luke, *it appears close by the Parables of the Mustard Seed and the Leaven*.)

To the Hindus the Pleiades were said to represent Agni, the god of fire, and Allen thinks that Divali, the great Hindu Feast of Lamps, is held in October-November in honour of this constellation. However, some confusion exists as to how many stars the naked eye can see in this group. Some say six, some seven. Keats calls them 'the Starry Seven' in *Endymion*, and in China they were worshipped by girls and young women as The Seven Sisters of Industry. Homer mentions six, Aratos seven, although he goes on:

Seven are they in the songs of men, albeit only six are visible to the eyes. Yet not a star, I ween, has perished from the sky unmarked since the earliest memory of man, but even so the tale is told. Those seven are called by name *Halcyone, Merope, Celaeno, Electra, Sterope, Taygete,* and queenly *Maia*. Small and dim are they all alike, but widely famed they wheel in heaven at morn and eventide, by the will of Zeus, who bade them tell of the beginning of Summer and of Winter and of the coming of the ploughing-time. (Aratus, page 227-8)

Ovid writes: *Quae septem dici, sex tamen esse solent* (Allen, page 411).

Eratosthenes called it *Pleias Eptasteros*, the Seven-starred Pleiad, although he said that one of them is *Panaphanes* – 'All-invisible'. *One of the stars of the Pleiades is hidden.* According to the myth, the Pleiades were the seven daughters of Atlas, who had been changed into stars by Pleione. Six of them had been married to gods, but the seventh, Merope, had married a mortal, so her light was dim and rarely seen. All of which strikingly reflects the Parable of the Lamp in Mark 4:21-22:

He said to them, 'Do you bring in a lamp to put it under a bowl or a bed? Instead, don't you put it on its stand? For whatever is hidden is meant to be disclosed [*phanerôthê*], and whatever is concealed is meant to be brought out into the open [*phaneron*]. If anyone has ears to hear, let them hear.'

(Notice how Mark uses the words *phanerôthê* and *phaneron*, verbs from the same root as *panophanes*, the word used by Eratosthenes to describe the invisible seventh Pleiad.)

Matthew's version, which is found in the Sermon on the Mount (5:14-16) is slightly different, but its verbs reflect the Greek name of Aldebaran, *Lampadias*, better than Mark's:

> You are the light of the world. A city on a hill cannot be hidden. Neither do people light a lamp and put it under a bowl. Instead they put it on a stand, and it gives light [*lampei*] to everyone in the house. In the same way, let your light shine [*lampsatō*] before men, that they may see your good deeds and praise your Father in heaven.

Since Aldebaran was called Oculus Tauri or The Bull's Eye, and even God's Eye, it is interesting to note that *immediately* after his version of the Parable of the Lamp, Luke adds:

> Your eye is the lamp of your body. When your eyes are good, your whole body also is full of light. But when they are bad, your body also is full of darkness. See to it, then, that the light within you is not darkness. Therefore, if your whole body is full of light, and no part of it dark, it will be completely lighted, as when the light of a lamp shines on you. (Luke 11: 34-36)

This Parable of the Lamp refers to the Taurean tendency to keep itself to itself. Gettings comments:

> On this level (the material), he is indeed the bull, guarding that which is his own, be it his pathetic strip of field, or his vast acres, his single cow or his herd ... He likes to be left alone in his field, lording it over his own, not caring over much for other people. (Gettings, 1972, page 39)

This proclivity towards insularity, the tendency to rest on laurels, and to be satisfied with the status quo, is not spiritually productive. To be effective, the lamp has to be seen. To be productive, our spiritual life has to be focused outward, away from our own petty concerns. To rest content with what we have achieved is to hide our light. We must press onward.

The two sayings which follow (Mark 4:24-25) continue the Taurean theme of growth and productivity. The first has a karmic ring to it, telling us that what we give out will be what we get back. The second is one of the most 'difficult' sayings in the New Testament:

> 'Consider carefully what you hear,' he continued. 'With the measure you use, it will be measured to you —and even more. Those who have will be given more; as for those who do not have, even what they have will be taken from them.' (Mark 4:24-5)

This seems to be a description of contemporary western economics, but we hardly expect to find it being endorsed by the Bible. However, the principle does not concern secular affairs. It relates to the laws of growth which govern the spiritual life, which do not favour an attitude of making do with what we have. The reward is to the one who is constantly discontented with his achievement and who presses on to even higher goals. As the medieval alchemists observed, 'You must have some gold before you can make more gold.'

Secrets and Parables

He also said, 'This is what the kingdom of God is like. A man scatters seed on the ground. Night and day, whether he sleeps or gets up, the seed sprouts and grows, though he does not know how. All by itself the soil produces grain — first the stalk, then the head, then the full kernel in the head. As soon as the grain is ripe, he puts the sickle to it, because the harvest has come.' Again he said, 'What shall we say the kingdom of God is like, or what parable shall we use to describe it? It is like a mustard seed, which is the smallest of all seeds on earth. Yet when planted, it grows and becomes the largest of all garden plants, with such big branches that the birds can perch in its shade.' (Mark 4:26-32)

The agricultural imagery pervades the next two little sub-sections, which refer specifically to the kingdom of God. To the Jewish people of the time this term would probably have been understood as a literal kingdom which would be set up, on earth, by the promised Messiah. This had been the united testimony of the Hebrew prophets. Such a kingdom would have an observable beginning and would be preceded by the kind of cosmic cataclysms that the apocalyptic literature (e.g. Joel 2) had so graphically described. However, these two similes in Mark seem to point in a different direction. The first one (Mark 4:26-29) tells us that the kingdom will grow in a way that defies our powers of observation and understanding, just as a seed grows in a field. The second (Mark 4:30-32) likens the kingdom to the tiny mustard seed which produces a plant of such prodigious size that all the 'birds of the air can settle in its shade'.

Christian scholars generally associate these parables with the slow but inevitable growth of the Church, and assume that, in some way, the kingdom of God and the Christian Church are virtually synonymous. This is an obvious inference to make, but the obvious inferences are the misleading ones, because earlier in the chapter Jesus explains that the parables were not intended to elucidate anything, but were deliberately used to *hide* meanings from profane ears. Strangely, Jesus was using parables to keep the crowd in the dark; he only explained the mysteries to his apostles:

> When he was alone, the Twelve and the others around him asked him about the parables. He told them, 'The secret of the kingdom of God has been given to you. But to those on the outside everything is said in parables so that, "they may be ever seeing but never perceiving, and ever hearing but never understanding; otherwise they might turn and be forgiven!"' (Mark 4:10-12)

Some scholars have suggested that Mark has mistaken the nature of the parable itself as a teaching vehicle, and saw it as a means of confusing rather than enlightening. This hardly seems plausible. The parable was a universally used teaching method of the Jewish rabbis. Its object was to startle the hearer into response and to entertain at the same time; it was not a riddle or puzzle intended to perplex. What seems far more likely is that Jesus' enigmatic remark is Mark's way of telling his reader that there is more in these stories than any purely exoteric interpretation can yield; that, as we saw in the Aries section, the kingdom is indeed within the individual and that the laws of its growth and cultivation are entirely different from those that operate within the secular world.

Jesus' words here are only intelligible if we assume that the mysteries of the kingdom of God formed part of a body of esoteric teachings which was transmitted to a few, those 'inside the house' (Mark 7:17), but kept from the many, 'those on the outside' (Mark 4:11). Such an understanding was not foreign to the Fathers of the early church. For example, Origen writes:

> I have not yet spoken of the observance of all that is written in the Gospels, each one of which contains much doctrine difficult to be understood not merely by the multitude, but even by certain of the more intelligent, which Jesus delivered to 'those without' while reserving the exhibition of their full meaning for those who had passed beyond the stage of exoteric teaching and who came to Him privately in the house. And when he comes to understand it, he will admire the reason why some are said to be 'without', and others 'in the house'. (Besant, page 63)

References to this esoteric teaching are also made by Polycarp of Smyrna and Clement of Alexandria. Their combined testimony seems to point towards a 'gnosis', a hidden (probably oral) spiritual wisdom kept from catechumens but preserved by initiates. If this is so, then the link between Gnosticism and the Gospels is more real than orthodox scholars are generally prepared to admit.

When Mark's two final Taurean parables are viewed as metaphors of the spiritual life, rather than as allegories about the growth of the church, the paradoxical nature of the kingdom becomes evident. The first one tells us that spiritual growth does not come by concentrating on its cultivation. It is a by-product of other things. Just as the seed grows while the farmer sleeps, so our spirituality increases as we go about our normal affairs. Victor Frankl has expressed this in psychological terms as follows:

> The more (a person) forgets himself – by giving himself to a cause to serve or another person to love – the more human he is and the more he actualizes himself. What is called self-actualization is not an attainable aim at all, for the simple reason that the more one would strive for it, the more he would miss it. In other words, self-actualization is possible only as a side-effect of self-transcendence. (Frankl, page 133)

Krishnamurti (born 12 May 1895) says much the same about true happiness which, like Frankl's 'self-transcendence', is a good secular synonym for what Mark understands by 'the kingdom of God'. Such states are not the product of material accumulation or of self-conscious spiritual 'development'. They come upon us unawares, but when they do they have enormous transforming power, not only for the one who experiences them, but for all with whom he or she comes into contact. The one in whom the seed of the spirit is planted can have an effect which transcends his own existence. He is truly 'a creative individual (in whose) action there will be the seed of a different culture' (Krishnamurti, page 155).

Gemini (Mark 4:35–6:29)
'My Name is Legion'

Do I contradict myself?
Very well then I contradict myself.
(I am large, I contain multitudes.)
  (Walt Whitman, born 31 May 1814)

Gemini and Mercury

'How significant it is,' writes Aldous Huxley in *The Perennial Philosophy*, 'that in the Indo-European languages, the root meaning of "two" should connote badness.' He goes on:

The Greek prefix dys- (as in dyspepsia) and the Latin dis- (as in dishon-ourable) are both derived from 'duo'. The cognate bis- gives a pejora-tive sense to such modern French words as bévue ('blunder', literally 'two-sight'). Traces of that 'second which leads you astray' can be found in 'dubious', 'doubt' and *Zweifel* – for to doubt is to be double-minded. Bunyan has his Mr Facing-both-ways, and modern American slang its 'two-timers'. Obscurely and unconsciously wise, our language confirms the findings of the mystics and proclaims the essential badness of division – a word, incidentally, in which our old enemy 'two' makes another decisive appearance. (Huxley, pages 11-12).

Since it is the primary contention of all mystical philosophy that reality is unitary, and the primary aim of all spiritual practice is to recognize this unity, it is fitting that any treatise on the spiritual life should contain a significant meditation on unity and division. Mark's Gospel contains such a meditation in its third section, where we are introduced to themes inspired by the constellation Gemini, the Twins, the first of those constellations called by Ptolemy 'bi-corporeal', 'double-bodied' (*disôma*), and by modern astrologers 'Mutable'. He describes them thus:

> The bicorporeal signs, Gemini, Virgo, Sagittarius, and Pisces, are those which follow the solid signs and are so called because they are between the solid and the solstitial and equinoctial signs and share, as it were, at end and beginning, the natural properties of the two states of weather ... The bicorporeal signs make souls complex, changeable, hard to apprehend, light, unstable, fickle, amorous, versatile, fond of music, lazy, easily acquisitive, prone to change their minds. (Ptolemy, pages 67-9)

Since these characteristics cover four zodiacal signs, we cannot claim that they all belong exclusively to Gemini. In fact, few astrologers today would accept that love of music, laziness, amorousness, or acquisitiveness were typically Geminian traits, but the rest seem particularly apt and feature prominently in any delineation of the Geminian type. Jeff Mayo lists the characteristics which most astrologers would accept as typifying this sign:

> Adaptable, communicative, versatile. Incessantly on the go, restless, inquisitive, liking variety and change, contriving ingenious methods for transmitting anything from here to there. In this way he is the ideal middle man, mediator. Nervously excitable, inconsistent, witty, chatty, never dull. (Mayo, 1964, page 43)

All these are really manifestations of 'duality', a factor present in all the mutable signs, but particularly evident in Gemini, because Gemini is also an Air sign, and Air is the element through which mutability or changeableness best expresses itself. The glyph of Gemini (♊) is a graphic representation of its nature: two poles, parallel but separate, joined at top and bottom, depicting a perpetual conflict between two quite distinct natures, and expressing the 'irrepressible restlessness by which man divides himself and widens his experience' (Jones, page 59). At its best it represents versatility, and the ability to be, with St Paul, all things to all men; at worst, inconstancy and even duplicity.

St Paul's Geminian qualities are further underlined by the numerous roles – spokesman, theologian, letter-writer, and missionary – which he played in the development of early Christianity, and by his *volte-face* on the road to Damascus which changed him from a fervent persecutor of the new faith to its most ardent devotee. His confession of moral turbulence in Romans 7 is a perfect expression of Geminian duality and Mercurial inconsistency.* He was even mistaken for an incarnation of Gemini's ruler, Mercury (Hermes in Greek), by the people of Lystra (Acts 14:12).

Mercury (☿) whose metal used to be called 'quicksilver', represents the whole of the cerebro-spinal system and the nerves, the 'message-bearers' of the body. It also rules the brain which, psychologists tell us, is 'bicameral', split into right and left hemispheres. The left hemisphere is rational and logical, the right affective and creative. Mercury is the fastest-moving planet in the solar system, which is probably why, in mythology, it came to represent the messenger of the gods. Ptolemy considers that when Mercury rules a horoscope the native will be 'thoughtful, learned, and inventive', but he also lists the potential negative qualities:

> ... utter rascals, precipitate, forgetful, impetuous, light-minded, fickle, prone to change their minds, foolish rogues, witless, sinful, liars, undiscriminating, unstable, undependable, avaricious, unjust, and, in general, unsteady in judgement and inclined to evil deeds. (Ptolemy, page 361)

The Spiritual Lessons of Gemini

He, the Highest Person, who is awake in us while we are asleep,
shaping one lovely bright sight after another; that indeed is the
Bright, that is Brahman, that alone is called the Immortal.
(Katha Upanishad)

This section of Mark's Gospel begins, in characteristic fashion, with a journey:

* 'I do not understand what I do. For what I want to do I do not do, but what I hate I do ... For I have the desire to do what is good, but I cannot carry it out. For what I do is not the good I want to do; no, the evil I do not want to do – this I keep on doing. Now if I do what I do not want to do, it is no longer I who do it, but sin living in me that does it.' (Romans 7: 18-20)

Geminian mutability is often expressed as mobility. Jesus has travelled before, but only in Galilee: now he and his disciples get in a boat in order to travel across the Sea of Galilee to the country of the Gerasenes, and apart from the fact that this incident takes place during a journey, there is little or nothing here that might immediately indicate the sign Gemini. However, our inability to detect the sign's presence really testifies to our ignorance of the iconography of the skies. The Hellenized audience for which Mark was writing would not have been as slow to understand as we are. Castor and Pollux, the twin stars of the constellation Gemini, *were the patrons of seafarers.* Seiss writes:

> In the Grecian temples they were represented as mounted on white horses, armed with spears, riding side by side, *crowned with the cap of the hunter, tipped with a glittering star.* ... After their return from Colchis it is said that they cleared the neighbouring seas from pirates and depredators and hence were honoured as the particular friends and protectors of navigation ... *It is further said that flames of fire were betimes seen playing around their heads,* and that when this occurred the tempest which was tossing the ocean ceased, and calm ensued ... They were assigned great power over good fortune, and particularly over the winds and waves of the sea. (Seiss, pages 112-3, emphasis added)

The ship which took St Paul from Malta to Syracuse (Acts 28:11) was called 'Castor and Pollux'. It is likely that this was a common name for vessels in view of the fact that these gods were supposedly favourable towards mariners. The constellation was often symbolized by two stars over a ship. Homer, in his *Hymn to Castor and Pollux*, wrote:

> Ye wild-eyed muses! sing the Twins of Jove,
> ... ... mild Pollux, void of blame,
> And steedsubduing Castor, heirs of fame.
> These are the Powers who earthborn mortals save
> And ships, whose flight is swift along the wave.
> When wintry tempests o'er the savage sea
> Are raging, and the sailors tremblingly
> Call on the Twins of Jove with prayers and vow,
> Gathered in fear upon the lofty prow,
> And sacrifice with snow-white lambs, the wind
> And the huge billow bursting close behind,
> Even then beneath the weltering waters bear
> The staggering ship – they suddenly appear,

Gemini (Mark 4:35–6:29)

On yellow wings rushing athwart the sky,
And lull the blasts in mute tranquillity,
And strew the waves on the white ocean's bed,
Fair omen of the voyage; from toil and dread,
The sailors rest rejoicing in the sight,
And plough the quiet sea in safe delight.
              (Translation by Shelley, Allen, pages 227-8)*

There are a few details in the story which underline its Geminian theme. The word for the storm used by Mark is *laelaps*, but Laelaps is also the name of the hound of Actaeon in Greek mythology, *a name associated with the constellation Canis Major, one of the decans of Gemini* (Allen, page 117). Jesus tells the storm to cease with the word *siôpa* – 'be quiet!' – echoing the Spartan name for Gemini, *to Siô*. And the 'cushion' upon which Jesus' head was resting – long believed to be a detail provided by Peter – echoes the headgear of the Geminian Twins, or the flames of fire which were supposed to issue from their heads. The Greek word generally translated 'cushion' is *proskephalaion*, which simply means '(that which is) towards the head'. In *The Golden Ass*, by Apuleius, Lucius recognizes that two young actors were playing Castor and Pollux by their helmets 'shaped like the halves of the egg-shell in which they were born to their mother Leda, and with spiky stars painted on them – the constellation of the Twins' (Apuleius, page 264).

The relationship of this story to Gemini does not end here, however. As a spiritual parable, this little incident expresses the notion of fragmentation and scattering that the sign symbolizes. The turbulent waters represent the emotional and spiritual turbulence that the neophyte experiences when faced with the diversity of life's options. This can result in action without direction, movement to no purpose, going fast only to be standing still. The parable teaches us that calm is a prerequisite for the spiritual life. The 'master', the Divine Self, within each of us is 'asleep' and needs to be awakened so that we can direct our attention towards our goal and not be caught in the frantic rush of activity which dissipates our energies and weakens our

---

* We might also note Macaulay's lines from *The Lays of Ancient Rome*:
    Back comes the chief in triumph,
    Who, in the hour of fight,
    Hath seen the great Twin Brethren
    In harness on his right.
    Safe comes the ship to haven
    Through billows and through gales,
    If once the great Twin Brethren
    Sit shining on the sails.

resolve. As Elijah discovered, God is not in the wind, or the earthquake, or the fire, but in 'the still small voice'. (1 Kings 19:11-12) Similar sentiments, with similar imagery, are expressed in the *Bhagavad Gita*:

> The mind
> That gives itself to follow shows of sense
> Seeth its helm of wisdom rent away,
> And, like a ship in waves of whirlwind, drives
> To wreck and death. Only with him, great Prince!
> Whose senses are not swayed by things of sense –
> Only with him who holds his mastery,
> Shows wisdom perfect.
>
> (Arnold, page 13)

This passage shows Jesus' power over the element of Air (the wind). During the course of the Gospel he will display his power over all four of the ancient elements.*

The Gerasene Demoniac

I was living an extremely burdensome life, because in prayer I understood more clearly my faults. On the one hand, God was calling me; on the other hand, I was following the world. All the things of God made me happy; those of the world held me bound. It seems I desired to harmonise these two contraries – so inimical to one another – such as the spiritual life and sensory joys, pleasures, and pastimes. In prayer I was having great trouble, for my spirit was not proceeding as lord but as slave. And so I was not able to shut myself within myself (which was my whole manner of procedure in prayer); instead, I shut within myself a thousand vanities. Thus I passed many years, for now I am surprised how I could have put up with both and not abandon either the one or the other. (Teresa of Avila, Bielecki, pages 43-4)

This same theme is explored in the next section, the story of the Gerasene Demoniac (Mark 5:1-20). As Jesus and his companions leave the boat, they are confronted by a man with 'an unclean spirit' who lives among the tombs, and is so violent that no chains are strong enough to bind him. Seeing Jesus in the distance, the man runs and worships him. Jesus commands the demon

---

* Air – The Calming of the Storm (Mark 4:35-41); Water – Walking on Water (Mark 6:45-52); Fire – Riding an Unbroken Horse (Mark 11:1-11); Earth – Cursing the Fig Tree (Mark 11:12-14, 20-25).

to leave, but the man cries out, 'I beg you, in God's name, don't torment me.' The story continues:

> Then Jesus asked him, 'What is your name?'
> 'My name is Legion,' he replied, 'for we are many.'
> And he begged Jesus again and again not to send
> them out of the area.
> A large herd of pigs was feeding on the nearby
> hillside. The demons begged Jesus, 'Send us
> among the pigs; allow us to go into them.' He gave
> them permission, and the evil spirits came out and
> went into the pigs. The herd, about two thousand in
> number, rushed down the steep bank into the lake
> and were drowned.
>
> (Mark 5:9-13)

It is significant that the number of pigs should be given as 2,000, since this does not correspond with the name 'Legion'. A Roman legion was normally 6,000 strong. It may well be that Geminian duality is reflected in the number, but the pig itself, while not generally associated with Gemini, does have one significant Geminian characteristic in that *it has a split hoof, completely divided* (Leviticus 11:7).

With the benefits of modern psychiatric knowledge, we cannot fail to see in the man with the two thousand demons an example of that most Geminian of conditions, schizophrenia, or split personality. In fact, the term 'multiple personality' would be a better description. This is an actual mental disorder, but we do not need to restrict the use of the term to describe those in whom the symptoms manifest so dramatically. We are all 'split personalities' since, as Aldous Huxley tells us, the complex human personality is made up of 'a quite astonishingly improbable combination of traits'. He goes on:

> Thus a man can be at once the craftiest of politicians and the dupe of his own verbiage, can have a passion, for brandy and money, and an equal passion for the poetry of George Meredith and under-age girls and his mother, for horse-racing and detective stories and the good of his country – the whole accompanied by a sneaking fear of hell-fire, a hatred of Spinoza and an unblemished record for Sunday church-going. (Huxley, page 48)

The character and career of British publisher Robert Maxwell (born 10 June 1923) provide a spectacular example of this. Following his death in

November 1991, the *Guardian* newspaper printed an assessment of the man by British journalist Geoffrey Goodman. Goodman asked how it had been possible for Maxwell to fool so many people for so long. He continues:

> My own theory from observations of the man at close quarters during the year and a half I worked for him at the *Daily Mirror* is that he was at all times at least 20 different people at once. It was usually impossible to know which one I was dealing with at any one moment – and I later came to the conclusion that he wasn't sure either. The 20 different personalities were in constant struggle with each other ... (The *Guardian* 6 December 1991, page 21)

The practitioners of Assagioli's system of personality integration, Psychosynthesis, often refer to the crowd-like nature of the human psyche. And Geminian Salman Rushdie (born 19 June 1947) writes:

> O, the dissociations of which the human mind is capable, marvelled Saladin gloomily. O, the conflicting selves jostling and joggling within these bags of skin. No wonder we are unable to remain focused on anything for long; no wonder we invent remote-control channel-hopping devices. If we turned these instruments on ourselves we'd discover more channels than a cable or satellite mogul ever dreamed of. (*Satanic Verses*, page 519).

P.D. Ouspensky, who claims to be following an ancient esoteric system, tells us that the fragmented personality is the normal condition of all human beings:

> Man is divided into different I's or groups of I's which are unconnected with one another. Then if one I knows one thing, a second I another thing, a third I yet another, and they never meet, what kind of understanding is possible? ... This is the state of an ordinary man's being, and it proves that as he is, he cannot have understanding. Understanding always means connecting things with the whole, and if one does not know the whole, how can one connect? (Ouspensky 1957, page 137)

Ouspensky likens this condition to a house full of servants without a master to control them. Each one does as he pleases, with no one performing the duty to which he was originally assigned: the cook works in the stable, the housemaid in the kitchen, the footman in the garden, and so on. What is required is a controlling 'I', a steward who will integrate the separate functions, and see that each is carried out correctly. This process of integration, says Ouspensky, is a lengthy one, but so important that it is a prerequisite of all spiritual progress.

Human inconsistency has fascinated and perplexed the more reflective among us since the beginning of time, and we can all say, 'My name is Legion', with the demon-possessed man, or 'I am large, I contain multitudes', with Walt Whitman. 'When a man lacks discrimination, his will wanders in all directions, after innumerable aims', says the Hindu classic the *Bhagavad Gita*. But the spiritual writers do not stop at mere observation; the object of all spiritual practice, whatever the tradition, is the transformation of Legion into Union, the fashioning of a coherent and consistent unity from the 'two thousand' fragments of the personality, the multiple diversions and distractions – both internal and external – which manifest as dilettantism and indecision. In doing so, however, one has not to destroy the individual elements: the glyph of Gemini, we remember, has parallel lines, separate, but joined. What is required is equilibrium and harmony among the warring members, not denial or sublimation. If we can achieve this, we can avoid the distorting and disfiguring effects of self-deception, symbolized so graphically in Mark's story as self-inflicted bruising and wounding. (The star *Saiph*, in the constellation Lepus, one of the decans of Gemini, is said by Fleming to mean 'Bruised'.)

This difficult movement towards simplicity, and not the pleasant cultivation of 'nice feelings', is what, in large part, any genuine spiritual practice attempts to effect. Aldous Huxley maintains that the saint is characterized by simplicity and singularity of purpose, qualities which are completely at odds with the lifestyle and appetites of sophisticated and mentally active people like us, who constantly seek novelty, diversity, and distraction. The actions of the saints, says Huxley, 'are as monotonously uniform as their thoughts; for in all circumstances they behave selflessly, patiently, and with indefatigable charity'. Their biographies, he goes on, are of no interest to us because 'Legion prefers to read about Legion' (Huxley, page 55); complexity and contradiction fascinate us; simplicity leaves us unmoved.

One final point: *Matthew has two demoniacs* in his version of this story (Matthew 8:28-34), which seems to be an even clearer indication of Gemini than Mark's one. This 'doubling' by Matthew is generally explained as deliberate exaggeration of the Markan account in order to emphasize the great power of Jesus. However, it might just be that Matthew is here drawing on a version of the story which preserves the original zodiacal motif in a more obvious way than that given by Mark.

Jairus's Daughter and the Woman with the Blood Flow

Upon Jesus' return to Galilee, he encounters Jairus, the synagogue official, whose *twelve*-year-old daughter is desperately ill. On the way to Jairus's house, Jesus is approached by a woman who has been suffering a vaginal blood flow for *twelve* years. She reaches out and touches his clothing, and is immediately cured. After commending the woman's faith, Jesus and his companions proceed to Jairus's house. On the way they are met by some people who report that the girl is now dead but, on arrival at the house, Jesus tells them all that she is not dead, she is asleep. The final part of the story runs as follows:

> After he put them all out, he took the child's father and mother and the disciples who were with him, and went in where the child was. He took her by the hand and said to her, *'Talitha koum!'* (which means 'Little girl, I say to you, get up!'). Immediately the girl stood up and began to walk around (she was twelve years old). At this they were completely astonished. He gave strict orders not to let anyone know about this, and told them to give her something to eat. (Mark 5:40-43)

This is one of the few places in the Gospel where Aramaic words (*Talitha koum*) are used. Aramaic would have been the first language of Jesus and the apostles, and this has given rise to the conventional idea that Mark is here preserving actual, remembered, words. There is, however, another possible explanation: Jesus' words are given in Aramaic *in order to emphasize them*. This command is not just to Jairus's daughter, but to us all. Like her, we are 'asleep'. We have no will, no resolve, no purpose. The Geminian fragmentation of our nature only exists because we are unaware of it. We believe we have a controlling centre, an 'I', when in fact we are composed of hundreds of I's, each with its own agenda. The first step in overcoming this is, as Ouspensky says, 'awakening, since the chief feature of our being is that we are asleep. By trying to awake we change our being, (Ouspensky, 1957, page 46).

Geminian Ralph Waldo Emerson (born 25 May 1803) puts it like this in his essay 'The Preacher':

> All that we call religion, all that saints and churches and Bibles from the beginning of the world have aimed at, is to suppress this impertinent surface-action, and animate man to central and entire action. The human race are afflicted with a St Vitus's dance; their fingers and toes, their members, their senses, their talents, are superfluously active,

while the torpid heart gives no oracle. When that wakes, it will revolutionise the world. Let that speak, and all these rebels will fly to their loyalty. Now every man defeats his own action, – professes this but practices the reverse; with one hand rows, but with the other backs water. A man acts not from one motive, but from many shifting fears and short motives; it is as if he were ten or twenty less men than himself, acting at discord with one another, so that the result of most lives is zero. But when he shall act from one motive, and all his faculties play true, it is clear mathematically, is it not, that this will tell in the result as if twenty men had co-operated, – will give new senses, new wisdom of its own kind; that is, not more facts, nor new combinations, but divination, or direct intuition of men and things?

'Awakening' is a consistent theme of all the world's spiritual traditions. The Buddha is 'the awakened one'. Huxley writes:

In one of the Pali scriptures there is a significant anecdote about the Brahman Drona who, 'seeing the Blessed One sitting at the foot of a tree, asked him: "Are you a deva?" And the Exalted One answered, "I am not." "Are you a gandharva?" "I am not." "Are you a yaksha?" "I am not." "Are you a man?" "I am not a man." On the Brahman asking what he might be, the Blessed One replied, "Those evil influences, those cravings, whose non-destruction would have individualised me as a deva, a gandharva, a yaksha (three types of supernatural being), or a man, I have completely annihilated. Know therefore that I am a Buddha"' (i.e. I am awake). (Huxley, page 54)

Enlightenment, for the Buddhists, is simply waking up.

The most obviously Geminian feature of the story of Jairus's Daughter is the way in which it is told: *it is the only miracle story in the Gospels which combines two quite separate elements.* Nineham writes:

What we have here is without precise parallel in the Gospel – an incident broken into by another incident which takes place in the middle of it. (Nineham, pages 156-7)

In addition, however, we should consider the name 'Jairus' (*Iaeirios*) which means, appropriately, 'Jehovah Enlightens', but which also bears more than a passing resemblance to the name of the brightest star in the night sky, Sirius (in Greek *Seirios*), the Dog Star, which is found in Canis Major, one of the Geminian decans, and whose name means *The Chief One, the Leader*. Jairus, we are told, is the *archisunagôgon, the Leader or Ruler of the Synagogue*. And, as Ptolemy reminds us, the heliacal rising of Sirius at the summer solstice presaged the beginning of the Egyptian New Year and *the flooding* of the Nile (Ptolemy, page 196), thus connecting this star with the constantly menstruating woman.

In addition to being a possible zodiacal reference, Mark's double use of the number twelve provides us with further evidence that we are meant to link the two females, and that this double story is not just a narrative accident. The woman with the blood-flow has been sick for twelve years (Mark 5:25), while the little girl is twelve years old (Mark 5:42). The contrast between the young girl and the older woman reflects two of the decans of Gemini, Canis Major and Canis Minor, The Big Dog and The Little Dog, but Mark's narrative is also playing with contrasting features of the astronomy and mythology of Gemini's stars, Castor and Pollux. Although 'twin' stars, Castor and Pollux differ in brilliancy, and at the time Mark was writing Castor was the brighter of the two, a situation which, strangely, has been reversed in the last three centuries. In the myth, they were the sons of Leda. Castor had a human father and was therefore mortal, but Pollux had been sired by Zeus and was immortal. Such was their love for each other that they eventually agreed to share immortality, living and dying alternately. In an ancient Euphratean representation they are depicted as the sun and moon, the one rising as the other sets: consequently, they came to symbolize the eternal battle between vitality and decay, youth and age, life and death, themes which are clearly echoed in Mark's narrative.

By linking the two stories Mark is once more emphasizing the theme of unity. The young girl is the daughter of a prominent official and so we can assume that her family is prosperous as well as powerful. The woman with the blood-flow is older and, what is more, on the lowest stratum of society. Because it was forbidden for a Jewish man to have any sexual relations with his wife during her menstrual period (Ezekiel 18:6), this lady would have had to forsake the society of men for the duration of her illness. The two women represent opposite poles of Jewish society: rich and poor, young and old, illustrious and outcast. In the power of the Christ they are united.*

---

* Immediately following his account of this dual miracle, Matthew tells two more stories which are not found in Mark but which express the Geminian theme: The Healing of the Two Blind Men (Matthew 9:27-31), and the Cure of the Mute (Matthew 9:32-34). Geminian duality is obvious in the first; the second relates to Gemini's rule over speech and communication generally. Luke does not have these two stories, probably because he copied from a version of Mark which, like canonical Mark, does not have them either. The fact that Matthew has them is yet another indication that the version of Mark that he used was longer and more comprehensive than canonical Mark and, what is more, at times more clearly zodiacal in its themes.

Gemini (Mark 4:35–6:29)

Kith and Kin

In classical astrology Gemini is associated with brothers and sisters. The third house of the horoscope, over which Gemini has 'natural' rulership, is generally consulted by astrologers for information about sibling relationships. Mayo writes of the Third House:

> Its sphere of life has a correspondence with the principle of Mercury and the adaptive and communicative attitude of Gemini. Hence, it relates to activities and matters connected with one's need to relate and adjust oneself to the immediate environment created by circumstances, *involving near relatives such as brothers and sisters, and casual acquaintances, neighbours.* Activities will be of a close communicative nature, short journeys, direct mental contact. (Mayo, 1964, page 78, emphasis added)

The symbolism is quite easy to understand: Gemini, the twin, represents all those who spring from the same source as ourselves, who are our 'twin selves', whether actual twins or not. In addition, since Gemini rules those who are separate but joined, its association with the immediate family becomes apparent. In view of this we can see the reason why Jesus rejects the demoniac's request to become his follower, and enjoins him instead to tell his friends (*tous sous* – 'all yours'), those closest to him, what the Lord has done for him (Mark 5:20). It also enables us to see the significance of the episode which opens chapter 6 of Mark. Jesus returns to his home town only to be rejected by those closest to him. The people who knew him as a boy cannot understand where his wisdom comes from, and even his own brothers and sisters were 'offended at him' (Mark 6:3). Jesus rebukes his critics with the famous words:

Jesus said to them, 'Only in their own towns, among their relatives and in their own homes are prophets without honour.' He could not do any miracles there, except lay his hands on a few sick people and heal them. He was amazed at their lack of faith. (Mark 6:4-6)

As we saw at the end of the Aries section, those who are bent on the spiritual life will meet most opposition from their closest kin. 'I am astonished by the harm that is caused by dealing with relatives,' writes St Teresa. She goes on: 'I know through my own experience, as well as that of others, that in time of trial my relatives helped me least.' (Bielecki, page 56) The 'true relatives'

97

of Jesus are not those who claim kinship by accident of birth. So, the true spiritual companion is one who shares our ideals, our attitudes and our aspirations: whether or not he shares our name is irrelevant.

'Two by Two'

The narrative continues with Jesus sending out the disciples *'two by two'* (Mark 6:7). Their mission is to preach repentance, to heal the sick, and to cast out demons. They are not to take anything with them for the journey except a staff, and they are to wear only sandals; they are not to wear *two* coats (Mark 6:8-9). It is appropriate that the apostles are sent out to proclaim the message of the kingdom in this section, since Gemini, and its ruler, Mercury, both concern communication. This passage might well describe an actual commissioning, but its position among so many incidents which express the duality-unity theme tends to lend it symbolic value. The apostles are to conduct their mission 'in twos', acknowledging, perhaps, the inherent duality of the individual, but the fact that they are not to wear two coats is a possible warning against double-mindedness and inconsistency. This is further emphasized in the command to 'remain in one house' in each city that they visit (Mark 6:10), not to flit about from place to place like those whose lives have no direction or purpose. The warning that those towns which reject the apostles' message will suffer a worse fate than Sodom and Gomorrah (Mark 6:11), contains another clear Geminian reference: Sodom and Gomorrah, known as the *twin* towns of the plains, are, like Castor and Pollux, always referred to together. They are not mentioned anywhere else in this Gospel.

The Death of John the Baptist

The final episode in the Gemini section illustrates the dangers of Geminian inconsistency. In the story of John the Baptist's death (Mark 6:14-29), we encounter King Herod, a man who cannot make up his mind.* With Gemini, says Carter, 'there is a lack of decision and a good deal of wavering' (Carter, 1925, page 69). He had married Herodias, the former wife of his brother, Philip, and had locked John the Baptist in prison for speaking out against such an illicit union. Herod was certainly ambivalent in his approach to

---

* Josephus in his History of the Jews (Book 18 chapter 5) mentions the death of John the Baptist at the hands of Herod, but he doesn't tell us how he died. The beheading – the division of the body into two pieces - is probably Mark's invention. Even the head on a platter looks like an astrological detail – the earth surrounded by the circle of the zodiac – rather than a historical one.

John: he feared and admired him, and would often listen to what he had to say, but his vanity and vacillation, twin pitfalls of Gemini, led him, at his birthday celebrations, to make the reckless promise which brought about John's death. He makes his step-daughter the Geminian offer of *half* his kingdom for dancing so well, but gives her John the Baptist's head instead. This is a cautionary tale depicting the catastrophic results which follow when we are incapable of exorcizing the legion of contradictions which inhabit our carnal selves.

Cancer (Mark 6:30-8:21)
'Be Thou Open!'

My religion is kindness. The Dalai Lama (born 6 July 1935)

John the Baptist and Jesus

The entry of the sun into Cancer, on or around 21 June each year, marks the
time of the summer solstice, the point of the sun's maximum northerly
declination, and the longest day of the year in the northern hemisphere.
From this point onwards the days will gradually, but inexorably, shorten as
the sun sinks lower in the sky. This is what Manilius calls 'the hinge of the
year, the blazing turning point' when the sun is 'recalled, and bends back the
length of day'. This notion of 'reversal' seems to be common to all the creatures – including the Tortoise, the Crayfish, and the Lobster, in addition to
the Crab – which have been held to represent this constellation. For
Christians, this time of year has always been associated with John the
Baptist, and his birth is celebrated on 24 June, three days after the summer
solstice, and six months before the celebration of the birth of Jesus at the time
of the winter solstice, on 25 December. John, we are told in Luke's Gospel,
was six months older than Jesus (Luke 1:36). Mark has nothing about the
birth of John, but it is curious that he should recount his death (see previous

chapter) *precisely at the point in the narrative when Gemini crosses into Cancer.* This could be purely fortuitous, of course, but it could well be, as I suspect, that mid-summer has been in some way connected with John from the very beginning of Christianity, at least from the time the Gospels were written. If this is so, then the implication is that Jesus was always associated with the mid-winter solstice, too, and that the celebration of his birth on 25 December was part of the Christian mysteries from the earliest days, and was not simply a later concession to paganism, as is generally thought. The association of the solstitial axis with the stories of the birth of Jesus undoubtedly owes something to the ancient name for the constellation Cancer, given by Aratos as *Karkinos*, and expanded by Eratosthenes to *Karkinos, Onoi kai Phatnê*, The Crab, the Asses and the Manger; and the Latin *Praesaepe*, often rendered as 'Beehive', but more appropriately as 'Manger' is still the conventional name of the cluster of stars in the centre of this otherwise inconspicuous constellation.

Jesus and John are always contrasted in the Gospels. In the first chapter of Mark, John represents the passing Age of Aries which is giving way to the new Age of Pisces, but there is also a contrast based upon the symbolism of the two solstice points. Jesus, 'the light of the world', is said to be born at the time of maximum darkness, when the light begins to grow; John is born when it starts to wane. Hence the Baptist's enigmatic words in John's Gospel, 'He must increase, I must decrease' (John 3:30)

In the ancient world, Cancer and Capricorn, the two solstitial signs, were considered the 'gates' of incarnation: the human soul incarnates in Cancer, the divine in Capricorn. Homer alludes to this in book 13 of the *Odyssey*, where Odysseus encounters two gates in the cave at Ithaca. Chapman translates the passage thus:

> (There) runs a cave......
> ....
> To which two entries were: the one for man,
> On which the North breath'd, the other for the gods,
> On which the South; and that bore no abodes
> For earthy men, but only deathless feet
> > Had there free way. (lines 164-7)

The neoplatonist Porphyry, in his commentary on Homer, expounds the astrological significance of this passage:

> These two gates are Cancer and Capricorn; but Plato calls them entrances. And of these theologists say that Cancer is the gate through

101

which souls descend; but Capricorn that through which they ascend. (Quoted in *The Astrological Journal*, volume 46 No. 2. page 59.)

If men are born in Cancer and gods are born in Capricorn, we can better understand the contrasting roles of John the Baptist and Jesus in the Gospel narrative. John represents everything that is good and noble in the human being. He preaches justice, equity, and stability, the sort of principles that any religious liberal might be expected to endorse. 'Among those born of women there is no-one greater than John the Baptist,' says Jesus, *'yet the one who is least in the kingdom of God is greater than he'* (Luke 7:28). John epitomizes the human virtues, but Jesus, who tells us not just to share what we have, as John does, but to give it all away, epitomizes a qualitatively different way of being. John shows us how to live a human life: Jesus shows us how to live the divine life. John represents the old covenant, the Mosaic Law which takes us to the borders of the Promised Land. But Moses and his Law do not take the people over the threshold; Joshua is the one who makes the final conquest, just as Jesus (whose name is a Greek version of the Hebrew name Joshua) leads us into the kingdom of God.

Cancer and the Moon

The signs which mark the solstices and the equinoxes – Aries, Cancer, Libra, and Capricorn - are called Cardinal signs, each one of them associated with a different element. Aries is Cardinal Fire; Cancer is Cardinal Water, Libra Cardinal Air, and Capricorn Cardinal Earth. In the beautiful, simple imagery of the zodiac we see the tension that is produced in Cancer by the union of Cardinality with Water: the Cardinal signs denote pioneering activity, leadership, whereas Water represents the 'shrinking, fearful, self-protective instinct' (Carter, 1925, page 64). Herein lies the paradox of Cancer, so familiar to all of us: just at the point of maximum opportunity to press forward and achieve our goals we retreat fearfully into the securities of the past. The Crab is the perfect symbol of this. It is one of the most absurdly constructed creatures, a walking paradox, with its skeletal system on the outside protecting its soft and vulnerable interior flesh. Its movement lacks the consistency of direction which marks the movement of most other creatures. Instead it scuttles, apparently uncertain of its destination, and, just to be on the safe side, it carries its house along with it. Its tenacious claws enable it to grab and hold all those things it needs to make its life bearable.

Such things give us a clue as to how the ancient world saw the Cancerian type: energetic but cautious; concerned with home and family; trapped in the past while constantly threatening to break away from it; sensitive and caring beneath a thin but hard shell of aggressive self-protection. Manilius, rather unkindly perhaps, dwells on Cancer's grasping nature, and its ability to 'sell the world's produce to the world, to establish commercial ties between so many unknown lands, and to search out under foreign skies fresh sources of gain' (Book 4, lines 165-71). Psychologically, says Mayo, Cancer represents 'the primitive urge to protect and to nourish, especially the feminine desire to receive into the womb and to possess'. (Mayo, 1964, page 45). The glyph of Cancer (♋) is generally thought to represent the crab's claws, but many see it as a representation of the breasts, symbols of nurture and care, and of the transmission of nourishment from one genera-tion to the next. Physiologically, it is said to rule the stomach and the digestive system generally.

These traits and concerns can often be detected in individuals who have Cancer strongly marked in their horoscope. They manifest in an astonishing variety of ways, but the underlying themes are evident and consistent. Boxer 'Iron' Mike Tyson (born 30 June) typifies the aggressive shell hiding the vul-nerable interior; in his *Metamorphosis*, Franz Kafka (born 3 July) describes the transformation of Gregor Hamsa into a giant hard-shelled beetle, and in *The Trial* he explores the essential isolation of the individual human being; Thoreau (born 12 July) lived the life of a recluse, barely moving from the place of his birth; and the British writer, Colin Wilson (born 26 June), attained some celebrity with his first book *The Outsider*. Even the philo-sopher Leibnitz (born 1 July) expressed Cancerian images in his 'monads', the theory that reality is composed of discrete and impermeable entities.

However, few people typify Cancer as completely as Marcel Proust (born 10 July), who spent much of his time in his room, wrapped in a cocoon of bedclothes, and was constantly troubled by his stomach. His great work is the multi-volume *Remembrance of Things Past*, a paean to reminiscence, sparked by eating a little cake called a *madeleine*, and when asked which manual profession he would take up should he need to, he replied, in true Cancerian fashion, 'I think I would become a baker. It is an honourable thing to give people their daily bread.' (de Botton, page 201)

Such traits can also be perceived in Cancerian nations. America, 'born on the fourth of July', seems to epitomize the sign. Reagan's 'Star Wars' pro-gramme, conceived as a 'protective shell' around the USA to keep out all enemy missiles, struck a Cancerian chord deep in the American psyche. The flag, mom, and apple-pie are all Cancerian themes, demonstrating a national commitment to collective security, family values, and a full stomach. Popcorn, that most American of foods, symbolizes the need for abundance

103

and the desire to be able to eat forever and never get full (or fat!). A talent for trade has enabled the American people to fill their coffers to overflowing, and to seek out new markets in an attempt to appease the god of economic growth. Add to this a tendency towards sentimentality, a preoccupation with genealogy and, at times, an insularity of which President Monroe would have approved, and you have all the major characteristics of the sign Cancer embodied in one nation.

The spiritual challenge of Cancer, then, lies in coming to terms with our own need for security, which tends to chain us fearfully to the past and renders us incapable of jettisoning all the accumulated detritus that we consider indispensable to our life. It challenges us to open ourselves up, to remove the shell of conditioning and expose our vulnerable underside, to break through the barrier which shuts out the unfamiliar, and which serves as a defence against novel and alien experience. We construct our personal carapace out of family, tradition, and fear and we keep it in place by averting our eyes from the horizon and fixing our gaze downward. We become fierce protectors of our inheritance and eager collectors of anything which might cushion us or our offspring against life's capricious reversals.

The symbolism of the moon (☽), which 'rules' Cancer, further underlines these themes. The sun and the moon are the two primary celestial symbols, representing opposed, but complementary, aspects of life. The sun is positive, shining with a light of its own; it is constant, always the same shape in the daytime sky. It is the yang or 'masculine' energy of the conscious mind which pushes outward. The moon, on the other hand, is negative, shining with reflected light; it seems inconstant, in a state of flux, and so has come to be associated with the 'feminine' yin energy of the turbulent, unpredictable unconscious. In classical astrology, the moon symbolizes the feminine side of us all, the tender, nurturing, protecting instinct. It particularly stands for the mother, our individual, personal mother, and the collective source of all life, Motherhood personified. The moon represents all organizations and institutions, such as churches and schools, which have a mothering role, and which we honour with such titles as Mother Church or Alma Mater. Mayo sees the moon as representing 'the mediator between past and present' by means of which 'are created protective forms of habit patterns, instinctive behaviour and response'. The moon's readily observable cyclic rhythm has led to its association with 'the ebb and flow of sensation and emotional experience .... that maintains the periodical need for a man to withdraw into past experience, memory, or to draw on the past'. In addition, and crucial to what follows, the moon is said to govern 'taste and drinking, the stomach, belly, and the womb' (Mayo, 1964, page 18).

Cancer (Mark 6:30-8:21)

The Spiritual Lessons of Cancer

This section begins, in characteristic Cancerian fashion, with a withdrawal. The apostles have returned from their mission and have begun to tell Jesus of their experiences. He senses their weariness and suggests that they accompany him into a secluded place to rest for a while (Mark 6:30-32). However, their movements are being monitored, and great crowds of people run ahead of them (Mark 6:33). The story continues.

> When Jesus landed and saw a large crowd, he had compassion on them, because they were like sheep without a shepherd. So he began teaching them many things. (Mark 6:34)

The crab-like urge to retreat into seclusion after an active sortie is in no sense a bad thing, and the text does not imply that it is. It simply suggests that it is impossible. For those on the spiritual path there can be no inactive period. Concern for those in need, and compassion for those in distress must take precedence over even legitimate personal requirements. This is Jesus at his most 'maternal', responding to the needs of others regardless of the cost to himself. The shepherd who, as John's Gospel tells us, will 'lay down his life for his sheep' (John 10:11), is as apt an expression of the essence of Cancerian protectiveness as it is possible for us to devise. Jesus has shown compassion before (Mark 1:41, 5:19), but only to individuals: now he takes pity on whole groups.

He tells his disciples to give the people something to eat but, on making enquiries about available food, they report that they only have five loaves and two fish (Mark 6:38). Jesus commands them to have the people sit down on the grass (Mark 6:39):

> So they sat down in groups of hundreds and fifties. Taking the five loaves and the two fish and looking up to heaven, he gave thanks and broke the loaves. Then he gave them to his disciples to set before the people. He also divided the two fish among them all. They all ate and were satisfied, and the disciples picked up twelve basketfuls of broken pieces of bread and fish. The number of the men who had eaten was five thousand. (Mark 6:40-44)

This remarkable miracle is repeated, almost verbatim, a little later in the Gospel (Mark 8:1-10). There are slight differences, however, and these help us to understand why two similar events (not two accounts of the same event, as some scholars suggest) should be placed so close together. To begin with, the two events occur in very different places. The first is in Galilee: no

105

change of location has been indicated since Jesus was preaching 'round about the villages' near his home town (6:6). However, the second feeding occurs in Gentile territory, 'on the coast of the Decapolis' (6:31). Furthermore, as if to underline that the Jew-Gentile theme is important, Mark uses two different words for 'basket' in his twin accounts. In the 'Jewish' feeding he uses the word *kophinos*, which Abbot-Smith informs us means 'a basket, probably of wicker-work, such as were carried by Jews for food'. In the 'Gentile' feeding, the word is *sphuris* which is a more generic term, with no Jewish connotations. The numbers also are different and, therefore, of significance. In the Feeding of the Five Thousand, twelve baskets of surplus are collected from five loaves; in the Feeding of the Four Thousand, seven baskets from seven loaves. It is more than likely that five and twelve specifically indicate Jews: the five books of Moses comprise the Pentateuch, the foundation of Jewish religious life, and the twelve is an obvious reference to the twelve tribes of Israel. Similarly, seven and four could obliquely refer to the 'seventy Gentile nations'* which were scattered around the 'four quadrants' of the earth.

Taken together, the two stories are designed to show that compassion has no racial boundaries. But there is more to them than this. In breaking the bread Jesus anticipates the actions he will perform at the Last Supper (Mark 14:22), when he gives his followers the spiritual food they will require to sustain them in tribulation. This link gives us a clue to the meaning of these two feeding stories: Jesus dispenses the spiritual manna to all who wish to receive it, regardless of religious affiliation, and there is such abundance that no one has to go hungry or to hoard provisions for future consumption. God's bounty is everywhere for those who have eyes to see.

The presence of fish in both these stories should alert us to the Piscean motif which runs through this Gospel, and which reaches a climax in the final section. Fish is the symbol of the new age of Pisces which the death of Jesus will inaugurate. To eat fish is to commune with Christ, a fact which was not lost on the early Christians who ate fish each week on Friday, the day of Venus, the planet exalted in the sign Pisces. The catacombs contain many examples of bread and fish as symbols of the Eucharist.

---

* Seventy Gentile nations are mentioned in Genesis 10. Seventy people went down into Egypt with Jacob (Exodus1:5), and seventy elders were appointed to assist Moses in his ministry (Numbers 11:25). This number has consistently been associated with universality. According to Ptolemy, the earth was divided into four quadrants, each under the influence of an astrological element – Earth, Fire, Air or Water (*Tetrabiblos*, pages 129-131).

The Decans of Cancer

The names of stars in the constellation Cancer and its decans seem, more than coincidentally, to be reflected in these stories. *Ma'alaph* in Cancer is said by Fleming to mean 'assembled thousands', and *Praesaepe*, Cancer's central cluster, which means 'the Manger', can also mean 'the Pen', 'the Fold', 'the Enclosure', 'the Beehive', a notion echoed in Ursa Major and Ursa Minor, two of Cancer's decans. Seiss contends that these two constellations, the Great and Little Bears, have been wrongly named by the Greeks because they confused the name of the principal star in Ursa Major, *Dubah*, with the word Dob, 'bear'. He continues:

> But 'Dubheh' or 'Dubah' does not mean bear, but a collection of domestic animals, 'a fold', as in the Hebrew word 'Dober'. The evidence is that, according to the original intent, we are to see in these constellations not two long-tailed bears but *two sheepfolds or flocks*, the collected and folded sheep of God's pasture. (Seiss, pages 125-6, emphasis added)

Alkaid, a star in Ursa Minor, means, according to Fleming, 'The Assembled', and Alpherkadain means 'The Redeemed Assembly'. The less fanciful Allen also notes that early commentators considered The Folds an appropriate title for these constellations (page 449).

Walking on the Water

The other decan of Cancer is Argo, the mythological ship which carried Jason (another variation of Jesus/Joshua) and the Argonauts in their quest for the golden fleece. Manilius, in his survey of the constellations, describes the Argo as the ship *quae vicerat aequor*, 'the ship which conquered the water' (Book 1, line 623), a feat which Jesus repeats by walking on the surface of the lake (Mark 6:45-53). Since water has perennially symbolized the emotional nature of the human being, this action shows that Jesus has conquered those irrational, turbulent forces which reside in the unconscious and constantly threaten to overwhelm us, and has attained that serenity of spirit which marks the enlightened individual, and which is the goal of all spiritual aspirants. As we read in the *Bhagavad Gita*:

> Not shaken by adversity,
> Not hankering after happiness;

107

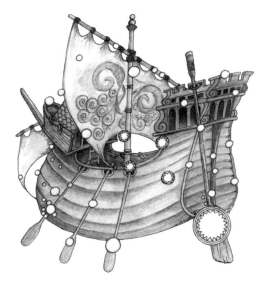

Fig. 10 Argo, 'the ship which conquered the waters'

Free from fear, free from anger,
Free from the things of desire.
I call him a seer, and illumined.
(*The World's Bible*, page 29)

The rest of the section faithfully reflects those Cancerian motifs which we outlined earlier. Jesus demonstrates his concern for others as he heals the sick in Gennesaret (Mark 6:53-56), and shows his contempt for man-made traditions in his argument with the Scribes and Pharisees over food laws. His opponents are scandalized by the fact that Jesus' disciples do not perform the ritual washings before they eat (Mark 7:1-5), but Jesus attacks them mercilessly, declaring their customs bogus and their motives mercenary (Mark 7:6-13). Nothing, he says, that a man puts into his stomach can render him defiled; defilement consists in what comes out of a man. His actions defile him, not his food (Mark 7:14-23).

The food motif is not exhausted yet. At the end of the Cancerian section, Jesus and his disciples once more put to sea in a boat (Mark 8:13). The disciples have only one loaf of bread with them. The story continues:

The disciples had forgotten to bring bread, except for one loaf they had with them in the boat. Be careful,' Jesus warned them. 'Watch out for the yeast of the Pharisees and that of Herod.'
They discussed this with one another and said, 'It is because we have no bread.'

> Aware of their discussion, Jesus asked them: 'Why are you talking about having no bread? Do you still not see or understand? Are your hearts hardened? Do you have eyes but fail to see, and ears but fail to hear? And don't you remember? When I broke the five loaves for the five thousand, how many basketfuls of pieces did you pick up?'
>
> 'Twelve,' they replied.
>
> 'And when I broke the seven loaves for the four thousand, how many basketfuls of pieces did you pick up?'
>
> They answered, 'Seven.'
>
> He said to them, 'Do you still not understand?'
>
> (Mark 8:14-21)

Nineham calls this 'a truly remarkable incident' (page 213) in view of the fact that the disciples are at their most obtuse and Jesus at his most enigmatic. They talk about loaves of bread after witnessing two stupendous feeding miracles; he refuses to give a direct answer to any of his own questions.

It hardly seems possible that, as it stands, this passage describes a real historical incident. Could even the dullest among us show so little insight as the apostles here display? What seems more likely is that this episode has been constructed by Mark along the lines of similar dialogues in John's Gospel (e.g. John 3) in which lack of comprehension is a literary device designed to prompt further elucidation. Here in Mark, however, there is no elucidation. In fact, Jesus himself, not some uncomprehending listener, is asking the questions. And, in the light of all that has preceded this incident, he cannot be asking these questions of the apostles. He is asking them of us. This discussion is not so much a record of the spiritual blindness exhibited on one particular occasion by a specific group of people. Instead, it describes the darkness and ignorance in which we all find ourselves as we try to assuage our spiritual hunger with physical food. This is the point at which Mark tells us that we do not live on bread alone, that our life is about more than food and our body about more than clothing (Matthew 6:25). But our carnal nature can only understand tangible, edible, saleable objects, the accumulation of which is the concern of the Pharisees and Herod, symbols here of materialism and greed. The yeast* symbolic of corruption, and of tradition, represents the insidious and subtly pervasive attractiveness of the world's commercial values which have perennially offered us a counterfeit of genuine spiritual sustenance. This passage asks us to consider whether we who have been apprised of the miracles of God, which are so abundantly evident

---

* Bread was leavened with dough from an old batch, so each new baking was linked with what had come before. 'Unleavened' bread, i.e. bread without yeast, symbolized a new start (hence its importance in both Passover and Eucharist).

in nature and in life, are still of the opinion that happiness consists in a full stomach.

Opening Up

This section also contains the lovely story of the Syro-Phoenician Woman who begs Jesus to heal her daughter. Jesus refuses at first, declaring that it is not right to give the children's food to the dogs (Mark 7:24-27). 'Yes,' she says, 'but even the little dogs under the table get to eat the children's crumbs' (Mark 7:28). Cancer 'rules' dogs, particularly the faithful, protective, domestic variety, and Alice O. Howell tells us that in the Glastonbury Zodiac 'it seems that instead of a crab for Cancer there was a dog' (Howell, 1990, page 136). The Greek text specifies that the woman was talking about 'little dogs' (*kunaria*), and it is interesting that Manilius considers the constellation Procyon, The Little Dog, to be a decan of Cancer and not, like Seiss *et al*, of Gemini. He says:

> But when the Crab hath doubled Ten Degrees,
> And rear'd seven more, bright Procyon leaves the Seas.
> Inclines to Weave strong Nets, to train the Hound,
> To know the Breed, and to improve the Sound.
>
> (page 161)

Could the woman's reply contain a veiled reference to a constellation that Mark considered a decan of Cancer? This is not unlikely. The decans loosely surround the zodiacal constellations and, in some cases, might be said to belong to one as to another. In fact, Manilius's list of decans is quite different from that of Seiss, and this discrepancy could indicate some measure of disagreement in the ancient world. However, as far as I am aware, this is the only occasion on which Mark seems to follow the tradition represented by Manilius over the one that Seiss inherited from the tenth-century Arab astronomer, Albumaser. There are, in fact, quite a number of 'dogs' in this part of the sky, and 'Caesius mentions *Catuli* and *Canes Laconicae*, the Lapdogs or Puppies, and the Spartan Dogs, as titles for both of the Bears' (Allen, page 450).

Jesus' Strange Journey

'And again, coming out of the region of Tyre he went through Sidon to the Sea of Galilee up (through) the middle of the region of the Decapolis' (Mark 7:31, my translation).

110

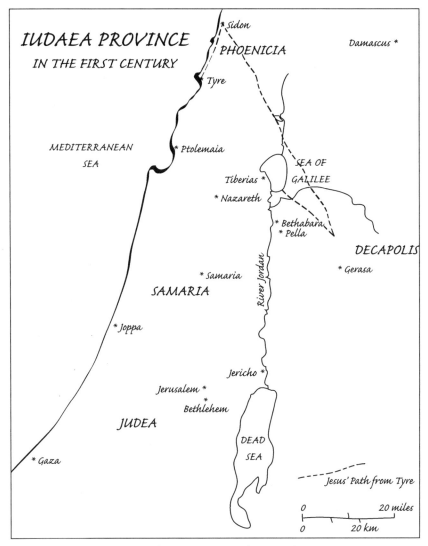

Fig. 11 Iudaea Province in the First Century

This roundabout journey (see map), which has been compared with travelling from London to Cornwall via Manchester, has given literalist commentators untold headaches. The general consensus seems to be that it shows Mark's lack of geographical knowledge and probably indicates that he was not a native of the area. However, it is quite obviously a joke by Mark – a reference to the scuttling crab's inability to get directly to its destination.

The NIV tries to make sense of it by translating it: 'Then Jesus left the vicinity of Tyre and went through Sidon, down to the Sea of Galilee and into the region of the Decapolis', but this is not completely faithful to the Greek.

Cracking the shell of exclusiveness is the theme of the next incident, the Cure of the Deaf and Dumb Man (Mark 7:31-37), which takes place after Jesus has made a curiously crab-like journey back to the sea of Galilee. Jesus' Aramaic command to the deaf man's ears expresses the hard task of the Cancerian phase of the spiritual life: '*Ephphatha*, that is, be opened.'

At first sight these two incidents – The Cure of the Syro-Phoenician Woman's Daughter and the Healing of the Deaf Mute – look like two separate miracle stories, and they are usually interpreted as such in conventional biblical commentaries. But they need to be taken together to get the full impact of what the Gospel writer is trying to convey.

The woman who approaches Jesus is a Gentile, i.e. a non-Jew. She asks Jesus to cast a demon from her daughter, but Jesus refuses her request initially because, he says, it is not right for him to give the children's food to the dogs. This, of course, is a terrible insult, and the fact that it is uttered by Jesus himself has proved quite embarrassing to Christian commentators, who try to soften it a little by saying that the word used is rather an affectionate term for a dog, and anyway, Jesus was really only testing the woman's faith. Does Jesus really come out of it better if we assume that he is playing some sort of game with this distressed woman? If she had been unable to respond cleverly to his insult, would he have refused to heal her daughter?

The significance of this story only becomes apparent when we read it in conjunction with the story which follows. After putting his fingers in the man's ears and touching his tongue with spittle, Jesus says the Aramaic word *Ephphatha*, and the man finds himself able to hear properly and to speak coherently.

It is unusual to find Aramaic words or phrases in the Synoptic Gospels. Aramaic was the first language of the Palestinian Jews, and so would have been the language of Jesus and the apostles, and commentators regularly point out that it is present in the Gospels – which were all originally written in Greek – because these would have been the actual words that Jesus said. But, as we noted in the story of Jairus's Daughter, it is possible that Aramaic is used *for emphasis* in the Gospel of Mark; that the Gospel writer is saying, 'I'm writing this word in another language, so pay attention to it. It's important.'

The word *Ephphatha* means 'Open up!' What Jesus is saying to this deaf man is what he is saying to all of us. This man was suffering from a physical deafness; we are suffering from spiritual deafness. Our ears are closed to the words of those who live in close proximity to us, but whose traditions are different from ours. We don't hear what they are saying, and so our opinions are garbled and worthless. The Jewish exclusiveness displayed by Jesus in his encounter with the Gentile woman dramatically illustrates our own clannishness, our refusal to listen attentively to the unfamiliar voices. It is only when we are prepared to open up that our prejudices can be eroded; and only then that the impediment in our speech will be removed and our opinions will be worth listening to.

This theme is explored further in the final scene of this section, the Cure of the Blind Man (Mark 8:22-26). As Jesus enters Bethsaida a blind man is brought to him and, in response to the man's entreaties, Jesus restores his sight. This seems to be just another example of Jesus' amazing power to heal. But the story is different from all the other miracles recounted in the Gospels, because it is the only one in which Jesus is shown failing at his first attempt. He takes the man to one side, rubs spittle on his eyes, and asks him, 'What do you see?' 'I see men but they look like walking trees,' the man replies. Jesus rubs the man's eyes again, and this time his sight is restored and he can see everything clearly.

This tiny little story was left out of the Gospels of Matthew and Luke even though the authors of these Gospels undoubtedly knew about it. They probably didn't include it because they seem to have had a pressing need to show Jesus in a favourable light, and giving an account of an incident in which he fails to achieve his purpose immediately does not do justice to his remarkable powers. But they failed to understand the significance of the story, as have numerous commentators who, for want of something relevant to say, spend their time explaining that Jesus took the man aside because he was concerned for his dignity, and how spittle was considered to have healing properties in the ancient world. Liberal commentators, desperate to find a naturalistic explanation for the miracle, will even suggest that Jesus had enough medical knowledge to realize that this man had cataracts, and that rubbing his eyes with spittle would remove them.

All of which miss the point. The blind man, like all the characters in the Gospels – when the Gospels are read as psychological, spiritual treatises and not as historical reminiscences – is you and I. We have received the first rub of the spittle, and we can see, but we don't see people, we see walking trees – or, in contemporary language, ciphers, zombies, humanoids. We recognize their general shape and their mobility, but we have yet to grant them fully human status. What we need is a second metaphorical rub of the eyes to correct our vision, to remove the residual film which prevents us seeing people as they really are, as ends in themselves, and not as means to our own ends. Einstein expresses the same sentiment as Mark, but less dramatically and more philosophically, as follows:

113

A human being is part of a whole called by us 'universe', a part limited in time and space. He experiences himself, his thoughts, and feelings as something separated from the rest, a kind of optical delusion of his consciousness. This delusion is a kind of prison for us, restricting us to our personal desires and to affection for a few persons nearest to us. Our task must be to free ourselves from this prison by widening our circle of compassion to embrace all living creatures and the whole of nature in its beauty. (Goldstein, page 126)

The function of all spiritual practice – from whatever tradition it comes – is to help us to narrow the gap between self-awareness and other-awareness, to remove that residual film from our eyes which is deluding our sight. And while it is important to stress that this applies to everyone, regardless of their zodiacal sun sign, it is appropriate to give the final word in this chapter to Helen Keller (born 27 June 1880), who bore the physical burden of Cancerian isolation in a way expected of few people. That she overcame it, both physically and spiritually, is wonderfully consoling – and challenging – to us all.

Those who have been mentally blinded 'in the gradual furnace of the world' can, and must, be pressed to look for new capabilities within themselves and work out new ways to happiness. They may even resent faith that expects nobler things from them. They say in effect, 'I will be content if you take me for what I am – dull, or mean, or hard, or selfish.' But it is an affront to them and to the eternal dignity of man so to acquiesce. How often it comes over us that there is much in us which our nearest friends cannot know – more than we dare or care or are able to lay bare, more of feelings, more of power, more of manhood. How little we know ourselves! We need limitations and temptations to open our inner selves, dispel our ignorance, tear off disguises, throw down old idols, and destroy false standards. Only by such rude awakenings can we be led to dwell in a place where we are less cramped, less hindered by the ever-insistent External. Only then do we discover a new capacity and appreciation of goodness and beauty and truth.
(Keller, pages 202-4)

Leo (Mark 8:22–9:29)
'Who Am I?'

Jesus said: 'One who knows everything else, but who does not know himself, knows nothing.' (Gospel of Thomas, Saying 67)

Leo and the Sun

'The sign of Leo,' says Ptolemy, 'as a whole is hot and stifling', and from a purely meteorological point of view, he is absolutely right. The days from late July to late August are the *dies caniculariae* of the Romans, the 'dog-days', named after Sirius, the Dog-star, whose heliacal rising, four hundred years before the Christian era, corresponded with the sun's entrance into the constellation Leo and marked the hottest time of the year. It is a time when we can do little more than follow the advice of Hesiod: 'When Sirius parches head and knees, and the body is dried up by reason of heat, then sit in the shade and drink.'

Leo, the second Fire sign, is the sign of the sunshine. It is the only one of the twelve zodiacal signs said to be 'ruled' by the sun, and although Cancer marks the point of the sun's greatest northerly declination, Leo marks its point of maximum power. Its metal is gold, the royal metal, and in the zodiacal man it corresponds with the heart, the 'central fire' of the body, upon which all the other organs depend. For the Jews it represented the tribe of Judah, 'the lion's whelp', according to Jacob's blessing (Genesis 49:9). Indeed the Lion, whose mane is reflected in the glyph of Leo (♌), has been associated with this constellation from the earliest times and in various cultures, in part no doubt because 'the sunne being in that signe is most raging and hot like a lion' (Allen, page 253), but also because the dignity, pride, indolence, individualism and sense of innate superiority which, in folklore at least, the lion displays are often manifest in those people who are born at this time of the year. The Greek solar hero, Hercules, whose twelve labours reflect the signs of the zodiac, wears the skin of a lion, and his most memorable labour is the slaying of the Nemean Lion. Hercules' Hebrew counterpart, Samson (whose Hebrew name means 'Sunny'), kills a lion with his bare hands in the vineyards of Timnath, and eats honey ('liquid sunshine' as it has been called) from its carcase (Judges 14: 5-9).

'The sons of the Lion,' writes Manilius, 'are filled with the urge to adorn their proud portals with pelts ... and (to) swagger about in the heart of the capital with droves of beasts', which, making concessions for cultural differences, agrees entirely with more modern assessments which detect in the sons and daughters of Leo a fondness for self-display, vanity, and aristocratic individualism. Charles Carter says that in Leo 'there is the temptation to say, "For *mine* is the kingdom, the power and the glory", to which the bombastic Italian dictator (Mussolini, born 29 July 1883) so completely succumbed'. But what sometimes manifests negatively at the level of human character is only a reflection of the essence of Leo, 'the sign of divine splendour', whose ruler, the sun, has ever been a symbol of deity 'not as a vain and self-seeking magnate but as a source of tender affection and loving fatherhood for all upon whom its rays may shine' (Carter, 1965, page 71).

In essence, then, Leo concerns identity; not just awareness of the ego and its constant struggle to draw attention to itself, nor even of the 'personality', the mask we wear in life's theatre, but the real identity of the human person as a child of God, as a soul of infinite value. 'We are stardust, we are golden', sang Joni Mitchell at Woodstock, echoing the Psalmist who tells us that we are 'a little lower than the angels' (Psalm 8).

This individuality is symbolized, astrologically, by the sun, the source of all life, which 'implants in the soul at length the mastery and direction of its actions, desire for substance, glory, and position, and a change from playful, ingenuous error to seriousness, decorum, and ambition' (Ptolemy, Book IV,

200-208). Its glyph is the circle with the dot in the centre (☉), the microcosm in the midst of the macrocosm, the tiny spark of divinity which awaits discovery in the depths of every human person.

The Spiritual Lessons of Leo

I am all at once what Christ is, since he was what I am, and
This Jack, joke, poor potsherd, patch, matchwood immortal diamond,
Is immortal diamond. (Gerard Manley Hopkins, born 28 July 1844)

On a journey to Caesarea Philippi,* Jesus asks his disciples, 'Who do people say that I am?' The text goes on:

> They replied, 'Some say John the Baptist; others say Elijah; and still others, one of the prophets.' 'But what about you?' he asked. 'Who do you say I am?' (Mark 8:28-29)

Conventionally, this episode is read as a record of an actual discussion between Jesus and his disciples in which the Lord reveals the secret of his own unique status as the Christ (or Messiah)† of Jewish expectation. But such an approach is fraught with problems, as scholars have discovered. To begin with, Mark's Jesus is manifestly *not* the Christ of Jewish expectation. Unlike Matthew and Luke, Mark does not say that Jesus was born in Bethlehem, the city of David, which Micah had predicted would be the Messiah's birthplace (Micah 5:2). In addition, it is unlikely that Jesus was of the Davidic line; as an inhabitant of Galilee in the north his ancestry would hardly be from the tribe of Judah which was located in the south of the country, around Jerusalem. The only individual who calls him 'Son of David' in Mark's Gospel is blind! (Mark 10:46-52), and Jesus seems to repudiate this title in chapter 12 (verses 35-37), a passage which has proved very problematical for most conventional exegetes.

Most telling of all, however, is the fact that Jesus does not fulfil the role of Messiah in any way that was even remotely comprehensible to the Jews, which is why the Jewish people to this day have difficulty in accepting him as such. The Messiah was to be a literal leader who, as Psalm 2 declares, would 'Break (the heathen nations) with a rod of iron, (and) dash them in

---

* Caesarea Philippi is the ideal place for the revelation of the 'deity' of Jesus. The legendary birthplace of the god Pan, it was littered with remains of at least a dozen temples to pagan deities, and it boasted a temple of white marble to the godhead of Caesar, which had been built by Herod the Great.

† 'Messiah' is Hebrew, 'Christ' is Greek. They both mean 'the anointed one'.

117

pieces like a potter's vessel' (verse 9), which the Jesus of the Gospels does not even attempt, let alone achieve. The conventional Christian response to this is to claim that the Jewish people were wrong to expect this kind of Messiah, and that the nature of the real Messiah is to be found in the Suffering Servant Songs of Isaiah 52–53. However, nowhere in Mark do we find references, other than exceedingly oblique ones, to this section of Isaiah. It is Matthew who quotes from these verses, in an attempt to give Jesus better Messianic credentials (Matthew 12:15-21). He makes Jesus a clear personification of the Suffering Servant, whereas for Jewish exegetes the whole nation of Israel was, and is, the embodiment of this Old Testament figure.

Such anomalies have led commentators to make all manner of speculation about Jesus' role as Messiah. Wrede, for instance, writing at the beginning of the twentieth century, considered that this section of Mark's Gospel was really an attempt to come to terms with the fact that Jesus had never claimed to be the Messiah in his lifetime, and the title had only been accorded him, by his followers, after his death. Hence the secrecy motif which pervades these verses. However, there is no need to resort to such reasoning, dependent as it is upon an overly literal view of what it means to be the Messiah. That there is secrecy here there can be no doubt, but it is not the secrecy born of expediency. Mark's secret is the same as Paul's:

> [It is] the mystery that has been kept hidden for ages and generations, but is now disclosed to the saints. To them God has chosen to make known among the Gentiles the glorious riches of this mystery, which is *Christ in you*, the hope of glory. (Colossians 1:26-27, emphasis added)

This section of the Gospel attempts to teach us that Messiahship is not embodied in one individual, historical character, but that it is a status which all potentially share. To be the Messiah, the Christ, to be agents of transformation in the world, we have to become fully persuaded of our relationship with God, and fully committed to the welfare of others who are equal sharers in divine sonship and daughtership. 'Who do you say that I am?' is not a question asked, once and for all, by Jesus of Peter; it is the question that all of us must ask ourselves at some time or another; and we must keep reminding ourselves of the correct answer.

The Fourth Gospel has no account of Jesus' question to Peter, but it explores the theme of identity even more comprehensively than the synoptics. Jesus uses the expression 'I am' on a number of occasions – 'I am the bread of life' (6:48); 'I am the Good Shepherd' (10:14); 'I am the resurrection and the life' (11:25); and, in conversation with the Jews, he makes the astonishing claim, 'Before Abraham was, I am (*ego eimi*)'. This is not just a claim to pre-existence; it is nothing short of a claim to identity with God who, in the Book of Exodus, had revealed himself to Moses as 'I am who I am' (Exodus 3:14).

Most of Christendom interprets this to mean that Jesus alone has this oneness with God, a position which undoubtedly hinders all genuine dialogue with non-Christian faiths. But this is not the only possible interpretation. For Gnostics, and for all who accept the perennial philosophy in one or other of its guises, 'I am' refers to the awareness of identity with God which can be experienced by all who discover the Christ within.*

On such an interpretation, 'the Christ' is not a single historical figure but the eternal principle of mystical unity with the divine which, says Thomas Hickey, has been discovered and proclaimed 'by saints and sages, poets and wise people, throughout history, and ... is recorded in the sacred books, mythologies and literatures of all cultures' (Hickey, page 33).

It can be found in the Hindu *Upanishads*, which came into existence hundreds of years before the Christian era. In the *Chandogya Upanishad* the seeker, Svetaketu, is informed by his father about the nature of the Self:

> In the beginning there was Existence alone – One only without a second.
> He, the One, thought to himself: Let me be many, let me grow forth.
> Thus out of himself he projected the universe; and having projected out
> of himself the universe, he entered into every being. All that is has its
> self in him alone. Of all things he is the subtle essence. He is the truth.
> and that, Svetaketu, THAT ART THOU. (Prabhavananda, pages 68-9)

Tat Tvam Asi, 'that art thou', expresses the identity of the Self with Brahman, Being itself, the source of all existence. The Gnostic Gospel of Thomas is firmly in this mystical tradition, teaching that 'we came from the light, the place where the light came into being on its own accord' (Barnstone, page 303). Later in the same document we read, 'Split a piece of wood and I am there. Lift up the stone and you will find me there' (i.e. there is nowhere that the Christ is not). The similarity between such ideas and eastern mystical philosophy can be clearly seen, and may give us a clue as to why the name of Thomas, who was traditionally considered to be the Apostle to India, came to be associated with this Gospel.

This essentially Gnostic viewpoint has been expressed in more recent

---

* John's Gospel gives an account of another occasion on which Jesus claims identity with God by declaring 'I and the Father are one' (John 10:30). When accused of blasphemy by the Jews, he quotes in his own defence Psalm 82 (verse 6), 'I have said you are gods', which is a clear statement of divine potential within all human beings.

times by ex-Dominican priest Matthew Fox, in terms which, no doubt unwittingly, reflect the leonine themes of this section of Mark's Gospel:

> 'What good is it to me if I am a king and do not know I am a king?' asks Meister Eckhart. The name 'Christ' means 'the anointed one'. All of us are anointed ones. We are all royal persons, creative, godly, divine, persons of beauty and of grace. We are all Cosmic Christs, 'other Christs'. But what good is this if we do not know it? Everyone is a sun of God as well as a son or daughter of God, but very few believe it or know it. The ones who do Meister Eckhart calls 'the enlightened ones'. (Fox, page 137)

'Son' and 'sun' are accidental homophones in English, but this is not their only connection. Leo, the fifth sign of the zodiac, ruled by the sun, has natural affinity with the fifth house of the horoscope, which in traditional astrology concerns offspring. It can be no accident that this Leo section of Mark contains a number of Father-Son references: the voice of God on the mount of Transfiguration declaring 'This is my beloved Son, listen to him,' (9:7), and the incident of the man with the demon-possessed son, which ends the section (9:14-29). God makes a similar claim to the paternity of Jesus in the Aries section (1:11), and Aries is the sign of the sun's exaltation. In Luke's genealogy of Jesus (Luke 3:23), Jesus' grandfather is said to be *Heli*, which is a contraction of the Greek word for 'sun' – *helios*.

Matthew, in his parallel account, has even more father-son references. He has Peter declare that Jesus is 'the son of the living God' (Matthew 16:16), and in the next verse Jesus calls Peter 'bar Jonah' – *son of Jonah*, named for the prophet of old who refused to obey God's command to preach to the people of Nineveh, and ended up in the belly of the great fish. This could be an allusion to Peter's Piscean character because, despite his ironic nickname 'Rocky', he displays all the characteristics of the vacillating Pisces. In this passage, Peter represents the sons and daughters of Pisces – the citizens of the new age – to whom Jesus is revealing the secrets of the kingdom of God. The 'rock' upon which Jesus will build his community (*ekklêsia*) is not the man, Peter, as generations of Roman Catholics have believed, *but the statement Peter makes about the identity of the Messiah:* 'You are the Christ, the son of the living God' is to be the unshakeable foundation of the new community, and is the key to the kingdom of God. Those who possess this knowledge of their own true identity transcend the conventions of inherited morality and live from their own divine centre, in accord with the values of the kingdom of God, but having a self-derived authority like that of Jesus who 'taught with authority, and not as the scribes'. Such people can make their own rules. As Edward Carpenter writes:

> Once you really appropriate this truth (i.e. your identity with God), and assimilate it in the depths of your mind, a vast change (you can easily imagine) will take place within you. The whole world will be transformed, and every thought and act of which you are capable will take on a different colour and complexion. (Carpenter, page 303)

The discovery of our own 'royal' nature, momentous though it is, is not the end of our efforts, as the Gospel goes on to show. Jesus predicts that suffering and death lie ahead, and not for him alone, but for all who would come after him (Mark 8:43). Paradoxically, the Leo phase of the spiritual journey does not involve aggrandizement but abasement. The Christ-like individual cannot pursue worldly wealth and glory: his treasure is his soul, his divine life, over which the things of the world will constantly try to throw a veil (Mark 8:35-37). As Alice Bailey points out, a prerequisite of living the divine life is 'the crucifixion of the lower self and the conquering of individual self assertion' (Bailey, 1974, page 74) symbolized mythologically by the slaying of the Nemean Lion, and by the destruction of 'the serpent of illusion', Hydra, one of Leo's decans, which represents that which 'veils and hides the soul'.

Fig. 12 Hydra, 'the fleeing serpent'

The lion and the serpent, Hercules' adversaries in the Greek myth, become the Devil, or Satan, in the Christian story. As we learn from the First Epistle of Peter, 'Your enemy the devil prowls around like a roaring lion looking for someone to devour' (1 Peter 5:8); and in the Book of Revelation we read about 'that ancient serpent called the devil or Satan, who leads the whole world astray' (Revelation 12:9). Unless the devil, the false, egotistical self, is conquered, no progress is possible in the spiritual life. As Leonine Carl Jung was wont to say: 'the death of the ego is the birth of everything else', a sentiment echoed by Aldous Huxley (another Leo, born 26 July 1894), who tells us that

> 'Our kingdom go' is the necessary and unavoidable corollary of 'Thy kingdom come'. For the more there is of self, the less there is of God. The divine eternal fullness of life can be gained only by those who have deliberately lost the partial, separative life of craving and self-interest, of egocentric thinking, feeling, wishing and acting. (Huxley, page 114)

This is the meaning of the 'crucifixion' predicted by Jesus.

Dane Rudhyar (page 71) says that a tendency to self-dramatization, to 'feeling quite special', accompanied by a growing sense of spiritual achievement, are the pitfalls associated with the Leonine phase of the spiritual journey (Rudhyar, page 71), which is why Jesus explains that suffering, not self-glorification, is a necessary consequence of Christhood. Peter's reluctance to accept this prompts Jesus to say 'Get behind me, Satan', and to tell him that his ideas are not of God but of men (Mark 8:33). Peter represents all those who have not yet moved beyond the point of 'feeling quite special'. Like the blind man (Mark 8:22-26), he can see, but not clearly; and like the rest of us, he has still to learn the lesson of self-crucifixion.

There may well be an allusion to the constellation Corvus, The Raven, one of the decans of Leo, in Jesus' rebuke of Peter. In his *Metamorphoses*, Ovid tells the story of the raven who, on reporting unwelcome news to his master, has his former silver colour changed to black. The story concludes:

> Then he turned upon the Raven,
> 'Wanton babbler! see thy fate!
> Messenger of mine no longer,
> Go to Hades with thy prate!'

According to Allen, it was from this story that the name *Garrulus Proditor* – 'Talkative Betrayer' – came to be associated with this constellation.

Son of Man

Throughout this section of the Gospel, Mark has Jesus refer to himself by this strange title which, originally, meant nothing more than 'human being'. In Psalm 8 (verse 4), for example, the psalmist asks:

> What is man, that you are mindful of him?
> The son of man, that you care for him?

This is a perfect example of 'parallelism', a consistent feature of Hebrew poetry, in which the second part of a statement echoes the first. These lines also reflect a Hebrew idiom in which 'son of' means 'one who exhibits the nature of', as in such expressions as 'son of kindness' (*ben chesed*) in the Old Testament, or 'Sons of Thunder' (*boanerges*, a Greek transliteration of an Aramaic word) in the New. In Ezekiel, the term 'son of man' is used on numerous occasions to mean nothing more than 'person' or 'human being'. Even in Daniel, where 'son of man' seems to take on an apocalyptic character (Daniel 7:18, 22, 27), there is still no indication that the term refers prophetically to an individual messianic figure. Indeed, as J.L. Mckenzie points out in his *Dictionary of the Bible*, 'son of man' refers to Israel in the Book of Daniel. Attribution of this title uniquely to Jesus is a development of later Christian theology, but this interpretation has its problems. The principal one concerns passages like Mark 8:38, which refers to the son of man 'coming in the glory of his Father with the holy angels'. If this foretells a literal second coming of a glorified Jesus, then it was not fulfilled since we are later informed that many present would not die until they had experienced this 'return' along with the coming of the kingdom of God 'with power' (Mark 9:1). Only by interpreting the 'coming of the son of man' and the 'coming of the kingdom' as poetic expressions of internal, spiritual transformations are we freed from the literalist's preoccupation with looking up at the sky.

The Transfiguration

Glory and faith, kingship and selfhood are the Leonine themes explored throughout this section of Mark, but nowhere more so than in the account of the Transfiguration. Six days* after the Caesarea Philippi episode, Jesus

* Since we are dealing with a document that is densely packed with symbolism, it would be rash of us to assume, as many commentators do, that 'after six days' is little more than an

takes Peter, James and John into a high mountain where he is transfigured
before them:

> And his clothes became dazzling white, like snow, whiter than anyone in the
> world could bleach them. And there appeared before them Elijah and Moses
> who were talking with Jesus. (Mark 9:3-4)

Jesus' true identity as God's son is made known in an unambiguous way to
the frightened and bewildered onlookers, who respond by asking whether
they should build three 'tabernacles', one each for Jesus, Moses and Elijah†
(Mark 9:5). These three 'tabernacles' (Greek *skênas* – tents, dwellings) reflect
the three-fold phases or locations of the sun: rising, midday and setting, and
so symbolize the three-fold nature of deity. Manly Hall writes:

> God the Father, the Creator of the world, is symbolized by the dawn.
> His colour is blue, because the sun rising in the morning is veiled in
> blue mist. God the son, the illuminating one sent to bear witness of His
> Father before all worlds, is the celestial globe at noonday, radiant and
> magnificent, the maned Lion of Judah, the Golden-haired Saviour of
> the world. Yellow is His colour and His power is without end. God the
> Holy Ghost is the sunset phase, when the orb of day, robed in flaming
> red, rests for a moment upon the horizon line then vanishes into the
> darkness of night to wander in the lower worlds and later rise again tri-
> umphant from the embrace of darkness. (Hall, pages 135-6)

In this wonderfully dramatic episode Mark declares that the Messianic status
of Jesus is ratified by two of the greatest figures from Jewish history, representing the Law and the Prophets, twin cornerstones of biblical religion.
Their endorsement is particularly important since both were supposed to
return to earth at the dawn of the Messianic age (see Deuteronomy 18:18,
and Malachi 4:5-6). But it is God himself who finally, and decisively, proclaims
Jesus as his son and tells the onlookers to listen to what he has to say (Mark 9:7).

---

editorial gloss, or an arbitrary linking phrase. According to Genesis, six is the number of creative days, and on the sixth day God created human beings (Gen 1:26-31). Six symbolizes
human nature in its original, 'unfallen' state, when our relationship with God, in whose image
we were created (Genesis 1:27), was most evident. Six is also the number of points on the Star
of David, which is composed of two con-penetrating triangles, one pointing up to heaven, the
other down to the earth, thus symbolizing the union of human and divine. The appearance of
the number six in a passage designed to teach us about the true nature of a human being is,
therefore, singularly appropriate.

† 'Elijah' is the common English translation of *Elias*, which in the original Greek sounds
very much like 'helios', the Greek word for the sun.

Fig. 13 The Transfiguration, by Raphael

In this poetic epiphany Mark is telling us that Jesus, in his true nature – the nature he shares with all of us – fulfils all the conditions of Christhood, and that the Jewish heritage, properly understood, points towards this, too. In this episode Matthew, once again, is more 'astrological' than Mark: he says (Matthew 17:2) that Jesus' face 'shone like the sun' (*elampsen to prosôpon autou hôs ho hêlios*), as clear a reference to Leo and its ruler as one could wish for.*

Fruitful comparison can be made between the Transfiguration and the revelation of Krishna's divine form in the Hindu classic the *Bhagavad Gita*, which was already about 400 years old by the time the Gospels were written, and would most certainly have been known to those sages from whom the Gospels eventually sprang. Its message is 'that each human life has but one ultimate end and purpose: to realize the Eternal Self within and thus to know, finally and fully, the joy of union with God, the Divine Ground of Being':

> O conqueror of sloth, this very day you shall behold the whole universe with all things animate and inert made one within this body of mine. And whatever else you desire to see, that you shall see also. But you cannot see me thus with those human eyes. Therefore, I give you divine sight. Behold, this is my yoga power. (Sanjaya, the narrator:) ... When he had spoken these words, Sri Krishna, master of all yogis, revealed to Arjuna his transcendent, divine Form, speaking from innumerable mouths, seeing with myriad eyes, of many marvellous aspects, adorned with countless divine ornaments, brandishing all kinds of heavenly weapons, celestial garlands and the raiment of paradise, anointed with perfumes of heavenly fragrance, full of revelations, resplendent, boundless, of ubiquitous regard. Suppose a thousand suns should rise together into the sky: such is the glory of the Shape of Infinite God. (Novak, page 24)

In the constellation Leo there are a number of stars whose names (as interpreted by Seiss *et al*) reflect the Transfiguration incident quite strikingly: the second star in Leo is Al Giebha, said to mean *the exalted, the exaltation*, while Zosma, situated near the lion's tail, is *the shining forth, the epiphany*, and while we may dismiss these as fanciful or anachronistic, there can be no doubt about the appropriateness of the name of the constellation's principal star, Regulus, *The King*, sometimes called 'Cor Leonis', 'the Heart of the Lion'. Allen writes:

* The Feast of the Transfiguration is celebrated in the Catholic tradition on 6 August, when the sun is in the centre of the sign of Leo.

Regulus was so called by Copernicus ... as a diminutive of the earlier *Rex*, equivalent to the βασιλισκος of Ptolemy ... Thus, as *Sharru*, the King, it marked the fifteenth ecliptic constellation of Babylonia; in India it was *Magha*, the Mighty; in Sogdiana, *Magh*, the Great; in Persia, *Miyan*, the centre; among the Turanian races, *Masu*, the Hero; and in Akkadia it was associated with the fifth antediluvian King-of-the-celestial-sphere, *Amil-gal-ur* ... In Arabia it was *Malikiyy*, Kingly; in Greece, βασιλισκος αστηρ; in Rome *Basilica Stella*; with Pliny, *Regia*; in the revival of European astronomy, *Rex*, and with Tycho, *Basiliscus*. (Allen, pages 255-6)

The very ancient and widespread association of this star with kingship and glory stems from its status as the leader of the so-called 'Royal Stars', Regulus, Formalhaut,* Aldebaran and Antares, which rise approximately six hours apart, and so seem to divide the sky into quadrants. According to Allen, in antiquity these stars were associated with the four climactic points of the year, the equinoxes and the solstices, and Regulus was associated with the summer solstice, when the sun is at the highest point in its annual journey through the heavens.

The Boy with the 'unclean spirit'

When Jesus comes down the mountain and returns to his disciples, he finds a great crowd has gathered. A man has brought his son to be healed, but the disciples of Jesus seem powerless, and the man approaches Jesus himself, begging him to cure his son who, he says, is oppressed by a 'dumb' (*alalos*) spirit, which regularly takes hold of him, causing him to foam at the mouth and to gnash his teeth. 'How long has this been going on?' asks Jesus. 'From childhood,' replies the man. 'It often throws him into the fire and into the water, trying to destroy him.' Jesus tells him that all things are possible to one who has faith, and the man utters the famous words, 'Lord, I believe, help thou mine unbelief.' Then Jesus rebukes the spirit, which convulses the lad, before coming out of him and leaving him as if dead. Jesus takes the young man by the hand and lifts him up, and then tells the astonished disciples that this kind of spirit can only be exorcized by prayer and fasting.

* Formalhaut is found in the constellation Piscis Australis, which lies opposite Leo, and is one of the decans of Aquarius. Its Arabic name means the Fish's Mouth, and while there is no corresponding Greek or Roman name in Ptolemy or Manilius, Allen says that the Fish's Mouth has long been the common name for this star. This helps to explain why Jesus tells Peter that he will find a coin in a fish's mouth with which to pay the temple tax. This curious story, found only in Matthew, comes just after his account of the Transfiguration (17:24-27).

Mark's version of this story illustrates the importance of faith – a characteristic quality of all three Fire signs, but particularly of Leo and Sagittarius. 'If the affirmation of Cancer is *I fear*, that of Leo is *I have faith*', writes Charles Carter (1965, page 71). But faith in this context cannot possibly mean 'faith in doctrines' or even 'faith in Jesus'. It refers to a particular kind of confidence in one's own power as a child of God, *the power of the Christ within*, in the light of which everything is possible. 'It's not a question of whether I can help you,' says Jesus to the man, 'it's more to do with whether you can help yourself' (verse 23), the implication being that any power Jesus might possess is available to anyone who, through spiritual discipline ('prayer and fasting'), comes to realize his or her own essential divinity. It is the paltriness of our self-understanding which renders us impotent, cowering in the face of adversity. 'Man is a god in ruins,' says Emerson, and only when we reacquaint ourselves with our true nature will we be able to exercise those powers which are our birthright.

In these days, when a reputable scientist can declare, 'I think we follow the basic law of nature, which is that we're a bunch of chemical reactions running around in a bag' (Dean Hamer, quoted in *Time* magazine, 29 November 2004), and when politicians of right and left can view people as expendable economic entities, the Gospel teaching about the inherent divinity of the human being needs to be affirmed with all the energy we can muster.

'Moonstruck'

Matthew's version of this story (Matthew 17: 14-21) adds another dimension. According to Matthew, the young man is not harbouring a 'dumb' spirit, as Mark says, he is 'moonstruck' (*selêniazetai*), a term which has perplexed commentators and translators, so much so that the boy's condition is generally considered to be epilepsy, since epileptic seizures were thought to be influenced by the moon. But the Greeks had a perfectly good word for epilepsy – epilepsy! – and, presumably, Matthew could have used this word if he had wanted to. However, there is the intriguing possibility that Matthew used this word for a different reason, a reason connected with Leo's principal star Regulus, which lies directly on the ecliptic, the sun's apparent path in the sky (and the belt of sky through which all the planets, including the sun and moon, seem to move), which means that it is occulted (hidden) by the sun every year (around 22 August) *and even more frequently by the moon*. Regulus, 'the little king', 'the prince', symbolizes the grandeur of the human soul, which perceives its own royal nature on the Mount of Transfiguration but which, on descending the mountain, is brought once more into the conflicts and uncertainties of daily life where it begins to doubt itself. After being illumined by the sun it is struck by the moon, tossed to the earth, buffeted 'between the fire (sun) and the water (moon)', losing faith in its own inherent divinity, as it becomes re-entangled in the minutiae of mundane existence. Whereas the sun rules maturity, 'giving mastery and direction to action,' the moon, by contrast, rules infancy, 'with its changeability and the imperfection and inarticulate state of its soul' (Ptolemy, IV, section 10). To the ancient astrologers the moon represented flux and inconstancy, but also habit, the instinctive, deadening, thoughtless, reactive, response to experience.

Whenever we are at the mercy of instinct or of habit, when we are swayed by prejudice, or when we act automatically and without thought, we are 'moonstruck'. Sadly, but realistically, this is the normal human condition, and it can only be overcome, as the Gospel text clearly tells us, by consistent spiritual practice.

Virgo (Mark 9:30–9:50)
Beginner's Mind

The sole meaning of life is to serve humanity.
(Leo Tolstoy, born 9 September 1828)

Virgo and Mercury

We noted in the chapter on Aries that in the ancient world, Virgo was considered to be the leading constellation in the zodiac circle. The association of Virgo with birth and children makes it an appropriate starting point for any symbolic account of the spiritual journey. Our spiritual life begins not with our natural birth, but with our *rebirth*, which is not brought about by physical urges but by the Spirit of God working within us. 'Unless a man is born again,' says Jesus to Nicodemus, 'he cannot see the kingdom of God' (John 3:3). The Jews called this harvest* constellation Bethulah and associated it with the tribe of Asher, of whom Jacob had declared 'his bread shall be fat' (Genesis 49:20). Symbolically, Virgo is the 'house of bread' which, in

---

* It could well be that in the 'original' Gospel the saying of Jesus concerning the harvest, 'The harvest truly is great, but the labourers are few; pray ye to the Lord of the harvest, that he would send forth labourers into his harvest,' occurred in this Virgo section. Luke has Jesus say this in chapter 10 (verse 2), just a little after Jesus has set a child before the disciples (Luke 9:46-48)

Fig. 14 Isis and Horus

Hebrew, is Bethlehem (*Beth* – 'house', *lechem* – 'bread'), where we become 'children' once more, stripped of our pretensions and our cynicism, and open to the promptings of the Spirit. The Gospels of Matthew and Luke are both prefaced by stories in which these themes are prominent. Mark, who has chosen to structure his narrative around the yearly cycle, beginning with Aries, has to introduce them halfway through.

The ancient zodiacs invariably depict Virgo as a woman holding something. In the Egyptian zodiac of Denderah, for example, the figure is drawn carrying a distaff, and when she represents the Egyptian goddess, Isis, she appears with wheat-ears in her hand, or clasping the young Horus in her arms. In the middle ages, this ancient figure reappeared as the Virgin Mary with the child Jesus, and in *Titus Andronicus* Shakespeare alludes to it as 'the good boy in Virgo's lap'.

The image of Isis with Horus in her arms has become, in Christian iconography, the Virgin Mary carrying the child Jesus. Joseph Campbell writes:

When you stand before the cathedral of Chartres, you will see over one of the portals of the western front an image of the Madonna as the throne upon which the child Jesus sits and blesses the world as its emperor. That is precisely the image that has come down to us from most ancient Egypt. The early fathers and the early artists took over these images intentionally. (Campbell, 1988, page 222)

Albertus Magnus (thirteenth century) thought that Jesus was born under the sign of Virgo. Equally ancient (and equally unlikely) is the idea that the glyph of Virgo (♍) is composed of the initials of the Blessed Virgin (MV, 'Maria Virgo'). But the association of this constellation with Mary is more ancient than either of these quaint notions, as the calendar of the Roman Catholic Church testifies. The Feast of the Assumption of the Virgin is celebrated on 15 August, and the Birth of the Virgin on 8 September. On or around the first of these dates, as the sun leaves the constellation Leo and approaches Virgo, the powerful rays of the rising sun apparently eliminate the fainter lights from Virgo's stars: the Virgin is 'assumed' into the glory of the sun, or as the Book of Revelation has it, she is '*clothed* with the sun, with the moon under her feet and a crown of twelve stars on her head' (Revelation 12:12, emphasis added). On 8 September, the Virgin is 'born' as her stars once more become visible at sunrise.*

Mary's 'Virgoan' qualities can be found in the Gospel of Luke, where she is portrayed as the 'handmaid' (*hê doulê* – 'slave') of the Lord' (Luke 1:38), one who embodies the great virtues of humility, service and self-effacement. Manilius gives us a picture of this aspect of the Virgo nature:

> But modest Virgo's Rays give polisht parts,
> And fill Men's Breasts with Honesty and Arts,
> No tricks for Gain, nor love of Wealth dispense,
> But piercing Thoughts, and winning eloquence …
> But bashful Modesty casts down their Eyes,
> The best of Vices, yet 'tis still a Vice,
> Because it stifles, checks or nips like Frost,
> A blooming Vertue, and the Fruit is lost.
>
> (Manilius, 1697, pages 125-6)

Modesty, which Manilius sees as both the strength and weakness of this sign, is a key characteristic of Virgo, sharply contrasting the assertiveness and bombast usually associated with Leo. Virgo is an Earth sign, connected with the harvest, but it is also a Mutable sign, and mutability and earth are strange bedfellows. Earth is the element that responds least well to change, and love of variety is not as evident in Virgo as it is in the other Mutable signs. Mayo considers that the Mutable-Earth combination produces people who are 'self-repressive, passive, restrained, with qualities of practicality, adaptability and variableness' (Mayo, 1964, page 46), qualities which manifest

---

* Owing to the precession of the equinoxes, these dates no longer apply. Now, the sun passes through this constellation from mid-September to late October.

132

Fig. 15 The Assumption of Mary, by Titian

as an ability 'to collate and catalogue, to create order, to systematize' (Carter, 1925, page 73). People in whom the Virgo principle operates strongly generally shun the limelight, but they are excellent workers, well able to provide a practical structure for someone else's grand, but hazy and unformed, idea. Manilius says that the stenographer (*scriptor*) comes under Virgo, 'one who can record in novel notation the long speech of a rapid speaker' (Book 4, line 199), and the association of Virgo with secretarial work continues down to the present day. This aspect of Virgo as the devoted servant has been well described by Charles Carter:

> It is not the sign of leadership but of service; it does not aim at brilliant results but at useful ones. It is patient and does not turn from routine drudgery; it hates show and shuns responsibility and publicity. It is not ambitious but is satisfied with a straight job and a fair wage. (Carter, 1965, page 73)

If we translate the elements of this somewhat unflattering psychological portrait into spiritual categories we can see that the Virgo phase of experience is characterized by service, discipleship, living out the precepts laid down by the spiritual master. In the modern era no one has exemplified these better than Mother Teresa of Calcutta (born 27 August 1910), whose practical, 'hands-on' approach to religion has had such a marked influence on the contemporary world. Although her shrewd self-promotion, her high profile and her considerable leadership qualities seem to indicate the importance of other factors, her image and her public utterances seem almost invariably to reflect her birth sign.

> A sacrifice to be real must cost, must hurt, must empty ourselves. The fruit of silence is prayer, the fruit of prayer is faith, the fruit of faith is love, the fruit of love is service, the fruit of service is peace. (Mullan, page 122)

Leo Tolstoy (born 9 September 1828), who in his later years was drawn towards an analysis of the religious nature of the human being, extolled the simple, rational, practical aspects of religion, free from supernaturalism, and concentrating almost exclusively on behaviour: 'Let all the world practise the [teaching] of Jesus and the reign of God will come upon earth,' he wrote.

The strongly developed critical faculties associated with Virgo manifest on the spiritual level as the principle of discrimination, of making those choices which will provide a secure foundation for the living out of the spiritual life. The making of such discriminations demands painstaking effort and it is often a very costly affair, since all choice involves loss. So, the Virgo phase of the spiritual life is not simply the passive acceptance of inherited principles, the sheep-like, unquestioning adherence to a system which will enable us to rest from the agonizing choices that life calls us to make. Genuine discipleship demands that we appropriate spiritual values by constantly re-evaluating them in the light of our growing knowledge and experience. The 'simple faith' which refuses to make such discriminations is not a commend-able spiritual state, but a manifestation of laziness masquerading as piety. Mark will address these issues in the Virgo section of his Gospel.

The 'ruler' of Virgo is the planet Mercury (☿), which is also said to be 'exalted' in this sign. Mercury, in fact, is the only planet which is exalted in a sign it is said to rule, and so it has a double connection with Virgo. Mercury, in either its Geminian or Virgoan guise, is the 'mental' planet since its operations are to do with the making of connections between the multi-farious aspects of experience, but, what is more to the point of our present study, it is the planet said to have affinity with childhood. Ptolemy writes:

> In the following period of ten years, Mercury, to whom falls the second place and the second age, that of childhood, for the period which is half the space of twenty years, begins to articulate and fashion the intelligent and logical part of the soul, to implant certain seeds and rudiments of learning, and to bring to light individual peculiarities of character and faculties, awaking the soul at this stage by instruction, tutelage, and the first gymnastic exercises. (Ptolemy, page 91)

In *As You Like It*, Shakespeare reflects the ancient tradition of the Seven Ages of Man, the idea that each period of life is governed by a particular planet. His 'young boy, creeping like snail unwillingly to school' is governed by Mercury, the god of learning and communication.

The Spiritual Lessons of Virgo

Heaven lies about us in our infancy!
Shades of the prison-house begin to close
Upon the growing Boy.
But He beholds the light, and whence it flows,
He sees it in his joy;
The Youth, who daily farther from the east
Must travel, still is Nature's Priest,

135

And by the Vision splendid
Is on his way attended;
At length the Man perceives it die away,
And fade into the light of common day.
(Wordsworth, *Intimations of Immortality*)

On a psychological level Virgo has little in common with Leo, the sign that precedes it in the zodiac. However, spiritually, they represent two sides of the same coin. We noted in the previous chapter that coming to a realization of our own divine nature necessitates accepting that other people share the same intrinsic status. Such a realization produces a sense of the immanence of God in all things and, especially, in all people, in the light of which we can only be humble. This is one of the numerous paradoxes of the spiritual life, whose laws operate in a manner quite different from the ordinary laws of physical life. In the Leo section, Jesus informs us that in order to save our life we must lose it (Mark 8:35), and that suffering and self-denial are a necessary part of following Christ (Mark 8:34): we can only realize our true divinity by relinquishing it. In the Letter to the Philippians (2:5-8), St Paul expresses it thus:

Your attitude should be the same as that of Christ Jesus, who, being in very nature God, did not consider equality with God something to be grasped, but made himself nothing, taking the very nature of a servant, being made in human likeness. And being found in appearance as a man, he humbled himself and became obedient to death – even death on a cross!

This is the principle of *kenôsis*, self-emptying: our divine nature is only realized to the extent that we serve the divine in other people. In the Gospel of Mark, no sooner are we apprised of Jesus' glory (Leo) than we are given clear instructions about the necessity of humility (Virgo).

These instructions appear in the form of a dialogue which takes place between Jesus and the apostles immediately after the Cure of the Boy with the Unclean Spirit (Mark 9:14-29), and the Second Prediction of Jesus' Passion and Death (Mark 9:30-32). The apostles have been arguing about which of them was most important. Jesus sits down and says to them:

'If anyone wants to be first, he must be the very last, and the servant of all.'
(Mark 9:35)

He further reduces their sense of self-importance by taking a child in his arms and explaining that receiving such a child is receiving Christ, and

136

receiving Christ is receiving God (Mark 8:36-37). The child stands as a perfect symbol of Virgo: Mercury rules childhood, and, as we have seen, the child is a central figure of this constellation. We might note that Matthew reflects the Virgoan character of this passage even more clearly than Mark:

'Therefore, whoever humbles himself like this child is the greatest in the kingdom of heaven.' (Matthew 18:4)

For both evangelists the child represents humanity in its simplest and least affected state. This was a particularly apt image at the time the Gospels were being written, when children had little or no status in the community, but it

Fig. 16 'Jesus and the Children', by Heinrich Hofman.

137

applies today too. Children are vulnerable, trusting, open, free from guile, until the 'shades of the prison-house' begin to form around them and they have to learn to compromise with the world.

Being childlike, and receiving the kingdom of heaven 'like a child' (Mark 10:13-16),* are central themes of this Gospel, and it might be as well to explore the meaning of these images in a little more depth, since it is likely that more than innocence and lack of guile is being alluded to.

Religious Experience and Childhood

In the mid-seventies, the Religious Experience Unit at Oxford University conducted a survey of (initially) 2,000 people, asking the question: 'Have you ever been aware of or influenced by a presence or power, whether you call it God or not, which is different from your everyday self?' Rather more than 36 per cent of the people approached answered affirmatively, from which figure it was predicted that 'about fifteen million adults in this country (England) would say the same; that is to say, over a third of the population aged sixteen or over' (Hay, page 113).

Edward Robinson was struck by the number of respondents, some 15 per cent, who claimed to have had such an experience in childhood, and this prompted him to compile a book containing dozens of examples of these early intimations of transcendence. For example, one 57-year-old lady writes:

> The most profound experience of my life came to me when I was very young – between four and five years old ... My mother and I were walking on a stretch of land in Pangbourne, Berks, known locally as 'the moors'. As the sun declined and the slight chill of evening came on, a pearly mist formed over the ground. My feet, with the favourite black shoes with silver buckles, were gradually hidden from sight until I stood ankle deep in gently swirling vapour. Here and there just the

* Mark 10:13-16. This occurs in what I have called the Libra section of the Gospel, which seems somewhat unfortunate from the point of view of my main thesis. This is one of the few places where the zodiacal themes appear slightly out of sequence, but I am reluctant to attribute this seeming discrepancy to some copyist's error, particularly since Matthew preserves the same general order (see Matthew 19). Libra is a comparative newcomer to the zodiacal circle, and its stars have been associated with both Virgo and Scorpio. The Roman goddess of Justice, Astraea, who is an obvious Libran figure, was frequently identified with Virgo, and Libra was originally known as the 'horn' or 'claw' of the Scorpion, so, as Deborah Houlding informs us, 'the symbolism of this constellation has swung between allegiance with the imagery of the Scorpion and the Maiden,' (http://www.skyscript.co.uk/libra_myth.html). By placing Virgoan themes in his Libran section Mark could well be demonstrating his awareness of this fact.

very tallest harebells appeared above the mist. I had a great love of these exquisitely formed flowers, and stood lost in wonder at the sight. Suddenly I seemed to see the mist as a shimmering gossamer tissue and the harebells, appearing here and there, seemed to shine with brilliant fire. Somehow I understood that this was the living tissue of life itself, in which that which we call consciousness was embedded, appearing here and there as a shining focus of energy in the more diffused whole. In that moment I knew that I had my own special place, as had all other things, animate and so-called inanimate, and that we were all part of a universal tissue which was both fragile yet immensely strong, and utterly good and beneficent ... This is without doubt the (experience) which has laid the deepest foundation of my life, and for which I feel the profoundest gratitude. (Robinson, E., page 11)

I have quoted this beautiful passage at length because it typifies so many of the experiences described in Robinson's book, and because it exemplifies so perfectly the book's main thesis: that in childhood we are as open to spiritual experience as at any other time of our life, but that such early experiences have a purity unsullied by adult rationalizations and untouched by the constraints of conventional religion. As Matthew informs us, God has kept the things of heaven from the wise and prudent, and revealed them to mere children (Matthew 11:25). This view of childhood as an exalted state is not a nostalgic denial of childhood's problems, but an affirmation of the sensitivity to the holiness of life which our growing involvement with the world tends to obscure. 'The child tends to grow out of his direct awareness of the one Ground of things; for the habit of analytical thought is fatal to the intuitions of integral thinking' (Huxley, page 22). As Jesus takes the child in his arms (Mark 9:36), echoing the oldest images of the constellation Virgo, he is, in yet another paradox, showing us that the world is best understood by those who have lived in it least; that this virginal, untainted state is a prerequisite for understanding the things of God. To become as little children is to cultivate what the Buddhists call 'beginner's mind', a willingness to look at the world with fresh eyes. This is well illustrated by the following Zen parable:

A very clever University professor went to visit Nan-in, a Buddhist holy man. The professor wanted some advice on how he should live a spiritual life. 'I have been studying for many years,' he told the holy man. 'I have read hundreds of books; I have sat at the feet of many gurus; and I have attended many different places of worship; but I have never found what I am looking for. So now I have come to see you.'

Nan-in looked kindly at the professor. 'Would you like a cup of tea?' he asked with a smile.

'Yes, please,' replied the professor.

Nan-in prepared the tea and began to pour. The professor's cup was filled to overflowing, but Nan-in continued to pour the tea until it spilled out on to the saucer, and then on to the table.

'What are you doing?' asked the astonished professor. 'The cup is full. No more will go in!'

'Just like you,' said Nan-in. 'Your head is so full of theories, scriptures, ceremonies, and philosophies that there is no room for anything else. Before I can start to teach you, you must empty your cup.'

The virginal, 'empty' state is necessary if we are to bring to birth the God who lies dormant within the soul. The ancient church called Mary *Theotokos*, a Greek term meaning 'God-bearer', and the Catholic Church, which preserves the vocabulary of these ancient mysteries but which has largely forgotten their meaning, honours her with that title today. But, as Meister Eckhart said in the twelfth century: 'Mary is blessed, not because she bore Christ physically, but because she bore him spiritually, and in this everyone can become like her' – a sentiment echoed by Angelus Silesius in the seventeenth century, who wrote: 'Though Christ were yearly born in Bethlehem and never had birth in you yourself, then were you lost forever' (Bailey, 1934, page 270).

Mark's text goes on to describe two dangers of the Virgoan stage. The first of these is perfectionism, which can manifest as insularity or the 'holier than thou' mentality. Mayo calls this the Virgoan need 'to be "pure" and free from the influence of others' (1964, page 47). The disciples tell Jesus that they have forbidden someone, not of their company, from casting out devils in Jesus' name. Jesus disapproves of their action and tells them to let the man alone, because 'whoever is not against us is for us' (Mark 9:40). He goes on to indicate that even the smallest gesture of support for the things of God will not go unrewarded (Mark 9:41). All expressions of service and humility, regardless of their motivation or origin, will foster the growth of the kingdom. Matthew preserves this saying of Jesus, but he places it in a different context, and in his zeal to preserve the purity and authority of the church, he completely reverses the sense: 'He that is not with me is against me' (Matthew 12:30), he has Jesus say. Virgoan exclusiveness, the need to stay aloof from the encroachments of 'paganism', started early on in the church's history, but it is a need that is totally absent from Mark, except insofar as he tells us to avoid indulging it.

The second warning of this section concerns Virgoan passivity or, as

Carter has it, 'lack of spiritual aspiration and appreciation' (Carter, 1968, page 29), and echoes the constellation Coma Berenice, 'Berenice's Hair'. Berenice was the wife of Eueregetes, an ancient king of Egypt. As her husband was preparing to set out on a perilous journey she vowed that, should he return safely, she would cut off her hair, of which she was extremely proud, and offer it as a sacrifice to Aphrodite. On the king's return, Berenice kept her promise, placing her shorn locks in the temple of the goddess. Mark's text, which makes much of sacrificing precious body parts, reads as follows:

> If anyone causes one of these little ones — those who believe in me — to stumble, it would be better for them if a large millstone were hung around their neck and they were thrown into the sea. If your hand causes you to stumble, cut it off. It is better for you to enter life maimed than with two hands to go into hell, where the fire never goes out. And if your foot causes you to stumble, cut it off. It is better for you to enter life crippled than to have two feet and be thrown into hell. And if your eye causes you to stumble, pluck it out. It is better for you to enter the kingdom of God with one eye than to have two eyes and be thrown into hell, where "their worm does not die, and the fire is not quenched". Everyone will be salted with fire. Salt is good, but if it loses its saltiness, how can you make it salty again? Have salt in yourselves, and be at peace with each other. (Mark 9:42-50)

In this series of blood-curdling sayings, Jesus informs his followers that discipleship demands the most strenuous exercise of the will in a constant battle to maintain spiritual integrity. It is not simply a matter of withdrawing from life and insulating oneself in the kind of religiosity which takes refuge in prudishness and convention; the kind of pseudo-spirituality which believes that cleanliness is next to godliness, and that going to bed early and disapproving of bad language fulfil the duties of the spiritual life. On the contrary, the spiritual life is a life of crisis – choice, discrimination, decision – which demands, in Dane Rudhyar's words, 'the purification of desire and the steeling of the essential will', as well as 'strength, courage, inner stillness, an unemotional and unglamorized type of devotion' (page 124). Without such qualities we are cold-blooded and insipid, and, like salt that has lost its saltiness, fit only to be discarded. With them we become suitably pure, virginal receptacles from which the Christ may be born in the soul.

The Parable of the Lost Sheep

Matthew adds the parable of the Lost Sheep (Matthew 18:11-14) immediately after these warnings about indifference

141

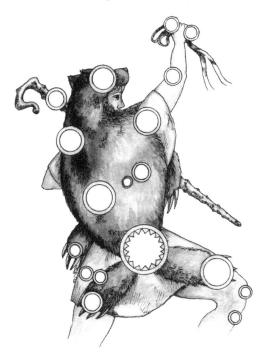

Fig. 17 Bootes, 'The Coming One, the Shepherd'

(For the son of man *has come* to save the lost.) What do you think? If a man has a hundred sheep and one of them is lost, won't he leave the ninety-nine and go *into the mountains* to look for the one that has gone astray? And believe me, if he happens to find it, he will rejoice more over that sheep than over the ninety-nine which didn't wander. (emphasis added)

This is a reference to the constellation Bootes, one of the decans of Virgo. Bootes, one of the oldest named constellations, is mentioned in the *Odyssey*, and has been identified for 3,000 years, and possibly longer. Its name has many possible derivations, but Pastor was one of its titles in the ancient world (the French still call it Bouvier), probably because the kite-like shape of the constellation resembles a human figure who seems to be eternally shepherding the stars around the North Pole. Its most prominent star, Arcturus, the fourth brightest star in the sky, was called the Shepherd of the Heavenly Flock, or the Shepherd of the Life of Heaven, in the ancient civilizations of the Euphrates.

In Greek mythology, Boeotus was one of the twin sons of Poseidon who were abandoned and left to die on Mount Pelion but who were rescued and raised by a herdsman. Boeotus was later reclaimed by his grandfather and went on to inherit part of his kingdom. Seiss writes:

> We have here the figure of a strong man, whom the Greeks named Bootes, the ploughman. But he and the so-called plough are set in opposite directions. Neither does a man plough with uplifted hand in the attitude of this figure. The name thus transformed into Greek has in it a Hebrew and Oriental root, *Bo*, which means coming; hence, the coming One or the One that was to come ... Bootes is not a ploughman at all, but the guardian and shepherd of the flocks ... The brightest star in the constellation of Bootes is also called Arcturus, the guardian or keeper of Arktos, a word which in its Oriental elements connects with the idea of enclosure, the ascending, the happy, *the going up upon the mountains*. (Seiss, page 32, emphasis added)

Seiss's etymology may be strange, but Jesus' statement 'For the Son of man *is come* (êlthen) to save that which was lost', which immediately precedes the parable, and the reference to the mountains within the parable, certainly seem to substantiate it. The story has an obvious relationship with the Virgoan concern for the details; most of us would be content that ninety-nine were safe, and we wouldn't be inclined to jeopardize that safety by seeking out the straying sheep. But God, who notices even the fall of a sparrow, and numbers the hairs on your head (Matthew 10:29-30) looks after the small matters as well as the bigger picture. As Virgoan Mother Teresa said, 'Little things are indeed little, but to be faithful in little things is a great thing.'

Libra (Mark 10:1–10:31)
Maintaining the Balance

Jesus said: 'When you make the two into one,
you will be called sons of men.'
(*Gospel of Thomas*, Saying 106)

Libra and Venus

The entry of the sun into Libra marks the autumnal equinox in the northern hemisphere, when day and night are equal once again. This is the mid-point of the year, the moment of equilibrium, when the forces symbolized by the day and the night are in perfect counterpoise. This has happened before, of course, when the sun entered Aries in the springtime, but there is a difference between these opposite but complementary points: at the spring equinox the point of poise occurs before the daylight begins to dominate; in the autumn this is reversed and the balance-point presages the forthcoming massing of the darkness.

The eternal interplay of light and darkness is symbolized in the zodiac itself, which, on one level, is nothing more than the yearly cycle projected on to the sky. The first six signs, then, come under the dominion of the daylight and can be said to represent the light of individual consciousness struggling

144

to establish its identity. This process is associated with the sun, the giver of light. It begins in Aries, the sign of the sun's exaltation, and reaches its climax in sun-ruled Leo. The signs which follow the autumnal equinox, however, are characterized by the gathering darkness and have to do with the group into which individuality has to be incorporated, if not submerged. These are the 'social' signs which begin with Libra, the sign of the sun's 'fall' or 'depression', and which reach their point of maximum power in Aquarius, the sign (in modern astrological jargon) of the sun's 'detriment'.

In ancient Egypt Libra was associated with Maat, the goddess of cosmic harmony and justice, whose special task was to weigh the hearts of the dead on the scales of justice balanced against an ostrich feather, and she is usually depicted with a feather in her headdress. Those who failed her test were 'heavy hearted'; those who passed, 'light hearted'.

Among the Greeks, notably Hipparchus, Libra was *Zugos, The Yoke*, the very word used by Matthew in a passage immediately following Jesus' declaration that God has revealed the secrets of the kingdom to infants (Matthew 11:25-30). Mark uses a word from the same root (*sunzeugnumi*) when he writes: 'What God has joined – *yoked* – together, let no man separate' (Mark 10:9).

Among the Jews, the tribe of Issachar, described in Jacob's blessing (Genesis 49:14) as 'a strong ass crouching down between two burdens', is generally associated with Libra. The glyph (♎) represents both the setting sun and the crossbeam of a pair of scales, reflecting Libra as the balance point or fulcrum of the year. It is not too difficult to see how this notion of balance can be extended to encompass such things as justice, the law, and paying one's debts, the very categories with which Manilius deals in his description of Libra:

> Libra, whose scales, when Autumn turns the Signs,
> And ruddy Bacchus treads the juicy Vines;
> In equal Balance, poise the Night and Day,
> Teach how to measure, and instruct to weigh …
> Besides, he'll know the Niceties of Law;
> What guard the Good, and what the Guilty awe,
> What vengeance wait on Crimes, with Skill declare,
> His private Chamber, still shall be the Bar.
> What he determines, that for Right shall stand,
> And Justice weigh'd her Balance in his Hand.
>
> (page 126)

Fig. 18 Justice carrying the Libran Scales above the
Old Bailey in London

But legal matters are not the only areas over which Libra is said to have dominion. The image of the balance can be applied to any sphere of life in which we find the interaction of complementary forces, principal among which is the relationship between male and female in marriage. Libra, the sign of the sun's fall, represents the subordination of one ego to another in a perpetual struggle to maintain a fragile harmony. As Aries represents the consciousness of self, Libra symbolizes 'the other', the one with whom our ego has to make the biggest compromise, the one with whom we have to learn the hard lessons of mutual concern and love. Mayo considers that Libra symbolizes 'the primitive urge for unity and relatedness with others ... and the need to conform to an ideal pattern of community life' (Mayo, 1964, page 49). The spiritual lesson of the Libra phase involves our willingness to move from isolation into participation, a movement symbolized by marriage but not restricted to it. Such primary unions are microcosms of the greater unity and harmony of the ideal society in which the Libran principle of justice operates to guarantee equity, fairness, and balance in all areas of communal life.

The 'ruler' of Libra is Venus (♀) called by astrologers 'the lesser benefic' (Jupiter is 'the greater benefic'), since it symbolizes good fortune, health, material prosperity, and physical beauty. In Greek mythology Venus is Aphrodite, the goddess of love, who rules young manhood and young

146

womanhood, the stage of Shakespeare's 'lover, sighing like a furnace'.* At this stage, says Ptolemy, there is 'an activity of the seminal passages' and 'an impulse toward the embrace of love' (page 445). However, the sensuality and materialism which characterize the planet's association with Taurus, while undoubtedly present in Libra, seem to manifest in a less gross form. In its Libran aspect, Venus is the planet of grace, art, style and refinement. Ptolemy gives us an exhaustive list of this planet's attributes:

> If Venus alone takes the domination of the soul, in an honourable position she makes her subjects pleasant, good, luxurious, eloquent, neat, cheerful, fond of dancing, eager for beauty, haters of evil, lovers of the arts, fond of spectacles, decorous, healthy, dreamers of pleasant dreams, affectionate, beneficent, compassionate, fastidious, easily conciliated, successful, and, in general, charming. (Ptolemy, page 357)

Although Ptolemy does go on to mention a few possible faults (such as 'erotic' and 'timid'), these are not of the worst kind. From the point of view of normal human society, then, Venus represents all those things we would consider desirable and praiseworthy. From the point of view of the spiritual life, however, these things are not enough, as we shall see.

The Spiritual Lessons of Libra

At the beginning of chapter 10 Mark takes up the Libran themes by describing an altercation between Jesus and some Pharisees over marriage. In an attempt to trap Jesus into making an injudicious reply, they ask him about the legality of divorcing one's wife (Mark 10:1-2):

> 'What did Moses command you?' he replied. They said, 'Moses permitted a man to write a certificate of divorce and send her away.' 'It was because your hearts were hard that Moses wrote you this law,' Jesus replied. 'But at the beginning of creation God "made them male and female". For this reason a man will leave his father and mother and be united to his wife, and the two will become one flesh. So they are no longer two, but one. Therefore what God has joined together (*sunezeuxen – yoked*), let man not separate.' (Mark 10:39)

*According to Allen (page 174), Venus was associated with Libra because the goddess bound together human couples under the yoke of matrimony. The planet came to be called Veneris Sidus. Some astrologers considered Mars to be the ruler of Libra, prompting the delightful line by some anonymous fourteenth-century writer: 'Whoso es born in yat syne sal be an ille doar and a traytor' (Allen, page 274). However, this has never been a common attribution.

For its time, this is indeed radical teaching. Marriage was not a sacred institution in the ancient world and divorce was commonplace, even among the Jews, for whom monogamy was the ideal. The Jewish scriptures compared Yahweh's fidelity to Israel with the tender concern of a loving husband for his wife (e.g. Hosea 2), and the prophet Malachi has God declare, 'I hate divorce' (Malachi 2:16). Such an ideal was, apparently, more honoured in the breach than in the observance, and Moses' teaching allowing divorce enabled the more unscrupulous to practise a kind of serial monogamy which would have had devastating consequences for the women involved.

Theoretically, divorce was open to both parties but, given the general status of women at that time, it was hardly an option for the female. William Barclay describes the situation as follows:

> One thing vitiated the whole marriage relationship. The woman in the eyes of the law was a thing. She was at the absolute disposal of her father or of her husband. She had virtually no legal rights at all. To all intents and purposes a woman could not divorce her husband for any reason, and a man could divorce his wife for any cause at all. 'A woman,' said the Rabbinic law, 'may be divorced with or without her will; but a man only with his will.' (Barclay, 1975, page 151)

Getting a divorce was very simple. The man had to give his wife a 'bill of divorcement' in the presence of two witnesses. This stated: 'Let this be from me thy writ of divorce and letter of dismissal and deed of liberation, that thou mayest marry whatsoever thou wilt.'

The passage from the Pentateuch to which the Pharisees refer in their discussion with Jesus can be found in Deuteronomy 24:1. The text states that a man may divorce his wife 'if she find no favour in his eyes, because he hath found some uncleanness in her'. The prevailing opinion among rabbis at the time of Jesus was that this was a specific reference to adultery, but certain rabbis, following Rabbi Akiba, considered that 'finding no favour' in one's wife could simply mean that one no longer thought her attractive. According to Barclay, the rabbinic school of Hillel taught that a man might divorce his wife if:

> she spoiled his dinner by putting too much salt in his food, if she went in public with her head uncovered, if she talked with men in the streets, if she was a brawling woman, if she spoke disrespectfully of her husband's parents in his presence, if she was troublesome or quarrelsome. (Barclay, 1975, page 152)

Divorce, it seems, was possible on the flimsiest of pretexts.

Whether Jesus' restatement of the ideal was intended to be a blanket condemnation of all divorce or, at least, all remarriage after divorce (Mark 10:11-12), as the Catholic Church has interpreted it, is difficult to say. It was obviously a point of contention within the early Church because Matthew's account of this event (Matthew 19:9) shows Jesus disapproving of divorce 'except for adultery' (*porneia*). This seems to be a concession, probably made as a result of top-level deliberation about the practicality of a total ban.

What is certain, however, is Mark's teaching that we cannot regulate our primary relationships simply by referring to what the law tolerates. There is a law that transcends the culturally conditioned statute book, a law that is written into our very being, which demands integrity in our intimate life as a condition of spiritual growth. Under this law we must relate to another as a 'thou' to be loved and cherished, not as an 'it' to be used and then discarded.

It is this obvious sense of the text that Christianity has proclaimed down the centuries, but the mystical traditions preserve another dimension to marriage which transcends its function as a social institution. The 'sacred marriage' symbolizes a return to a supposed prelapsarian condition of the human race when, 'in the beginning, God created them male and female' (Genesis 1:27), when the twin principles of spirit (male) and matter (female) were joined in harmonious unity and balance – the image of God – before being sundered by the Fall. A secular version of this myth of primordial unity is found in Plato's *Symposium* in which a certain Aristophanes refers to a time when humans were androgynous, male and female physically joined together in one circular whole, until their powers became so great they had to be cut in two by Zeus; human love, says Aristophanes, is the attraction between the separated halves. But joining the separate parts of the self is, in the Mysteries, a spiritual not a physical quest, in which each individual strives to balance the various polarities within him or her self, to become a complete human being 'in whose nature spirit and matter are both completely developed and perfectly balanced, the divine man who unites in his own person husband and wife, the male and female elements in nature, as God and man are one in Christ' (Besant, page 270). This 'sacred marriage' was the goal of the Gnostic aspirant. In the Gospel of Thomas, Jesus teaches his disciples:

> When you make the two one, and when you make the outside like the inside, and the above like the below, and when you make the male and female one and the same, so that the male be not male nor the female female then will you enter the Kingdom. (Saying 22)

This is the teaching that would have been imparted to those 'inside the house', i.e. to initiates, but it has been lost in the legalism of Christian orthodoxy's literal approach to the text.

Balance

The importance of personal balance is stressed in Taoism, the most Libran of the world religions, in which the unity of opposites, the yang and the yin, within the psyche is a condition of personal growth and social harmony. In the teaching of Hua Hu Ching we read:

> In ancient times, people lived holistic lives.
> They didn't over-emphasise the intellect, but
> integrated mind, body, and spirit in all things.
> Understand that true growth comes from meeting and
> solving the problems of life in a way that is
> harmonising to yourself and to others. If you can follow these
> simple ways, you will be continually renewed.
> Unless the mind, body, and spirit are equally developed
> and fully integrated, no (wisdom) ... can be sustained.
> When the body is emphasised to the exclusion of the
> mind and spirit, they become like trapped snakes:
> frantic, explosive, poisonous to one's person.
> All such imbalances inevitably lead to exhaustion and
> expiration of the life force.
>
> (Novak, pages 171-2)

The Rich Young Man

The more goods people possess, the greater the tedium.
(St Teresa of Avila)

The section devoted to marriage is followed by the story of the Rich Young Man (Mark 10:17-31). He comes running up to Jesus, kneels before him, and asks, 'Good teacher, what must I do to inherit eternal life?' Jesus says to him: 'Why do you call me "good"? Only God is good' (Mark 10:18). This reply has been a source of acute embarrassment to the Church, since it seems to undermine the status of Jesus as 'God incarnate'. And the embarrassment was felt early on. Matthew has Jesus say, 'Why do you ask me about what is good?' (Matthew 19:17), a slight but significant change, which does less damage to

Jesus' image as a divine figure. But this passage has nothing to do with Jesus' ontological status, and Mark's version is absolutely crucial to a proper understanding of the text. By repudiating all claim to 'goodness' which, in its conventional sense, is used to describe someone who operates comfortably within the mores of society, Jesus is teaching that 'becoming good', while it might be a by-product of the spiritual life, is not the object of it. This is precisely the lesson he wants to teach the young man. The story continues:

> 'You know the commandments: "Do not murder, do not commit adultery, do not steal, do not give false testimony, do not defraud, honour your father and mother."' 'Teacher,' he declared, 'all these I have kept since I was a boy.' Jesus looked at him and loved him. 'One thing you lack,' he said. 'Go, sell everything you have and give to the poor, and you will have treasure in heaven. Then come, follow me.' At this the man's face fell. He went away sad, because he had great wealth. (Mark 10:19-22)

This young man epitomizes everything that is noble and virtuous in Judaism. According to the conventional wisdom of the time, his prosperity is a reward for his scrupulous observance of the law, and stands as a guarantee that he is speaking the truth about honouring his contractual agreement with God: as Psalm 37 testifies, the Lord is good to the righteous. Moreover, the man is lovable. Jesus instantly recognizes that his dutiful approach to life has in no way diminished his attractiveness as a human being. We might assume that he possesses all the characteristics of the Libra-Venus personality as outlined above, and today the man would be hailed as a great model of religious piety, an enviable figure, an exemplary citizen.

For Jesus, however, the man has one major failing: he is too committed to a life of ease to be a serious candidate for the spiritual life which demands that we relinquish our attachments to fleshly pleasures, even the innocent ones. Jesus would have agreed with Wittgenstein, who said somewhere that whatever life is about, it certainly isn't about having a good time.

Contemporary Christianity is as astonished by this teaching as Jesus' apostles were (Mark 10:24). Throughout history, worldly success has been considered a reward for virtue, and the evangelists of today who condemn what they consider the 'paganism' of modern society while preaching that 'God wants us to be prosperous' might well reflect on this passage in Mark. In recent years, it would seem that every single TV evangelist in America has produced a book or a series of tapes with some variation on the title 'The Bible's Plan For Your Prosperity', each of which no doubt includes something about God's plan for the evangelist's prosperity, too. For Jesus, however, riches, while not wicked, are inimical to real discipleship (10:24), and

151

to the rewards that such discipleship will bring (Mark 10:30). The spiritual life cannot be lived amidst the distractions and temptations that invariably accompany wealth. As Schopenhauer says, 'People need external activity because they have no internal activity. Where, on the contrary, the latter does exist, the former is likely to be a very troublesome, indeed execrable annoyance and impediment'(Schopenhauer, page 178). A similar sentiment was expressed by St Teresa of Avila:

> It's as if a person were to enter a place where the sun is shining but be hardly able to open his eyes because of the mud in them. The room is bright, but he doesn't enjoy it because of the impediment of things like these wild animals or beasts that make him close his eyes to everything but them. So, I think, must be the condition of the soul. Even though it may not be in a bad state, it is so involved in worldly affairs and so absorbed with its possessions, honour, or business affairs, that even though as a matter of fact it would want to see and enjoy its beauty, these things do not allow it to; nor does it seem that it can slip free from so many impediments. If a person is to enter the second dwelling place, it is important that he strive to give up unnecessary things and business affairs. Each one should do this in conformity with his state of life. (Bielecki, page 49)

When Jesus told the rich young man to give his wealth to the poor he was not thinking so much about the material advantage to the poor, as about the spiritual advantages to the man himself. In losing his living he would find his life. There would follow, says Annie Besant, 'the joyous discovery that the life thus won is won for all, not for the separated self, that the abandoning of the separated self has meant the realizing of the Self in man, and that the resignation of the limit which alone seemed to make life possible has meant the pouring out into myriad forms, an undreamed vividness and fullness' (Besant pages 149-50).*

* Annie Besant comments on the story of the Rich Young Man:

'This text has been variously explained away, it being obviously impossible to take it in its surface meaning, that a rich man cannot enter a post mortem state of happiness. Into that state the rich man may enter as well as the poor, and the universal practice of Christians shows that they do not for one moment believe that riches imperil their happiness after death. But if the real meaning of the Kingdom of Heaven be taken, we have the expression of a simple and direct fact. For the knowledge of God which is Eternal Life (John 17:3) cannot be gained till everything earthly is surrendered, cannot be learned until everything has been sacrificed. The man must give up not only earthly wealth, which henceforth may only pass through his hands as steward, but he must give up his inner wealth as well, as far as he holds it as his own against the narrow gateway. Such has ever been a condition for initiation, and poverty, obedience, chastity, has been the vow of the candidate.' (page 39)

The spiritual message of Libra, then, is not just that we should strive for harmony in our social relations. The harder, and the higher, call of this sign bids us leave everything, husband, wife, mother, father, land, business (Mark 10:29), in order that we may enter into a newer, nobler relationship with all things and all people. In such a relationship we participate in the world's redemption by suffering with and on behalf of others and so bringing into our daily waking life 'that sense of unity with others which (we) experience in the higher realms of being' (Besant, page 151). In such a relationship the paradox of the Gospel is realized and the spiritual reward far outweighs the material sacrifice (Mark 10:30).

The life and work of Mahatma Gandhi (born 2 October 1869) is almost a textbook example of Libran preoccupations. He trained as a lawyer, was obsessed with matters of justice, and lived a life of such frugality that, at his death in January 1948, his possessions, which were worth no more than a few pounds, could be contained in a couple of plastic bags. Although a Hindu, he was a lover of the Gospels and this (potentially) very rich man gave everything to the poor and followed the Christ with a light heart.

The Decans of Libra

Fig. 19 The Cross

153

In addition to the Libran themes of law, relationships and wealth, this section of Mark's Gospel reflects the decans of the constellation Libra quite clearly. These are The Cross, The Crown, and Lupus, The Wolf or The Victim. The Cross is the Southern Cross, not visible in northern latitudes today because of the gradual shifting of the heavens. It was last seen in the horizon of Jerusalem about the time that the Gospels were written, and although neither Ptolemy nor Manilius refer to it (Ptolemy considered it part of Centaurus), Allen says that it was well known to the 'early races of mankind who 5,000 years ago could see the Cross from latitudes very much higher even than that of Italy' (page 186), and that 'the ancient Persians, who knew the Cross well, celebrated a feast by its name' (page 190). The Crown is Corona Borealis which, in Greek mythology, was the crown given to Ariadne by Dionysus. There is a possible allusion to these two constellations in Mark 10:21, where taking up the cross and 'treasure in heaven' (a 'crown of glory'?) are linked.

Fig. 20 The Crown

Matthew's parallel account does promise the apostles that they will 'sit on twelve thrones' (Matthew 19:28), which seems a little closer to the idea of a crown than Mark's version. Matthew also mentions that the apostles will judge* the twelve tribes of Israel (Matthew 19:28), reflecting the legal aspect

---

* Addison devoted the 100th number of the *Tatler* – that of 29 November 1709 – to 'that sign in the heaven which is called by the name of the Balance', and to his dream therof in which he saw the Goddess of Justice descending from the constellation to regulate the affairs of men; the

of Libra more specifically than Mark, and carrying more than a hint of the Egyptian goddess of justice Maat, whose task it was to judge the dead.

The third decan of Libra is Lupus, the Wolf, but Seiss tells us that the ancient world was in some doubt as to what it represented, and that the Arabs used a word in connection with it which means to be slain, destroyed. When the young man walks away from Jesus he is said to be *lupomenos* – 'dejected', 'pained', 'grieved', ('heavy-hearted'?) – a participle of the Greek verb *lupeo*. *Lupus* is Latin, of course, but such a cross-language pun is not out of the question since Mark and his audience would be familiar with both languages. This may not be a veiled reference to Lupus, but it does seem rather an odd coincidence that one of Mark's few uses of this word (another is in 14:19) can be found so close to ideas which can readily be associated with the other two decans of Libra.

The Three Predictions of the Passion

Mark's use of *lupeo* in these two separate contexts could also be a means of linking the two sections. The Rich Man walks away 'grieved' (Mark 10:22); at the Last Supper the apostles are said to be 'sorrowful' (Mark 14:19) when they hear that one of their number would betray Jesus; and, using a word from the same root (*perilupos*) Jesus is described as 'deeply grieved' in the Garden of Gethsemane (Mark 14:34). What makes it likely that such an echoing of themes is deliberate is the fact that the decans of this whole central section contain nine images, most, if not all, of which are taken up in the final drama of the Gospel. The table on the next page illustrates this.

The three predictions of the Passion, Death, and Resurrection of Jesus are found in these three central sections of the Gospel. It is likely that Mark has placed them here because the decans of these three signs seem to point us forward to the actual Passion narrative. I admit that some of the correspondences seem a little strained, but most are peculiarly apt. In addition, no other decan groups contain such striking echoes of the events of Holy Week, as a glance at Appendix 2 will show. If Mark did have some such idea in mind it may help us explain why the three very similar predictions of the Passion come so close together in the narrative. It may also help us to understand that the major themes of these three sections – identity, service,

----

whole a very beautiful rendering of the ancient thought connecting the Virgin Astraea with Libra. He may have been thus inspired by recollections of his student days at Oxford, where he must have often seen this sign, as a judge in full robes, sculptured on the front of Merton College (Allen, page 172).

and sacrifice – are intimately involved with the events of Holy Week (See Figure 19).

LEO

Hydra	The Fleeing Serpent	16:1ff.	Jesus defeats death(?)
Crater	The Cup	14:23	'And he took the cup ...'
Corvus	The Raven (Crow)	14:30	'Before the cock crows ... '*

VIRGO

Coma	The Infant, The Branch, The Desired One.	11:8-9	'and others cut down branches ... ' 'Blessed is he ... '
Centaurus	The Centaur	11:7ff.	Jesus enters Jerusalem on a colt.
Bootes	The Great Shepherd	14:27	'I will smite the shepherd ... '

LIBRA

Crux	The Cross	15:21ff.	Jesus is crucified.
Lupus	The Victim/The Slain	15:37	Jesus dies.
Corona	The Crown	15:17	'they plaited a crown of thorns ... '

Fig. 21 Decans of the three central sections of Mark's Gospel and their correspondence with later themes.

* It must be admitted that this correspondence is more impressive in English than in Greek. The bird that does the crowing is not a crow (*korax*), but a cock (*alektor*). The verb generally translated 'crow' is from the Greek *phôneo*, meaning 'to call out', and can be used of people as well as of animals. It has no specific connection with crows. The cock is, however, the bird of the sun (announcing the sunrise) and this is important, as we shall see in the Pisces section.

Scorpio (Mark 10:32–10:52)
Paths of Glory

The desire for fame tempts even noble minds.
(St Augustine, born 13 November 354)

Scorpio and Mars

The scorpion, says Seiss, 'is the most irascible and malignant insect that lives, and its poison is like itself'. Whatever the truth of this, there can be no doubt that the zodiacal sign Scorpio has something of a corresponding reputation for evil, which astrological writers throughout the ages have tended to express in the most uncompromising terms. For example, John Gadbury, writing in 1675, tells us that the person in whom Scorpio manifests strongly will display 'falsity, arrogance, ambition, ingratitude, boasting, lying, lechery, perjury, revenge, (and) all manners of vice and lewdness' (Gettings, 1972, page 96). Shakespeare's Macbeth, and Iago with his 'motiveless malignity' seem to embody at least some of these characteristics but, fortunately, in real life, such types are rare, and certainly do not constitute one twelfth of the human race! What Gadbury's list describes is not an individual but a series of potential manifestations of the primary principle of Scorpio: intensity of emotion.

157

Scorpio is a Water sign, and Water symbolizes the affectional nature, that part of us that operates more by instinct than by judgement. It represents the repository of all those unconscious urges and desires over which our conscious control is limited. If we add to this the principle of Fixity, we can see how Scorpio comes to represent these unconscious forces at their most ungovernable. It is the sign of intensity, of power, of the irrational impulse which can be enormously creative or destructive. Scorpio symbolizes the depths, the interior caverns of the personality into which we have barely even begun to shine a light.

The glyph of Scorpio (♏) 'vaguely resembles the legs and tail of the scorpion, which is essentially a creature of darkness, secretive, hiding in the shadows' (Mayo, 1964, page 49). The glyph is also similar to that of Virgo, (♍), with which sign it has much in common and 'with which, according to legend, it was at one time united, the sign Libra not having at that time been introduced into the zodiac' (Carter, 1965, page 78). (This may well be the reason why Virgoan themes of service are reiterated in the Scorpio section of the Gospel.)

Mythologically, the sign is associated with the underworld, the place of the dead, Sheol, the tomb to which we go, and the womb from which we come. It symbolizes the profound mystery of life and death which eludes all ratiocination, and so has come to symbolize rebirth, resurrection. The ancient northern peoples celebrated their festivals of death at this time of the year, and these linger still in Hallowe'en, and in their Christian counterparts, All Souls' Day and All Saints' Day; November, the Scorpio month is, in Catholicism, the month of the 'Holy Souls', when Catholics are encouraged to pray for the dead. It is supposedly the time when the veil between the world of the living and the world of the dead is at its thinnest.

Scorpio is the polar opposite of Taurus. In Taurus (April-May) the blooming crops appear above ground; in Scorpio (October-November), the dying vegetation is ploughed back into the earth where it rots to produce the nutrients in which the new seeds can take root. In Taurus, we were taught in parables; in Scorpio, we are introduced to the deeper mysteries of the kingdom of God, mysteries which are foreclosed to all who stand 'outside'.

The snake is often taken as a symbol of this sign: in the Egyptian Zodiac it is represented by the huge serpent, Typhon, and in Hebrew mythology it is associated with the tribe of Dan, 'a serpent by the way, an adder in the path' (Genesis 49:16), and the constellation Serpens is one of the decans of Scorpio. The snake epitomizes the Scorpionic dimension of human life, its ability to emerge from its own skin symbolizing our own mysterious origins from the womb, our inevitable descent into death, and our potential for rebirth into new life. Campbell says that the serpent:

represents immortal energy and consciousness engaged in the field of time, constantly throwing off death and being born again. There is something tremendously terrifying about life when you look at it that way. And so the serpent carries in itself the sense of both the fascination and the terror of life. (Campbell, 1988, page 53)

To the Jews, Scorpio was also represented by the eagle, which was thought to be capable of 'renewing its youth' (Psalm 103:5) and which 'symbolizes the power within man ... to rise above the temptations of his lower nature' (Mayo, 1964, page 49). Scorpio writers like Robert Louis Stevenson, Albert Camus, Fyodor Dostoyevsky and Sylvia Plath* seem particularly concerned to explore 'the lower nature' of the human being, but always with the realization that 'evil and darkness have to be redeemed and not simply censured or legislated away' (Wright, page 133). Redemption through suffering – personal or vicarious – is a consistent theme of Scorpio writers of both literature and theology.

Sexuality, generation, death and regeneration are obviously part of this matrix of associations, and it is interesting that the ancient world perceived a connection between sexuality, power and death which it has taken depth-psychology to rediscover. In Shakespeare's time, the orgasm was called a 'little death', and today feminists are telling us that many sex-acts have more to do with power and domination than with pleasure.

Power, in fact, is a central theme of Scorpio: power to destroy, power to recreate. Manilius tells us that:

> ... Scorpio's Tayl displays
> A double Influence from his forked Rays:
> For when that first appears, the peaceful Child
> Shall Cities raise, and be inclin'd to build;
> The World shall see him with his Plow surround
> The Place design'd, and mark the fatal Bound;
> Or he shall wast what others Pains did raise,
> Where populous Cities stood, there Beasts shall graze
> Or Harvest grow; he leads to these extreams,
> And Power, agreeing, waits upon his Beams.

> (page 136)

---

* Robert Louis Stevenson, born 13 November 1850.
  Albert Camus, born 7 November 1913.
  Fyodor Dostoyevsky, born 11 November 1821.
  Sylvia Plath, born 27 October 1932.

Even Gettings, who deplores the negative associations that have gathered round this sign, will admit that the Scorpionic type is 'essentially practical, jealous of honour, tending to be domineering ... (who) can relate perfectly when it is a matter of leading or dominating ... (and) who can never take second place' (Gettings, 1972, pages 97-8).

Such power is not always negative, of course. Surgery and medicine come under Scorpio, too, for obvious reasons. The physician, whose symbol is the Scorpionic serpent twined round the caduceus, is the one who has power over life and death, who can restore the weak to health and give vitality to the moribund. Like Pluto, he guards the way to the underworld and lets enter whom he will.

In modern astrology, the planet Pluto (♀) is said to be the 'ruler' of Scorpio, but this planet was unknown to the ancient world and Mars (♂) was considered the ruler. For Ptolemy, the 'destructive and inharmonious' qualities of Mars are consistent with the fact that the two signs it rules, Aries and Scorpio, are in 'square' (90-degree) relationship with Cancer and Leo, the signs ruled, respectively, by the moon and the sun (Ptolemy, page 81). We noted the characteristics of Mars in the chapter on Aries, and these apply as much to Scorpio as they do to Aries, but the Fixed Water sign has difficulty externalizing them and so they tend to operate more covertly than in Aries. In its Scorpionic mode of expression, Mars has less of an outlet and this is symbolic of explosive power, at times as deadly as the scorpion's sting.

Ptolemy also tells us that Mars rules the genitals, and that it:

assumes command of manhood for the space of fifteen years ... He introduces severity and misery into life, and implants cares and troubles in the soul and in the body, giving it, as it were, some sense and notion of passing its prime and urging it, before it approaches its end, by labour to accomplish something among its undertakings that is worthy of note. (Ptolemy, page 81)

The Spiritual Lessons of Scorpio

Power, whether vested in many or a few, is ever grasping
and, like the grave, cries, 'Give, give!'
(Abigail Adams, born 11 November, 1744)

This desire to 'accomplish something worthy of note' characterizes the challenge of the Scorpio phase of the spiritual life. It is a natural human need to be first and to achieve some measure of celebrity for our efforts, and in the secular world such ambitions are lauded and encouraged. However, as this section in Mark teaches us, such things are not to play a part in our spiritual life. James and John approach Jesus, asking that he do for them whatever they request. He asks what they want, and they reply:

'Let one of us sit at your right and the other at your left in your glory.' (Mark 10:37)

This is a clear expression of the Scorpionic reluctance to play second fiddle, and Jesus roundly condemns it. He tells them that spiritual reward is not simply conferred, like a knighthood; it has to be earned through suffering. If they wish to share his glory they have to follow his path, 'to drink from my cup and be baptized with my baptism' (Mark 10:38). The path of discipleship is not an easy one to tread.

The nature of this path has been explained three times now. These three predictions of the Passion, Death and Resurrection (Mark 8:31; 9:30-32; 10:32-34) are set pivotally in the Gospel, in order to emphasize the underlying Piscean character of the narrative as a whole. Pisces is the sign of the new age which will be characterized by the Piscean qualities of suffering and renunciation. Every human being ('son of man') has to be tried by suffering in order to share in the glory of Christ. We all have our own route to Calvary, 'the place of the skull'. Suffering and death are a condition of our human nature, part of what Wordsworth calls 'the still, sad music of humanity'. Our mortality guarantees our suffering, and the lesson of this Gospel is that we must accept that this is so and go on anyway. Out of it comes new life, not necessarily a life beyond the grave, although this is not ruled out, but a new awareness of, and a new response to, the life we are presently living. The moon, which spends three days in shadow before it emerges new once more, is a symbol of the indomitable and heroic urge of all life to renew itself in spite of the inevitability of death.

At the end of Dostoyevsky's masterpiece *Crime and Punishment*, Raskolnikov muses on his sufferings in precisely these terms:

He did not know that the new life would not be given him for nothing, that he would have to pay dearly for it, that it would cost him great striving and suffering. But this is the beginning of a new story – the story of the gradual renewal of a man, the story of his gradual regeneration, of his passing from one world into another, of his initiation into a new unknown life.

161

The lesson of Scorpio is that before we can ascend we have to descend, and it is significant that the Scorpio section of the Gospel takes place as Jesus and his apostles approach Jericho (Mark 10:46). Jericho is the ideal place for teaching about 'descending' and 'ascending', since it is the lowest place on earth, 825 feet below sea level. Before the ascent to Jerusalem (2,500 feet above sea level), comes the descent into Jericho.

In the light of such considerations, the urge to grasp for the ephemeral and tawdry baubles of the secular world is indeed vain. Jesus has already taught us that we need to renounce our attachment to our sense of self-importance (Leo), and to wealth (Libra), and he has advocated the virtue of self-abnegation (Virgo). In the Scorpio section, he teaches us to renounce our need for power over others. The apostles are indignant at James and John's request, presumably because they coveted seats in glory for themselves, and so Jesus calls them to him and explains:

> You know that those who are regarded as rulers of the Gentiles lord it over them, and their high officials exercise authority over them. Not so with you. Instead, whoever wants to become great among you must be your servant, and whoever wants to be first must be slave of all. For even the Son of Man did not come to be served, but to serve, and to give his life as a ransom for many. (Mark 10:42-45)

The word 'ransom' (*lutron*) has been taken by later Christian theology to refer to Christ's sacrificial death on the cross by which the price of men's sins is paid to God, but such an idea owes little to Mark and more to Paul, and to those Scorpionic theologians St Augustine (born 13 November, 354) and Martin Luther (born 10 November 1483) for whom a once-and-for-all transaction seemed very appealing. But, in the Gospel context, it is more likely to refer to the redemptive nature of all suffering, and to the nobility – and possibility – of suffering on behalf of someone else. Since Scorpio is related to 'shared resources' and 'inheritance' it concerns those intimate, unseen bonds by which living and dead are connected to each other, which ensure that 'no man is an island', that karma is a reality, and that the effects of our thoughts and actions extend beyond ourselves in time and in space.

Our call, then, is not to personal ambition and power, but to service and to suffering which are the only means by which any kind of transformation – individual or collective – can be effected. Dane Rudhyar addresses these very themes in his chapter on Scorpio:

> (The mystical way) ... asks moreover that all forms of ambition be relin-
> quished – and 'spiritual' ambition may be the most dangerous, withal

most subtle, kind of ambition ... There should be no feeling whatsoever of competition in one's endeavours, especially if one is part of a group of seekers or disciples. It does not matter if one appears to be first or last, for the competitive spirit is a form of violence, and there can be no violence in the soul of the true disciple on the spiritual Path. The zodiacal sign Scorpio tends to be associated with violence and competition, because the Scorpio type of person is often too emotionally and personally involved in making of human relationships what to him or her is a 'success'. (Rudhyar, pages 75-6)

It is entirely consistent with the rest of the Gospel story that James and John should be the ones to request positions of power in the kingdom. They were nicknamed 'sons of thunder' by Jesus (Mark 3:17), and they are the ones who, in Luke's Gospel, ask Jesus to command fire from heaven to consume the inhospitable Samaritan villages (Luke 9:54). They appear to be true sons of Mars! We might also note that Matthew tells the story of their request for power rather differently from Mark: in his desire to present the apostles as worthy characters, he has their mother make the request on their behalf (Matthew 20:20-28).

Blind Bartimaeus

Before Jesus reveals his true identity at Caesarea Philippi he cures a blind man whose perception of human nature is faulty (Mark 8:22-26). Before 'riding triumphantly into Jerusalem,' he performs a similar miracle. Bartimaeus is begging by the roadside outside Jericho, crying out: 'Jesus, Son of David, have mercy on me!' (Mark 10:47). It is significant that a man making such a cry is *blind*. His name is also significant. *Bartimaeus* means 'son of Timaeus', which, in Aramaic, would mean 'son of defilement', but *timê*, in Greek, means 'honour' and Mark is obviously capitalizing upon the ambiguity. 'Son of David!' is a conventional messianic title, and the blind Bartimeaus sees Jesus as a candidate for the role of literal Messiah, the one who will save Israel from her enemies. But, as Mark will later explain (12:35-7), the Messiah is not a specific historical figure descended from David. The whole of this Gospel is designed to teach us that salvation does not come through military victory but through the Piscean virtue of self-sacrifice. Nor is it delivered through the agency of any one person, but achieved by all who are prepared to take the way of the cross. Disabused of his erroneous ideas, symbolized both by the regaining of his sight and by the discarding of his cloak, 'the son of defilement' is transformed into a 'son of honour'. The beggar has become a disciple, and Bartimaeus is now able to move out of the depths of Scorpionic Jericho and 'follow Jesus in the way' (Mark 10:52).

Scorpio Themes in the 'Secret' Gospel of Mark

The Scorpio section of the Gospel is quite short, which is surprising when we consider that Scorpio symbolizes a number of matters – life, death, healing, initiation, regeneration – which are of great relevance to major themes of this Gospel. It could well be that something is missing from our version of Mark. Could it be sheer coincidence, then, that the letter of Clement of Alexandria (second century AD), which was discovered by Professor Morton Smith at the Monastery of Mar Saba, should mention, and quote, a passage from another version of Mark which deals explicitly with the raising up of a dead man, and which, Clement tells us, was to be found just before the words 'And James and John come to him' (Mark 10:34, i.e. the beginning of the Scorpio section)? The passage is quoted above in full (page 24). It seems authentic, reflecting many of Mark's stylistic idiosyncrasies. For example, the word 'straightway' (*euthus*), a favourite of Mark's, appears twice in this short narrative, and his habit of stringing his sentences together with 'and' ... 'and' ... 'and' is clearly evident. Why some versions of the Gospel would omit it is not immediately apparent; after all, John gives an account of the raising of Lazarus (John 11), and the synoptic Gospels all mention the raising of Jairus's daughter, and so the objection cannot have been to the idea of raising someone from death. Intriguingly, Clement himself gives us a clue: at the end of the account of the young man's resurrection from death, Clement, still quoting from the 'Secret' Gospel, goes on:

And going out of the tomb they came into the house of the youth, for he was rich. And after six days Jesus told him what to do and in the evening the youth comes to him, wearing a linen cloth over his naked body. And he remained with him that night, for Jesus taught him the mysteries of the kingdom of God. And thence, arising, he returned to the other side of the Jordan. (Barnstone, page 342)

'Resurrection from death' is not to be taken literally. Within the pagan mysteries, and within Gnosticism, it was an allegory for spiritual rebirth through initiation. The young man is taught 'the mysteries of the Kingdom of God', echoing Jesus' statement to the apostles in the Taurus section of the Gospel – Taurus is the polar opposite of Scorpio – that 'the secret of the Kingdom of God has been given to you, but to those on the outside, everything is said in parables' (Mark 4:11-12). 'The other side of the Jordan', to which the young man repairs, is the 'Promised Land', Gnostic enlightenment. Perhaps this 'initiation allegory' was considered too sacred to be seen by profane eyes. Perhaps, too, certain people had been misinterpreting the nakedness. This is suggested by what Clement writes next:

> After these words follows the text, 'And James and John come to him', and all that section. But 'naked man with naked man', and all the other things about which you wrote, are not found. (Barnstone, page 342)

What these 'other things' might be we have no way of telling, but since Clement refers earlier to the 'unspeakable teachings of the Carpocrations' and their 'blasphemous and carnal doctrines', we can legitimately conclude that some people saw hints of sexual activity here. It could well be, then, that Mark's Gospel originally explored the themes of Scorpio more extensively than our present version of the Gospel would suggest, but that certain passages were excised to prevent their being interpreted in ways that were potentially damaging to a nascent orthodoxy.

The Serpent Holder

Fig. 22 Ophiuchus

165

One of the decans of Scorpio is Ophiuchus, The Serpent Holder,* the mythology of which seems to be reflected in this 'secret' passage of Mark. Ophiuchus is Aesculapius, the son of Apollo, and Coronis, who was famed for restoring Hippolytus to life, using blood from the side of the goddess of justice and from the Gorgon. Ovid's hymn in honour of Aesculapius brings out the Scorpionic themes of death and rebirth admirably:

> Hail, great Physician of the world! All hail!
> Hail, mighty infant, who in years to come
> Shall heal the nations and defraud the tomb!
> Swift be thy growth! Thy triumphs unconfined!
> Make kingdoms thicker and increase mankind:
> Thy daring art shall animate the dead,
> And draw the thunder on Thy guilty head:
> For thou shalt rise, but from the dark abode
> Rise up victorious, and be twice a god.
> (*Metamorphoses*, Book 2, Dryden's Translation)

In the 'secret' Gospel of Mark, the Christ is the 'great physician of the world', the one who 'defrauds the tomb' and who 'animates the dead' by initiating the young man into the secrets of the Kingdom of God.

---

* Ophiuchus and Serpens are always taken together in the ancient authors. Manilius says that those born when Ophiuchus, 'encircled by the serpent's great coils, rises ... will receive snakes into the folds of their flowing robes, and will exchange kisses with these poisonous monsters and suffer no harm' (*Astronomica*, Book 5, lines 389-393). This seems highly reminiscent of the promise given by the resurrected Jesus in the so-called 'longer ending' of Mark, which does not appear in the earliest manuscripts. Could this be a misplaced fragment from a more comprehensive Mark, and did it originally appear in the Scorpio section? The text reads: 'These signs will accompany believers: in my name they will cast out demons, speak in new tongues, take snakes in their hands, even if they drink deadly poison, it will not harm them, and they will place their hands on sick people, and they will get well' (Mark 16:17-18). Some of these promised powers are clearly related to Scorpio and Ophiuchus.

Sagittarius (Mark 11:1–11:26)
'Zeal for thy House'

Bring me my bow of burning gold!
Bring me my arrows of desire!
Bring me my spear! O clouds unfold!
Bring me my chariot of fire!
I will not cease from mental fight,
Nor shall my sword sleep in my hand,
Till we have built Jerusalem
In England's green and pleasant land
　　　　　　　(from *Milton*, by William Blake,
　　　　　　　　　　born 28 November 1757)

Sagittarius and Jupiter

Sagittarius is the third sign in the Fire triplicity, and it shares the ardour and passion of Aries and Leo, the Fire signs which precede it in the zodiacal circle. As the Mutable Fire sign, however, it represents a combination of passion and mobility and so has come to symbolize the fervent urge to transcend the barriers of convention, to move outwards and onwards in the search for wisdom and truth. Its glyph ($\nearrow$) expresses this perfectly: the arrow directed to the heavens, symbolizing the power of man's aspirations and the deadly earnestness of his quest. Ptolemy designated Sagittarius a 'bi-corporeal' sign, 'two-bodied', a concept that had mythological expression in the Centaur, half man, half horse, a symbol of the warfare between the spiritual and carnal aspects of the individual person. These weird creatures were almost always considered to be savage, with the exception of Aesculapius's teacher, Chiron, who was renowned for his kindness and wisdom, who gave his life to save Prometheus, and who represents the eventual triumph of the human over the bestial.

What separates the human from the beast is, in part, what Sagittarius represents: the restless pursuit of spiritual values which constantly presents the seeker with new challenges and new journeys. Emily Dickinson (born 10 December 1830), who travelled little physically, but whose mental voyages were extensive, summed up the Sagittarian quest in this lovely poem:

This world is not conclusion.
A Species stands beyond –
Invisible, as Music –
But positive, as Sound –
It beckons, and it baffles –
Philosophy, don't know –
And through a Riddle, at the last –
Sagacity, must go –
To guess it, puzzles scholars –
To gain it, Men have borne
Contempt of Generations
And Crucifixion, shown –
Faith slips – and laughs, and rallies –
Blushes, if any see –
Plucks at a twig of Evidence –
And asks a Vane the Way –
Much Gesture, from the Pulpit –
Strong Hallelujahs roll –
Narcotics cannot still the Tooth
That nibbles at the soul – ...

Sagittarius (Mark 11:1–11:26)

On a less soul-nibbling level, however, Sagittarius represents acts of derring-do, swashbuckling heroism, taking a chance, having a gamble, anything, in fact, which takes the individual out of convention's groove and gives a bit of momentum to his life. All long 'journeys' – spiritual, religious, philosophical, as well as physical – are Sagittarian, so it is entirely appropriate that Sagittarius came to be associated with the horse, the primary means of all long-distance land travel in the ancient world, and Hippotês, 'On Horseback', was one of its names among the Greeks.

It is this connection with the horse that Manilius concentrates on in his description of the Sagittarian type, but he also gives us a hint of the sign's reputation for being undaunted, and for pressing onwards heedless of danger:

> The double Centaur different Tempers breeds,
> They break the Horse, and tame the fiery Steeds;
> They love the sounding Whip, the Race, the Rein,
> And whirl the Chariot o'er the dusty Plain:
> Nor is their Humour to the Fields confin'd,
> They range the Woods, and tame the Savage Kind.
> …
> For in the Frame, in double forms exprest,
> The Man is uppermost, and rules the Beast;
> His bow full drawn implies, his Rays impart,
> Strength to the Limbs, and Vigour to the Heart.
> Quick active Motions, full of warmth and heat,
> Still pressing on, unknowing to retreat.
>
> (page 127)

Eleanor Kirk, writing in 1894, explores the fiery nature of Sagittarius in the following terms:

People born in this sign have a tendency to fly all to pieces over a small matter, are quick to anger, but quickly over it, combative and determined to have their own way. As enemies Sagittarius people go to extremes … They are unreasonable in their desire to help those they love, and zealous and over-sanguine in whatever they undertake. They are unwilling to wait for proper times and seasons, and desire to rush through every piece of work as soon as it presents itself. (Gettings 1972, page 162)

It is not too difficult to translate these characteristics into spiritual categories.

169

The Sagittarian phase of the spiritual life is the point at which we learn to act confidently and courageously to make our vision a reality. Blake's 'New Jerusalem' can only be created by means of the bows, arrows, spears, chariots and swords which symbolize the Sagittarian challenge to all those powers, like sloth, indifference and habit, which enslave the human spirit, and with which we are called to do battle. This requires the other Fire-sign virtue, faith, because all ventures of this kind must be undertaken without any certainty as to their eventual outcome. As Blake puts it in *Auguries of Innocence*:

> He who doubts from what he sees
> Will ne'er Believe, do what you Please.
> If the Sun & Moon should doubt,
> They'd immediately go out.

'The Sagittarian Higher Mind,' says Dane Rudhyar, is 'mind plus will, plus faith and vibrant openness to ever-new possibilities' (Rudhyar, page 77). The one who enables himself to become a vehicle for the Sagittarian 'Higher Mind' becomes a genuine avatar, one who can 'stimulate, mobilize or fascinate human beings into doing what the latter would otherwise be unwilling and too inert to do'.

Sagittarius is ruled by Jupiter (♃), which in classical astrology is called 'the Greater Benefic' because of its association with all things that expand the mind and which lift us out of our spiritual torpor. Ptolemy considered Jupiter to be associated with elderly age, when wisdom brings 'honour, praise, and independence'. When this planet governs the soul:

> he makes his subjects magnanimous, generous, god-fearing, honourable, pleasure-loving, kind, magnificent, liberal, just, high-minded, dignified, minding their own business, compassionate, fond of discussion, beneficent, affectionate, with qualities of leadership. (page 447)

There is a negative side to Jupiter and to Sagittarius, however. Since they both represent the desire to expand the horizons of the human person, they have an obvious connection with religion, but all religion can lose its exploratory character and degenerate into ritualism and formalism. When it does so, the spiritual aspirations of the genuine seeker can be lost in the pseudo-spirituality of ecclesiasticism and sacerdotalism: Jupiter is as much the planet of pomp and hierarchy as it is of quest and faith.

The Spiritual Lessons of Sagittarius

This section begins with a striking and dramatic presentation of the Sagittarian symbol as Jesus, astride a colt, becomes the embodiment of the Centaur. Jesus sends two of his disciples into the village where they are to find a colt 'on which no one has ever sat', and bring it to him. The text continues:

> They went and found a colt outside in the street, ('where two roads meet' – *amphodon*) tied at a doorway. As they untied it, some people standing there asked, 'What are you doing, untying that colt?' They answered as Jesus had told them to, and the people let them go. When they brought the colt to Jesus and threw their cloaks over it, he sat on it. Many people spread their cloaks on the road, while others spread branches they had cut* in the fields. Those who went ahead and those who followed shouted, 'Hosanna! Blessed is he who comes in the name of the Lord! Blessed is the coming kingdom of our father David! Hosanna in the highest!' (Mark 11:7-10)

The cry of the people, 'Hosanna', means 'Save, we pray' in Hebrew, but the salvation they seek is not the kind that Jesus will offer. Jesus brings the salvation of the wise teacher, Chiron, who died that Prometheus might live, not the bogus salvation wrought by insurrection and war.

Mark has married Hebrew and Greek motifs extremely successfully in this incident. In addition to the image of Chiron, he has woven into the text strands from Psalm 45, the Royal Wedding Song, in which the bridegroom, with his sword upon his thigh, rides to meet his bride (verse 3). The shouts of the people echo the psalm's exhortation (verses 4-5).

> In your majesty ride forth victoriously
> On behalf of truth, humility and righteousness;
> Let your right hand display awesome deeds.
> Let your sharp arrows pierce the heart of the king's
> enemies.

This psalm abounds in Sagittarian images. The principal one, of course, is the horse, but the arrow is mentioned, and even the thigh, on which the bridegroom wears his sword, is ruled by Sagittarius, as Manilius tells us (see Appendix 2). Mark's original readers would undoubtedly have been aware of these associations, and they would also have made the connection between Jesus' ride into Jerusalem and the passage in the prophet Zechariah, which runs:

* Curiously, an early Chinese name for Sagittarius is Seih Muh, The Cleft Tree, or Branches Cut for Firewood (Allen, page 356).

Rejoice greatly O Daughter of Zion! Shout, Daughter of Jerusalem! See, your king comes to you, righteous and having salvation, gentle and riding on a donkey, on a colt, the foal of a donkey. (Zechariah 9:9)

It is interesting to note that Mark's version of Jesus' journey into Jerusalem does not refer specifically to any Old Testament passage. Instead, he lets our imagination and our memory work on the image. Matthew, however, sees this incident as a fulfilment of Zechariah's prophecy (Matthew 21:1-11), and even has Jesus ride, absurdly, on two animals ('an ass and a colt') to make sure Zechariah's words are fulfilled to the letter. It is from Matthew's fidelity to Zechariah that we get the image of Jesus riding on a donkey or ass (*onos*). Mark uses the word *pôlos*, which is much more generic, and which is always translated 'colt': it could as well be the horse of Sagittarius as the donkey of Zechariah.*

We generally interpret this scene through the eyes of popular piety which has robbed it of its powerful spiritual message. We are taught that riding on a donkey shows Jesus at his most humble, but we forget that the animal Jesus rode – whether donkey or horse does not really matter – was 'one on which no one has ever sat' i.e. an *unbroken* animal. Jesus was riding sedately on a 'bucking bronco'! Members of the horse family are not born as our natural allies. They are born wild and turbulent; they instinctively rebel against human dominance, and in order for them to be any use to us at all they have to be brought into subjection. Their natural, uncontrollable energies have to be harnessed to a will that is stronger than their own. They have to be 'broken' and when raw power is brought under the control of intelligence, a formidable alliance is formed.

In such a context was born the mythological image of the centaur – half man, half horse – which married the twin qualities of intelligence and strength. And it is not too difficult to see how the centaur came to symbolize the human being – part god, part animal; part creative intelligence, part destructive passion. The great artist Picasso was asked, toward the end of his long life, how he felt now that age had robbed him of his not inconsiderable physical passions. 'It's like being unchained from a wild animal,' he replied.

* Abbot-Smith gives for *pôlos*: 'a foal, colt, properly of a horse, then the young of other animals'. For onos: 'an ass'. From *A Manual Lexicon of the New Testament,* 1986 edition. T. and T. Clark Ltd, Edinburgh. Arndt and Gingrich, following Bauer, consider that *pôlos* simply means 'horse': 'W. Bauer has made more extensive researches ... (in which) he shows that *pôlos* in Greek literature from Homer down means young animal when another animal is named in its context ... but simply 'horse' (not 'colt') when no other animal is so found. With this as background, Bauer prefers horse also for the passages in Mark and Luke.' Arndt and Gingrich: *The Greek-English Lexicon of the New Testament and Other Early Christian Literature,* University of Chicago Press, Chicago, Illinois, 1957, page 739.

'Chained to a wild animal' is not a bad description of any human being in the full flush of youthful vigour; some of the animals to which we are chained are wilder than others, but all of us must admit that there are parts of our nature which are difficult to integrate, that we are complex, composite, ambiguous creatures. The eighteenth-century English poet Alexander Pope describes this dual nature of the human being in his *Essay on Man*:

> Plac'd on this isthmus of a middle state,
> A being darkly wise and rudely great;
>
> He hangs between; in doubt to act, or rest,
> In doubt to deem himself a God, or Beast;
> In doubt his Mind or Body to prefer,
> Born but to die, and reas'ning but to err.
>
> Chaos of thought and passion, all confus'd;
> Still by himself abus'd, or disabus'd;
> Created half to rise and half to fall;
> Great lord of all things, yet a prey to all;
> Sole judge of Truth, in endless Error hurl'd;
> The glory, jest, and riddle of the world.
> (from *Essay on Man*, by Alexander Pope,
> born 21 May 1688)

No one has described the ambiguous, centaur nature of the human being better. We are all centaurs. For the most part, the centaurs were portrayed in mythology as wild and savage creatures, all the more dangerous because their dominant bestial power was mixed with human ingenuity; but one of their number, Chiron, was a friend to humans, and so great was his wisdom that many young people were entrusted to his care. Indeed, Chiron taught what he himself had accomplished: the marriage of passion with intelligence, which produces the outstanding, heroic, undaunted, creative human being. Significantly, the apostles found the horse at a place 'where two roads meet' (verse 4).

It is images such as this which will enable us to understand the spiritual meaning of Jesus' entry into Jerusalem. In calmly riding an unbroken horse into the holy city, Jesus is shown to be capable of dominating the forces of the Fire element, the animal passions. His action symbolizes the mastery of the bestial by the spiritual, the mastery of what we might today call the ego (or, in Freudian terms, the Id) with its selfish cravings, by the powerful forces of self-knowledge and self-control. Jerusalem is the city of peace – *salem* is the same word as 'shalom' in Hebrew and 'salaam' in Arabic – and in order for us to enter symbolically into the holy city of peace, individually and collectively, we must attain the same level of mastery over those troublesome aspects of our animal nature that Jesus is shown exercising in this little story. And it is the objective of all spiritual practice, in whatever tradition it comes down to us, to attain this level of control over the wilder aspects of our nature. The greater jihad (holy war), said Muhammad, 'is the struggle against the lower self'. In short, we should strive to become creatures of will, not of whim. As Blake realized:

> To be in a Passion you Good may do,
> But no good if a Passion is in you.
>
> (*Auguries of Innocence*)

The Cursing of the Fig Tree and the Cleansing of the Temple

After visiting the Temple, Jesus leaves the city and spends the night in Bethany. He returns in the morning and, being hungry, looks for some fruit on a leafy fig tree. Finding none, he curses the tree with the words: 'Let no one eat fruit from you ever again!' (Mark 11:13). This seems almost a spiteful, pointless act, particularly so when we consider that figs were not in season (verse 13). Later in the text, however, we learn the real significance of Jesus' action.* The next day they find the fig tree 'withered from the roots' (verse 20), and Jesus uses the whole incident to give a lesson in faith. Whoever has faith in God, believing with his whole heart, can even move a mountain into the sea (verse 23). Hyperbole, of course, but a saying of great importance because it illustrates the power of the human mind to achieve even seemingly impossible goals. When we pray we must believe that we already have what we are praying for and it will be ours. This is much more than 'positive thinking'; it is what Dane Rudhyar (page 77) calls 'creative visualization', and it is one aim of the Sagittarian phase of the spiritual life. Its object is not to attract material success to our life: its application is principally to the spiritual life, operating as a kind of spiritual alchemy, by which the vague outlines of our aspirations are transformed by prayer, meditation and spiritual exercise into solid reality.

However, the lessons of the fig tree are not exclusively concerned with the

---

* As with the story of Jairus's Daughter and the Woman with the Blood Flow in the Gemini section, this story of the Fig Tree is told in two parts – appropriate for the 'bi-corporeal' Sagittarius.

spiritual life. The text implies that human beings can effect changes in the physical world; that persistent prayer involving mind, will and faith can achieve, in Tennyson's words, 'more than this world dreams of'. Such thinking is anathema to the materialistic philosophies of the contemporary world, which consider mind to be an epiphenomenon, a by-product, of matter. For Gnostics, however, consciousness is primary, and the material universe is a 'crystallization' of mind, the last in a long line of increasingly dense emanations from the Divine. In such a system of thought, matter can be made to respond to the dictates of mind. This is the basis of the magical world view, which can accommodate the gardener's green fingers, the shaman's raindance and the healing prayer with relative ease. In cursing the fig tree Jesus masters those things symbolized by the Earth, and so has now demonstrated control over all four Elements.

Ara – The Altar and the Curse

The relationship between the fig tree incident and the Sagittarian decan, Ara, is quite striking. To the Romans the word *Ara* meant 'altar' and, according to Caesius, the constellation Ara represented *one of the altars raised by Moses*, or the permanent *golden altar in the Temple at Jerusalem*. Some thought it represented the Altar erected by Noah after the Flood. Allen reckons that this association with this 'first' Altar helps to account for the prominence given to this visually unimportant constellation, and explains why Manilius calls it *Mundi Templum*, 'The Temple of the World' (Allen, page 63). But in Greek, the word *ara* means 'curse'. Seiss writes of this constellation:

> The Greeks used the word *ara* sometimes in the sense of prayer, but more frequently in the sense of an imprecation, a curse, or the *effect of a curse* – bane, ruin, destruction ... In Aeschylus it is the name of the *actual curse* of Oedipus personified. (Seiss, pages 56-7; emphasis added)

Seiss informs us that the constellation Ara also has association with the altar of sacrifice, and this links the whole incident of the fig tree with the story of the Cleansing of the Temple (Mark 11:15-19). The Jerusalem Temple was the centre of Jewish sacrificial worship, the excesses of which are attacked by Jesus in heroic Sagittarian fashion. He casts out the merchants, overturns the tables of the money-changers and the seats* of the dove-sellers. He prevents

---

* 'In ancient Arabia the two small groups of stars now marking the head and the vane of the Archer's arrows were of much note as relics of still earlier asterisms, as well as a lunar station ... and Al Jauhari compared these figures to an Overturned Chair, which these stars may represent' (Allen, page 355).

people using the Temple precincts as a thoroughfare, and he declares the place a den of thieves. The Temple no longer serves any valid religious function. Like the fig tree whose leaves deceive by promising fruit when no fruit exists, the Temple's beauty and ostensible commitment to spiritual values are mere hypocritical sham. It is not 'a house of prayer for all nations' (note the Sagittarian expansiveness, echoing Manilius's *Mundi Templum*), but a commercial enterprise based on the notion that God is to be approached through the killing of animals.

This incident has long proved troublesome to the conventional commentator, for a number of reasons. The first concerns its sequence in the narrative. Matthew and Luke, following Mark, place it at the end of Jesus' ministry, just before his Passion and Death. John, on the other hand, puts it right at the beginning, just after the miracle in Cana (John 2:13-17). Did Jesus do it twice? Is John's placement of the incident 'purely symbolic'? For the historically-minded these are not easy questions to answer, but the problem is compounded even further when we consider that Jesus would not have been able to accomplish this feat very easily: the Temple precincts were very heavily guarded, and a trouble-maker would have been whisked away at the first hint of a disturbance.

The incident's most problematic aspect, however, concerns the unfamiliar side of Jesus' character that it seems to show. Did he really, as John says, take a whip to these people (John 2:15)? What happened to turning the other cheek? Could Jesus get angry? Mark makes no specific mention of anger, but Jesus' actions here are not those of a restrained and passive person. He is indeed angry, justifiably so, righteously so, as he defends the cause of real religion against the charlatans, incurring the wrath of the authorities in the process (Mark 11:18), and demonstrating that the Sagittarian phase of the spiritual life demands tireless warfare against all religious cant and spiritual quackery. It is a task that Sagittarians, who seem to have almost a monopoly on satirical writing, have taken upon themselves with relish. Voltaire in *Candide*, Jonathan Swift in *Gulliver's Travels*, Samuel Butler in *Hudibras* and *The Way of all Flesh*, and the comedian Bill Hicks in numerous stand-up routines, mercilessly take the Sagittarian 'scourge' to all manifestations of irrational, divisive, cruel, myopic religion – as does Mark Twain, whose biting words are a fitting end to this Sagittarian chapter:*

Man is the Religious Animal. He is the only Religious Animal. He is the only animal that has the True Religion – several of them. He is the only

---

* Voltaire, 21 November 1694; Jonathan Swift, 30 November 1667; Samuel Butler, 4 December 1835; Mark Twain, 30 November 1835; Bill Hicks, 16 December, 1961.

animal that loves his neighbour as himself, and cuts his throat if his theology isn't straight. He has made a graveyard of the globe in trying his honest best to smooth his brother's path to happiness and heaven ... The higher animals have no religion. And we are told they are going to be left out in the Hereafter. I wonder why? It seems questionable taste.

Ah, human nature. What a study! I heard that there was a considerable amount of discord among God's creatures and so I decided to take the matter in hand. So I built a cage, and in it I put a dog and a cat. And after a little training I got the dog and the cat to the point where they lived peaceably together. Then I introduced a pig, a goat, a kangaroo, some birds and a monkey. And after a few adjustments, they learned to live in harmony.

So encouraged was I by such successes that I added an Irish Catholic, a Presbyterian, a Jew, a Muslim from Turkestan, and a Buddhist from China, along with a Baptist missionary that I captured on the same trip. And in a very short while there wasn't a single living thing left in the cage.*

---

* Compiled by Richard Gilbert. See:
http://unitarian.ithaca.ny.us/sermons/RSG20040104.html

Capricorn (Mark 11:27–12:44)
'Call No Man Father'

'So, Ananda, you must be your own lamps, be your own refuges ... Hold firm to the truth as a lamp and a refuge and do not look for refuge to anything besides yourselves.' (The Buddha)

Capricorn and Saturn

Capricorn is the sign of the winter solstice, the point of the sun's maximum southerly declination, when nights are at their longest in the northern hemisphere. The sun, symbolic of individual consciousness, is now at its weakest and the forces of darkness, symbolizing the collective, predominate. This is when 'institutions freeze into systems' (Rudhyar, page 29), when the demands of society and its laws take precedence over individual initiative, and the major organizations of collective endeavour begin their task of regulation and control. Capricorn symbolizes organizational man, the company, the state, the team, any area of life in which the individual is a participating member or, worse, a computer-generated number. Some hint of this polarity between the individual and the community is preserved in the ancient symbol of Capricorn, the Goat-Fish, which is half one creature, half another, just as the human person lives partly as an individual, partly as a member of a group. The sign's glyph (♑) supposedly resembles the horns of a goat with a curling fish tail.

Dane Rudhyar (page 29) tells us that this is the phase of life in which the state assumes control over the individual, and in which an individual ruler can become totally subservient to his office. Capricorn is a sign of power and authority, but it is not the innate authority of the individual that we find in Leo, but the conferred authority of the figurehead, the authority that springs from the office and not from the soul. The mountain-goat, slowly but sure-footedly climbing up the steep slope is an appropriate symbol for this sign's association with the relentless pursuit of office by painstaking ascent through the ranks.

Capricorn's commitment to society also finds expression in terms of the tokens of success which, collectively, we prize. This is the stage of accumulation, not as a protection against possible reversal of fortune, as in Cancer, but as a mark of achievement. Capricorn is the sign of the status-symbol: the private parking space, the second home. It is the sign of rigid social divisions, of knowing one's place. England, with its ludicrous social stratifications and its tradition of deferential forelock-tugging, is a heavily Capricornian country, as is caste-ridden India. Like Cancer, its polar opposite, Capricorn recognizes its debt to the past and finds solace in tradition, order, and continuity. It is the sign of the Father, our first authority symbol, who connects us with the past, who embodies all the accumulated wisdom of the race, and who teaches us the great Capricornian virtues of social responsibility and self-control.

Vesta (sometimes Hestia), the Roman goddess of the hearth, was considered to be especially associated with Capricorn as its 'tutelary deity'. Every new-born child was carried round the hearth as an initiation into the family, and each meal began and ended with an invocation to the goddess. Every Roman city would have a public hearth sacred to Vesta, tended by the vestal virgins who had to ensure, on pain of death, that the fire never went out. Coals from the hearth of the parent city would be carried to kindle a fire in the hearth of any newly founded city.

The hearth, then, symbolizes the family and the nation, the link between present and past, the role of the individual in the greater community, defined either spatially or temporally. That this should be associated with Capricorn serves to underline this sign's connection with lineage, centralized authority, convention, propriety, and social conformity.

179

It should not be assumed from the foregoing that these are in any sense undesirable elements of human experience. Even designating them the symbolic products of the Night Force is in no sense meant to imply disapproval. The collective dimension of life is not an option: we are called to live it whether we like it or not, and it is as well to remember that Capricorn characteristics, when embodied in an individual, can contribute markedly to the collective good. As Gettings says:

> Capricorn may often appear rather dominating to those who do not like being controlled, but someone has to shoulder life's responsibilities ... the Capricornian gives structure to the human world – he is the force which prevents us all from being lost in mere anarchy, the great stabilizer in the world of man. (Gettings, 1972, page 118)

Order and stability are essential to the proper management of any aspect of our life, and this is especially true of the spiritual life which is intrinsically turbulent, and which needs the support of tradition, and the consolations of company. However, it is our relationship to these structures that the Capricornian phase calls us to examine. We need to determine how far our commitment to spiritual authority, church doctrines, charismatic figures, holy books, group membership, and the like has affected our sense of self-reliance. How far have we turned over our spiritual life to the regulation of some outside agency or other so that we may be spared the problems associated with thinking for ourselves? 'The tragedy of the ... religious life is that it fosters dependence upon an intermediary,' says Dane Rudhyar (page 78), and the challenge of Capricorn is to develop a sense of spiritual self-determination so that, whether inside or outside of a recognized group, we may relinquish our need to place others between ourselves and the divine.

The ruler of Capricorn is Saturn, the furthest away from the earth of all the planets visible to the naked eye. To the ancient world, Saturn marked the boundary of our planetary system, and so came to represent all boundaries and limits, principal among these being death. Ptolemy associates this planet with old age, when a man becomes 'worn down ... dispirited, weak, easily offended, and hard to please in all situations, in keeping with the sluggishness of his movements' (page 447). Together with the sun, Saturn represents the father and, alone, it has rulership over the bones. The skeletal system defines and maintains the structure of the body, giving it form and durability, and persisting even after the body's demise as a universal symbol of mortality and decay. In Greek mythology Saturn is Cronos, Time, who decrees the limits of all things, and who stands with his scythe to announce impending death. The glyph of Saturn (♄) resembles the scythe of Cronos.

When Saturn rules the soul, says Ptolemy,

> he makes his subjects lovers of the body, strong-minded, deep thinkers, austere, of a single purpose, laborious, dictatorial, ready to punish, lovers of property, avaricious, violent, amassing treasure, and jealous. (page 241)

The above gives Ptolemy's view of the Saturnian influence when Saturn's position in the horoscope is 'dignified'! His list of epithets for an unfavourable position is even more colourful. However, Ptolemy's favourable list shows us quite clearly how the planet Saturn was viewed as a malign and sinister influence in the ancient world. The 'Lord of Capricorn', who crystallizes all things into form, and holds them together by force, is himself the symbol of their inevitable collapse.

It is important to realize that the sun's entry into Capricorn in December marks another reversal of direction. In Cancer, the northerly sun began to move south; in Capricorn it reaches its southerly limit and begins its movement northward. This was always a time of rejoicing among the ancient peoples of the northern hemisphere, and the Romans celebrated the Saturnalia, named in honour of Capricorn's ruling planet, between 17 and 23 December. It was a time when the customary roles were reversed – masters and servants changing places, for example – and when the moral conventions were relaxed a little. The tradition survives today in the office party! On a more exalted level, this reversal 'relates to the idea of a shift in value, a turning away from the values of the outer world to those within. In one sense it is the reawakening of the personal' (Wright, page 160).

Among the Jews, Capricorn was said to be the emblem of the tribe of Naphtali, but Jacob's description – 'Naphtali is a hind let loose' (Genesis 49:21) – is hardly unambiguous, and some have claimed Benjamin or Reuben for Capricorn. However, there seems little doubt that the Jewish people as a whole have affinity with this sign and with its ruler, Saturn.* Charles Carter writes:

* The Jewish Sabbath is Saturday – Saturn's Day. We noted earlier that Judaism was born when the equinoctial point entered the constellation Aries, and there is no doubt that Arien imagery of rams, goats, sheep, sacrifices and circumcision play a major role in the liturgical practices of Judaism. But the other Cardinal signs – Cancer, Libra, Capricorn – feature prominently in the development of Judaism. Libra, the polar opposite of Aries, is the sign of covenants and law, Cancer the sign of home, diet and mother, and Capricorn the sign of duty, social responsibility and the father. While Libra is the sign which symbolizes the Law's origin and

The Jews are principally under Capricorn ... and the New Testament does contain condemnations of the leaders of Jewry that certainly sound like attacks upon the traditional Capricorn – the love of high places, hypocritical formalism in religion, the desecration of holy places in pursuit of gain. (Carter 1965, page 83)

These condemnations take up a good proportion of the Capricorn section of Mark's Gospel.

The Spiritual Lessons of Capricorn

Lawyers are all right, I guess ... I mean they're all right if they go around saving innocent guys' lives all the time, and like that, but you don't 'do' that kind of stuff if you're a lawyer. All you do is make a lot of dough and play golf and play bridge and buy cars and drink Martinis and look like a hot shot. And besides. Even if you did go around saving guys' lives and all, how would you know if you did it because you really wanted to save the guys' lives, or you did it because what you really wanted to be was a terrific lawyer ... How would you know you weren't being a phoney? The trouble is, you wouldn't. (*The Catcher in the Rye* by J.D. Salinger, born 1 January 1919)

It is the question of spiritual authority that Mark addresses first in the Capricorn section of his Gospel. A group of 'chief priests, scribes and elders' approach Jesus and ask him by what authority (*exousia*) he does the things he does (Mark 11:27-28). Jesus replies with a question of his own:

'I will ask you one question. Answer me, and I will tell you by what authority I am doing these things. John's baptism – was it from heaven, or from men? Tell me!' They discussed it among themselves and said, 'If we say, "From heaven", he will ask, "Then why didn't you believe him?" But if we say, "From men" ...' (They feared the people, for everyone held that John really was a prophet.) (Mark 11:29-32)

They have fallen into Jesus' trap. Since any opinion they might voice would be based on social expediency and not on any objective assessment of the

----

purpose, Capricorn symbolizes its operation and enforcement; *legalism,* concern for the letter of the law, is, therefore, Capricornian. Similarly, while Christianity is a Piscean religion, it also relates clearly to the other Mutable signs – Virgo, Gemini and Sagittarius. Its emphasis on virginity and celibacy are Virgoan, its elaborate and divisive theology is Geminian (as are the Letters which constitute a good proportion of the Christian scriptures!), and its missionary zeal and sacerdotalism are Sagittarian.

evidence, they are unable to answer without incriminating themselves and so they admit that the question has defeated them. Jesus' response is wonderfully audacious, and provides one of the few occasions on which the reader is forced to smile. 'If you can't answer my question,' he says, 'I won't tell you where my authority comes from' (Mark 12:33).

It is as well for us to remember that these men are the sources of authority in Israel. They are not simply market-place debaters. The chief priests, who would almost certainly have been from the powerful and influential Sadducean party, are accompanied by those Saturnian figures 'the elders' (*hoi presbuteroi*), the older men, the pillars of the community, the sage and venerable counsellors of the people. Also present are some scribes, legal experts who were generally associated with the Pharisees, who could quote the Law of Moses verbatim, and who could cite precedent and precept on all matters pertaining to religious affairs. Jesus' handling of his interrogation at their hands shows his contempt for their supposed wisdom, and for the whole system of spiritual authority on which their combined status as teachers of the people is based.

The next passage, the Parable of the Tenants (Mark 12:1-12), is a blistering attack upon all the leaders of Israel, past and present, who have consistently maltreated or killed God's messengers. These are the wicked 'husbandmen' (*georgoi*) of Israel, the ones to whom God has entrusted his vineyard, but who, by their treachery, have forfeited the right to exercise any authority in spiritual matters (Mark 12:9-11).

Hard on the heels of this collective denunciation comes a series of encounters with the various separate groups of mentors within Judaism, the first of which involves the Pharisees and the Herodians. It is historically very unlikely that these two parties would be united on any issue, but it is their mutual animosity that Mark exploits as they frame a question for Jesus which, however he might answer it, would be sure to alienate one group or the other. 'Should we pay tribute to Caesar?' they ask (Mark 12:15). The Herodians, so named because they supported the puppet regime set up by the Romans, would want to hear an affirmative answer. The Pharisees, fiercely conscious of Israel's unique status as God's people, and opposed to Roman authority, would want to hear him say 'No'. Jesus' reply surprises them both: 'Give to Caesar what belongs to Caesar, and give to God what belongs to God' (Mark 12:17). This simple little saying expresses concisely what the Christian attitude to authority should be: where it makes legitimate demands we should obey, but we must not assume that our civic duties and our spiritual duties are the same thing. There is the clear implication, too, that our duty to God is more important than our duty to systems, be these secular or religious.

It is worth noting that a denarius minted in Spain during the reign of Augustus actually displayed an image of Capricorn on the reverse side. MacNeice tells us:

> The young Augustus, though a hard-headed and calculating person, was so impressed by the glorious future foretold for him (by an astrologer named Theagenes) that he published his horoscope and struck a silver coin stamped with Capricorn, the sign under which he was born.* (MacNeice, page 122)

Fig. 23 Roman Coin showing Augustus and Capricorn

Although Augustus was dead when Mark was writing it is possible that the text here alludes to an image of imperial power with which his earliest readers would have been familiar. After all, coins do not go out of circulation upon the death of the monarch whose likeness they bear.†

Some Sadducees bring the next question. These were the aristocratic, priestly party within Judaism, distinguished theologically from the Pharisees by their disbelief in resurrection. They held that the Pentateuch alone ('the Book of Moses', 12:26) was authoritatively from God, and any doctrine which could not be clearly found therein was not to be believed. Since there is no unambiguous reference to an afterlife in these five books, they rejected the notion of physical resurrection. Their question to Jesus concerns seven brothers who were married successively to the same woman. Although unusual, this would have been hypothetically possible, since under the law of levirate marriage, a man was obliged to marry his sister-in-

---

* The moon, not the sun, was in Capricorn when Augustus was born.

† Titus also issued a denarius with Capricorn on the reverse in 79 C.E. He was born on 30th December 39 C.E.

law in order to raise up children in his dead brother's name. In the resurrection, the Sadducees ask, whose wife this woman would be? (Mark 12:23). Jesus tells them that she won't be the wife of any of them because, in the resurrection, marriage does not exist and men and women will be 'like the angels in heaven' (Mark 12:25). However, it is Jesus' reasoning, rather than his answer, which is interesting from our point of view. He argues:

> 'Now about the dead rising – have you not read in the book of Moses, in the account of the bush, how God said to him, "I am the God of Abraham, the God of Isaac, and the God of Jacob?" He is not the God of the dead, but of the living. You are badly mistaken!' (Mark 12:26-7)

Here Jesus is shown arguing on the Sadducees' own terms, demonstrating how a text from the very books that they considered to be inspired could be used to refute the position they were defending. This is an attack upon all bibliolatry in whatever guise it may appear. Except perhaps for insurance policies, there are no unambiguous documents. We bring our prejudices and our background to everything we read, and differences of opinion over meaning are inevitable. The warring sects of Christendom are sufficient proof that this is so. In pointing out the faulty exegesis of the Sadducees (by means, we might add, of a very specious argument on his part), Jesus is not advocating that they go back and study the text more carefully, as is generally supposed: he is demonstrating to them the futility of all argumentation based on personal interpretations of sacred texts. Our religious life must never be entirely focused on any book, no matter how exalted the claims made for its origin. Scriptures may inspire us, and they may educate us; they may point us in the direction we must follow but they must never be allowed to usurp our sense of self-determination, which relies on the internal light and not the external text.

Jesus continues his parody of scripturalism a little later in this section when he refutes the notion that the Messiah was to be a 'son of David'. Quoting from Psalm 110, he asks:

> How is it that the teachers of the law say that the Christ is the son of David? David himself, speaking by the Holy Spirit, declared: 'The Lord said to my Lord: Sit at my right hand until I put your enemies under your feet.'
> David himself calls him 'Lord'. How then can he be his son? (Mark 12:367)

Again, specious reasoning, designed, I am sure, to raise a chuckle. Here the text of Mark is itself delightfully ambiguous: are we meant to infer that the Messiah was *not* to be a son of David; or are we meant to deduce that, given enough time and a sharp enough wit, we can prove anything we like from scripture? I leave the reader to judge.

The Sufis tell an illuminating and humorous story which suggests a more liberal attitude to scripture than that of the literalists. A preacher, renowned for his wisdom, drew large crowds wherever he went. At the end of his sermons he would often be asked the secret of his great wisdom. He always replied, 'I am wise because I know what is in the Koran.' One day, a questioner decided to probe further: 'Tell us, then. Just what is in the Koran?' 'In the Koran,' replied the preacher, 'there are two pressed flowers and a letter from my friend Abdullah.' Received texts can only be useful to us when they are examined in conjunction with our experience of living. Isolate a text from life, extol it as inerrant revelation, and it becomes a tyrant.

Sandwiched between these two scripture lessons is an encounter with a scribe whose faith Jesus commends. This man, in a spirit of genuine enquiry, asks Jesus which commandment is the most important. In reply, Jesus quotes the Shema, the prayer derived from Deuteronomy 6 that is central to all Judaism, and which runs:

> 'The most important one,' answered Jesus, 'is this: "Hear, O Israel, the Lord our God, the Lord is one. Love the Lord your God with all your heart and with all your soul and with all your mind and with all your strength." The second is this: "Love your neighbour as yourself." There is no commandment greater than these.' (Mark 12:29-31)

The scribe accepts what Jesus says, and his integrity is rewarded with the words, 'You are not far from the kingdom of God' (Mark 12:34). This passage illustrates the fact that Jesus does not condemn all Jewish leaders. It clearly implies that there were some, of whom this man was a representative, who accepted and practised the essential core of Judaism and who were unaffected by factionalism and casuistic squabbling.

This section of the Gospel ends with Jesus contrasting the spiritual vacuousness of certain scribes who parade their pseudo-piety for all to see, with the humble actions of a poor widow who puts all she has into the Temple treasury. The status-conscious scribes, who scrabble for the best seats in the synagogue (Mark 12:39), reflect everything that is reprehensible about Capricorn. Real religion, we learn, is not about putting on a display, but about the simple acts of generosity which are motivated by love.

Matthew's condemnation of the Pharisees is much longer than Mark's, comprising the whole of chapter 23. It is the most comprehensive and uncompromising attack upon hypocrisy anywhere in the Christian scriptures, but we must be very careful not to assume that it is directed only at a particular set of people living at a particular time. Pharisaism is endemic to the human condition. The 'whited sepulchres' of Jesus' time are just the 'phoneys' of our own.

In the passage from Matthew 23 which parallels the Markan section, Jesus denounces the Pharisees' clamouring for exalted titles with the words:

> But you are not to be called 'Rabbi', for you have only one Master and you are all brothers. And do not call anyone on earth 'father', for you have one Father, and he is in heaven. Nor are you to be called 'teacher', for you have one Teacher, the Christ. (Matthew 23:8-10)

This seems like a strange saying to Judaeo-Christian ears; after all, Jews call their ministers 'Rabbi', and Catholics call their priest 'Father', but it is perfectly comprehensible to adherents of less authoritarian religious systems. The Zen Buddhist master Dae Kwang, for instance, said, 'If you meet the Buddha on the road, kill him. If you meet the Patriarch, kill the Patriarch.' What he means by this is that nothing – books, gurus, traditions – should be allowed to usurp the individual's responsibility for his or her own enlightenment. The Buddha, who described himself as merely a finger pointing at the moon, says:

> It is proper ... to doubt ... to be uncertain ... Do not go upon what has been acquired by repeated hearing; nor upon tradition; nor upon rumour; nor upon what is in scripture; nor upon the consideration, 'The monk is our teacher'. [Rather] when you yourselves know: 'These things are bad; [when] undertaken and observed, these things lead to harm and ill', abandon them. [Likewise] when you yourselves know: 'These things are good; [when] undertaken and observed, these things lead to benefit and happiness', enter on and abide in them. (Novak, page 62)

Most religions confuse the finger pointing at the moon with the moon itself, keeping their adherents in the darkness of spiritual slavery. Capricorn, the time of maximum darkness, represents the power of the organization and the system over the individual, but, as all the mystical traditions remind us, Capricorn is also the Southern Gate of the Sun through which human souls ascend to heaven, because it is at this time of the winter solstice that the light of Christ-consciousness, the realization that the Teacher is *within*, is born.

Capricornian Khalil Gibran (born 6 January 1883) has expressed this autonomy of the human soul in this celebrated passage from his book *The Prophet*:

And a woman who held a babe against her bosom said, 'Speak to us of
Children.'

And he said:

'Your children are not your children.

They are the sons and daughters of Life's longing for itself.

They come through you but not from you,

And though they are with you, yet they belong not to you.

You may give them your love but not your thoughts.

For they have their own thoughts.

You may house their bodies but not their souls,

For their souls dwell in the house of tomorrow, which you cannot visit,
not even in your dreams.

You may strive to be like them, but seek not to make them like you.

For life goes not backward nor tarries with yesterday.

You are the bows from which your children as living arrows are sent
forth.

The archer sees the mark upon the path of the infinite, and He bends
you with His might that His arrows may go swift and far.

Let your bending in the archer's hand be for gladness;

For even as He loves the arrow that flies, so He loves also the bow that
is stable.'

Aquarius (Mark 13:1–14:16)
The Man Carrying a Jar of Water

Things fall apart; the centre cannot hold;
Mere anarchy is loosed upon the world,
The blood-dimmed tide is loosed, and everywhere
The ceremony of innocence is drowned;
       (*The Second Coming,* W. B. Yeats)

Aquarius and Saturn

When the musical *Hair* was first produced in 1968 the term 'The Age of Aquarius' entered popular consciousness for the first time, and people began singing about a supposed utopian future in which we would all take off our clothes, practise free love, and live in peace and harmony. Few understood the astrology behind it all. Even the writers of the musical had no real idea. The lines 'When the moon is in the seventh house / And Jupiter aligns with Mars' show astonishing astrological ignorance: Jupiter aligns with Mars frequently, and the moon is in the seventh house every day. And the rest of the stanza – 'Then peace will guide the planets, and love will steer the stars' – is more an expression of naive sixties optimism than a faithful account of esoteric tradition. If the writers had investigated this tradition they would have found that the 'dawning' of the Age of Aquarius would be anything but tranquil, harmonious and loving. As we shall see, one of the documents they could have consulted was Mark's Gospel.

'Capricorn and Aquarius,' says Ptolemy, ' ... are cold and wintry, ... and their diametrical aspect is not consistent with beneficence' (page 81). By 'diametrical aspect' he means their opposition to the signs Cancer and Leo in which the power of the sun is at its strongest. Cancer, though ruled by the moon, is the sign of the summer solstice, when the sun reaches its highest point in the sky; Leo, ruled by the sun, symbolizes the glory of the individual, the consciousness of selfhood, and personal uniqueness. Capricorn and Aquarius, on the other hand, are both ruled by Saturn, the planet which 'occupies the orbit highest and farthest from the luminaries', and in whose nature 'cold prevails'. 'Cold' and 'darkness' symbolize the collective; the light of self-hood is all but extinguished, and we are more conscious of our group orientation. Winter is the time of huddling together for warmth, of relying on our fellows to provide protection against predators, of sharing what we have to ensure the welfare of the community. Today, we have all but lost an awareness of these things and they survive, in somewhat mangled form, only in our celebration of Christmas at the time of the winter solstice. But, to our ancestors they would have been real indeed, and the symbolism of light and dark would have had much more meaning for them than it possibly can for us with our central heating and electric lights.

In the story of Samson's first haircut (Judges 16:17-19), the Jewish scriptures present us with a delightful poetic account of the sun's weakness when it is placed in the sign of Aquarius. The name Samson (see 'The Forgotten Language of the Stars'), comes from the Hebrew word *shemesh*, which means 'sun', and so his name is equivalent to our 'Sonny'. His nemesis is Delilah, whose name comes from the Hebrew word *deliy*, which means 'water-bucket'. Delilah is Aquarius, in which the sun loses its strength, a process symbolized by the clipping of Samson's locks (the sun's rays).

For Ptolemy, Capricorn and Aquarius lacked 'beneficence', then, not because people born under these signs were without benevolence, but because the signs themselves represent the bleakness and blackness of winter, when life was hard and dangers were many. Such hardship, however, makes us conscious of our vulnerability, of our need for others, of our responsibilities within the groups to which we belong: as our sense of individuality diminishes, our sense of communal responsibility increases.

190

In Capricorn, this manifested as authority, as the power of the state to subjugate and regulate the rights of the individual. In Aquarius, however, group-consciousness is expressed as co-operation among free individuals who have sublimated the demands of the ego in order to facilitate the highest good of the greatest number. Aquarius is the Fixed Air sign, and although fixity reflects something of its Saturnian inflexibility, Air is the medium of ideas, of debate, of intellectual exploration. Consequently, Aquarius has come to be associated with the democratic spirit, with free participation by equals in the governing process. The autocracy and patriarchy expressed by Capricorn has yielded to the egalitarianism of Aquarius, reflected no doubt in the curious fact that many of the twentieth century's most prominent feminist thinkers have been born under Aquarius.*

At its best, Aquarius symbolizes the ideal society, in which the proper balance between the rights of the individual and the rights of the group is established and maintained. People in whom the Aquarian vision seems most evident are socially committed, concerned for the welfare of the wider community. Manilius claims that Aquarius, when rising in the east at the time of birth, signifies a model citizen:

> The Good, the Pious, and the Just are born
> When first Aquarius pours out his Urn.
>
> (page 137)

Such sentiments are echoed in more modern delineations of the Aquarian type. Charles Carter, writing in 1925, has this to say:

> ... there is nearly always much kindness, sympathy, and refinement, together with an intense love for the feeling of kinship with wild nature. There is generally artistic ability. The love of friends is very marked, and the native is attracted to societies, clubs, associations, groups of people, and 'movements' of all sorts, easily merging his own personality in 'causes'. (Carter, 1925, page 8)

This easy merging with the group reflects the lack of commitment to a possessive individualism which also gives rise to that other Aquarian quality, detachment. This has led to an association of this sign with science, with the cool objectivity of the observer who is prepared to go wherever the evidence

* Virginia Woolf, 25 January 1882; Angela Davis, 26 January 1944; Susan Sontag, 28 January 1933; Germaine Greer, 29 January 1939; Vanessa Redgrave, 30 January 1937; Gertrude Stein, 3 February 1874; Betty Frieden, 4 February 1921.

leads. Manilius credits Aquarius with inventiveness, particularly with regard to aquatic machines; he also tells us that:

> To his Births the World oblig'd shall owe
> Spheres, Cycles, Orns, and turn new Skies below.
>
> (page 128)

This is a picture of the astronomer complete with the accoutrements of his vocation, observing and mapping the cycles of the heavens and interpreting their meaning for us who live beneath the skies. Here is the true 'Water-Bearer', then, who patiently gleans wisdom from heaven and earth and who pours it out for all humanity to share in and to benefit from. He is the one who lives a life dedicated to bringing refreshment to all, the selfless one who contributes unstintingly to the public good, and who embodies and fosters the ideals of brotherhood and equality.

These are noble ideals and, as we mentioned above, many people think that they will characterize the Age of Aquarius, on the threshold of which we now stand. But there is nothing automatic about these things. We may be experiencing a new awareness of our inter-relatedness, but the experience has to be appropriated, individually and collectively, if it is to become anything more than just sentimental longing for justice and equity. In order to become vehicles for the transformation of society, we have first to transform ourselves: we cannot pour out what we don't possess. Such transformation is the goal of the spiritual life *in toto*, but it has particular application in the Aquarius phase where we are called to assess our contribution to the collective and, more importantly, our willingness to offer it. So drastic is the change implied here that it cannot be achieved without turmoil. As Liz Greene tells us, before we can experience brotherhood we must:

> first go through the long and bloody process of discovering why we have never been able to experience brotherhood. No individual becomes conscious of himself instantaneously and without suffering, and no collective does either. If something must die, then it's going to raise a hell of a fuss in the process, and if something is being born, it's going to cause pain to the thing giving it birth ... It may be that Aquarius will bring us the awareness that we are indeed part of a vast interconnected life entity, both biologically and psychologically. But the awareness is going to force up everything in us which obstructs us from living our vision. (Greene, pages 172-3)

The trauma produced by radically changing the focus of our life is evident whenever there is a change of human consciousness, as symbolized by the concept of astrological ages (see 'The Forgotten Language of the Stars'). Whenever the equinoctial point moves from one constellation to another we are collectively obliged to come to terms with the principles embodied in the new constellation. This inevitably means radically breaking with the past, a process which can never occur painlessly. This applies to the ending of any cycle of human life, including the tiny cycles of an individual existence: the new can only be accepted if the old is allowed to die. But Aquarius, the penultimate sign, does not symbolize the end of a cycle. It really signifies openness to the end, preparedness for it, willingness to accept the pain that the end will involve.

These ideas are reflected in the Saturnian rulership of Aquarius. In the last chapter we noted how Saturn (♄) symbolized structure and order and how this was in keeping with its rulership of Capricorn. But Saturn is also the planet of decay and death, and there is a certain appropriateness in its ruling two signs together. Like Janus, it seems to face both ways: in Capricorn it represents the building up of structures; in Aquarius, it represents their dissolution. In modern astrology, this aspect of Aquarius has been appropriated by Uranus (♅), the planet of violent disruption and radical change, whose existence was unknown to the ancient world, but whose principle seems to have been associated with Aquarius from the earliest times.* Together, Saturn and Uranus are said to rule Aquarius, the one signifying gradual erosion, the other sudden and unexpected destruction.

In the Greek myths Saturn is the child of Uranus, but he eventually eats his own children and castrates his father. As Cronos, or Time, Saturn does indeed 'eat' his children, and as the symbol of structure and order he frustrates the chaos and creativity symbolized by Uranus.

The tension between structure and anarchy which Aquarius symbolizes can be detected in the work of Aquarian writers, who often seem to be breaking the stylistic conventions. James Joyce (born 2 February 1882) is an obvious example, but Joyce's literary iconoclasm was anticipated by fellow Aquarian Lewis Carroll (27 January 1832), who invented the anarchic Wonderland, in which 'the laws of space, time and logic that govern our familiar world are absent', and where 'there is no system, no logic, and language itself is a slippery and ambiguous medium'. Alice's adventure is a

---

* The astronomer William Herschel discovered Uranus in 1781, but there is some evidence to suggest that 'at certain times and from certain points of the earth's surface, it is discernible with the naked eye' (Reid, page 95). So it may well have been known to ancient initiates.

Fig. 24 'Saturn Devouring His Son', by Goya

'grimly comic trip through the lawless underground that lies just beneath the surface of our constructed universe' (Wright, page 182).

The world that confronts us in Mark 13 bears some of the qualities of Wonderland, but without the 'grim humour'.

194

The Spiritual Lessons of Aquarius

O wonder,
How many goodly creatures are there here!
How beauteous mankind is. O brave new world
That has such people in't!
(Miranda in Shakespeare's *The Tempest*,
Act 5, Scene 1)

Chapter 13 of Mark presents more difficulties to the commentator than any other passage in the Gospel. To begin with, the whole chapter takes the form of a single discourse, familiar enough to the reader of John's Gospel, but completely different from anything previously encountered in Mark. In addition there seems, at first sight, to be a change of emphasis. No longer is the kingdom of God seen simply as an interior state, growing within the individual like the mustard seed (Mark 4:30-32); instead, a cosmic dimension is introduced and the son of man, hitherto simply 'man', becomes a celestial, apocalyptic figure who, at the appointed time, will make his presence felt upon the earth. There are many statements which appear to be prophecies of some future time, and these have fuelled millenarian expectation throughout the centuries. In fact this chapter in Mark, along with the corresponding chapters in Matthew (chapter 24) and Luke (chapter 21), the Book of Revelation and the Book of Daniel, all notoriously difficult to interpret, seem to be the basic textbooks of contemporary sectarianism. Many people within mainstream Christianity, too, consider that these particular parts of the Bible provide us with a timetable of events leading up to the battle of Armageddon and the end of the world. When President Reagan announced, way before Perestroika, that Russia was the 'evil empire' and that the biblical signs of the end seemed to be evident, he sent a chill down every liberal spine in the western world. Even St Augustine believed in a literal, visible 'second coming' of Christ, and he used his belief to counter the arguments of those who held that the earth was round: it couldn't be, he said, because a returning Jesus would not be visible to those 'underneath'.

As a series of prophecies, however, chapter 13 of Mark is an obvious failure. Even the initial statement that none of the stones of the Temple would be left standing was not fulfilled to the letter (Mark 13:2), as the Wailing Wall, which still stands today, bears testimony. Add to this the promise found in verse 30 that 'this generation will not pass away until all these things

195

happen' and we can see why it is futile to interpret these verses as literal prophecies.

Literalism, in fact, inhibits any meaningful analysis of this chapter. Taking each verse and declaring it a 'scripture', one piece of God's great revelatory jigsaw puzzle, misses the point of the whole. We can only get some idea of the author's purpose if we allow his poetic images to work on us, and if we try to understand the sources of that imagery and the part that it plays in the complete sweep of the Gospel's narrative.

However, since the Jerusalem Temple was destroyed by the Romans in 70 CE it is possible that at least the first part of chapter 13 (1-23) reflects the situation immediately preceding this event, and that the warnings in these verses and the mention of the 'abomination which causes desolation' (thought by scholars to be the Roman standards in the Temple precincts) refer to actual historical incidents, in addition to any other reference they may have. Whatever the truth of this, there is no doubt that Mark has put it in the right place because, while the imagery is apocalyptic, and therefore conventionally Jewish, it is woven together with zodiacal references which are entirely Aquarian.

The Jewish ideas spring from the concept of the 'Day of the Lord', a time in the future when God would intervene dramatically in world history and act as champion of Israel. Whenever this is referred to in the Old Testament the imagery is invariably cosmic, catastrophic, and bloody. Joel's description (quoted in 'The Forgotten Language of the Stars') is a classic example of this kind of writing. For the Jewish people, history was divided into two periods: a time of anguish and strife, followed by a time of peace when Isaiah's vision would become a reality:

> They will beat their swords into ploughshares, and their spears into pruning hooks: nation will not take up sword against nation, nor will they train for war any more. (Isaiah 2:4)

The point of division between these two periods would be the 'Day of the Lord', the approach of which would be signalled by a variety of disasters, and by the coming of the Messiah.

Mark's Gospel reflects this notion faithfully. Before the 'end' occurs we are told that:

> ... in those days, following that distress, the sun will be darkened, and the moon will not give its light; the stars will fall from the sky and the heavenly bodies will be shaken. (Mark 13:24-5)

Fig. 25 The 'Wailing Wall', Jerusalem

Mixed with this conventional Jewish imagery, however, are astrological concepts which involve not one time of cosmic upheaval, but a series. As explained in 'The Forgotten Language of the Stars', the ancient world believed that when the equinoctial point moved from one constellation of the zodiac to another, a new age was born. This was not just a 'pagan' belief; both the story of Abraham and the story of the Exodus* show that this type

* The whole story of Abraham seems to reflect the movement of the equinoctial point from Taurus to Aries. He is supposed to have lived around 2,000 BCE, at the beginning of the Arien Age, and he is instructed by God to move out of the familiar territory of his homeland and go

197

of thinking was not foreign to the Jews. Mark was living at a time when the equinox was about to move from Aries to Pisces, from the Ram to the Fish, with all the attendant calamities that such a dramatic change in human consciousness was expected to bring. So Mark is writing about the end of the age (of Aries), *and* the approaching end of the individual's spiritual cycle, in terms drawn from Jewish apocalyptic writing which was the conventional way of describing catastrophic upheavals.

But there are astrological images too, and, for some reason we find, yet again, that the zodiacal motifs are less clear in Mark than in Matthew. In verse 26 Mark writes:

> At that time men will see the Son of Man coming in clouds with great power and glory.

Clouds, of course, are 'water-bearers'(!) but the parallel passage in Matthew is even more explicitly Aquarian:

> At that time the sign of the Son of Man will appear in the sky, and all the nations of the earth will mourn. They will see the Son of Man coming on the clouds of the sky, with power and great glory. (Matthew 24:30)

A little earlier Matthew reports that the question which prompts this whole discourse is, 'Tell us, when will these things be, what will be the sign of your coming (*parousia*, literally 'presence'), and the completion of the age?' The Authorized Version translates this last phrase 'the end of the world', but the Greek word is the genitive form of *aiôn* which means 'a space of time ... a lifetime, generation, period of history, an indefinitely long period, an age' (Abbot-Smith, page 15). There is more than a hint here of the end of one astrological age and the beginning of another. That the new age referred to is Aquarius is confirmed a little further on in the text, where we read:

> For as lightning that comes from the east is visible even in the west, so will be the coming of the Son of Man. (Matthew 24:27)

This little simile captures the very glyph of Aquarius (♒), the twin flashes of

---

to an unknown country. His experience is representative of all new beginnings, when we are called to proceed 'in faith' to an unknown future with no certainties and few landmarks. It is the ram of Aries that Abraham finds in the thicket as he prepares to sacrifice Isaac (Genesis 22:6ff.).

lightning.* The reference to the 'sign of the Son of Man in heaven' (verse 30) confirms the Aquarian signature on this whole section. Aquarius is the only 'sign of the man' in the zodiac, and whenever we have encountered 'the man' in this kind of symbolic context it has invariably been associated with the three other Fixed signs of the zodiac: Taurus, Leo, and Scorpio. This quaternity appears in the Book of Ezekiel (1:10) as the 'four living creatures' in the prophet's vision, and in the Book of Revelation as the four beasts around the throne of God (Revelation 4:7). They are the lion, the calf, the man and the eagle: Leo, Taurus, Aquarius and Scorpio.

This part of Matthew's Gospel seems to point towards our own day, the 'dawning' of the Age of Aquarius, when the old structures would be torn down and a new order would arise from the smoking ashes. W.B. Yeats, who was well versed in esoteric lore, describes the birth of the new age in his poem *The Second Coming*. It is a time when 'things fall apart' and 'the centre cannot hold'; when 'mere anarchy is loosed upon the world'. And the image from the *spiritus mundi* which will accompany these events is that of a beast 'with lion body and the head of man', Aquarius and its polar opposite sign Leo, the two signs which will characterize the new epoch. Peter Lemesurier has written about these Matthaean symbols in the following, rather colourful, terms:

And as he (Uranus) brandished his new-found powers, flexed his cosmic muscles, she, the Earth-Mother, would suffer violent convulsions. The planet would be sent reeling by disturbances in deep space. There would be planetary collisions – a comet, or worse. Earthquakes would follow. Volcanic dust would hood the moon and turn the sun to blood. Famine and pestilence would stalk the lands. Wars would rage. The very survival of life on earth would be threatened. Such would be the birth-pangs of the new age, the advent of the long-awaited sky-kingdom. And then, in the aftermath of the twilight of the gods, the promised new dawn. The coming of the Son of Man. The birth of Aquarius. (Lemesurier, page 40)

---

* Allen quotes Mr C.W. King: '"As for the source of these hieroglyphics, I have never been able to trace it. They are found exactly as we see them in every old medieval MSS"; and Mr King is inclined, in default of any other origin, to "suspect they were devised by Arab sages" – an opinion which I do not follow. The subject is shrouded in great obscurity; and even Professor Sayce recently informed me that he had been unable to trace the history of the zodiacal symbols up to their first appearance in Western literature.' (Allen footnote, page 49) However, there is little doubt that the Aquarius hieroglyph appears, just as we have it, except with three lines instead of two, on the Egyptian zodiac of Denderah.

But the turmoil and chaos of our own turbulent time of transition from Pisces to Aquarius – perfectly predictable on the basis of the ancient theory of Astrological Ages – echoes the time of transition from Aries to Pisces during which the Gospels were written. The age of the Fish is beginning; the age of the Ram – symbolized by the Temple in Jerusalem – is ending, and the old order will resist so strongly that the universe itself will reflect the tension between new and old (Mark 13:7-8). When these things will occur, no one knows, but Jesus' followers are called upon to hold out to the end (Mark 13:13), to look for the signs (Mark 13:28-31). One thing is certain: 'this generation will not pass away until all these things have happened' (verse 30), i.e. the time of transition will take place within the lifetime of people then alive.

The Decans of Aquarius

Pegasus and Cygnus, two of the decans of Aquarius, seem to be reflected in this apocalyptic chapter of Mark, since both are concerned with the sky. Pegasus, the Winged Horse, whose name probably derives from the Greek *pegai*, the Springs of the Ocean, was the steed of Bellerophon, and eventually became the Thundering Horse of Jove that carried the divine lightning. Seiss sees a different derivation for the name, and once again the names of some of the stars in the constellation seem so astonishingly appropriate to this chapter of Mark that, despite the fact that Allen would consider their etymology dubious, they are worth mentioning here:

> The first part of his or his rider's name, Pega, Peka, or Pecha, in the Noetic dialects means 'the chief'; and the latter part, sus, means, not only 'a horse', but *swiftly coming* or *returning* with the idea of joy-bringing; hence *the chief, coming forth again in great victory, and with good tidings and blessing to those to whom he comes.* The ancient names of the stars which make up this constellation are – Markab, *the returning,* Scheat, *he who goeth and returneth.* (Pages 76-7, emphasis added)

Of the third Aquarian decan, Cygnus, the Swan, Fleming writes:

> Cygnus was called Tesark, meaning *This from Afar* ... Its name in both Greek and Latin means *Circling and Returning.* The brightest star is Deneb *The Lord Comes* ... This star is also called Arided, which means *He Shall Come Down* ... The two stars in the tail, Azel and Fafage, have names meaning *Who Returns Quickly* and *Shining Forth.* (Fleming, page 84, emphasis added)

200

(The first Aquarian decan is *Piscis Australis*, the Southern Fish, whose principal star is *Formalhaut*, the Fish's Mouth, which we mentioned in connection with Matthew 17:24-27 in the Leo chapter.)

If the author of the original Gospel was familiar with this kind of star lore, and it seems to me very likely that he was, then we have some understanding of why he chose to weave the Aquarian section of his Gospel around the imagery of a returning saviour. To consider the 'returning saviour' motif as a poetic image used to describe the shifting of the Ages is to speculate, of course, but it does seem truer to what we know of history and astronomy than St Augustine's expectation of a visible Jesus appearing in glory at the end of time.

Awakening

There is also the likelihood of a personal spiritual dimension to this strange and complex chapter, i.e. that elements of it describe the 'awakening' of the individual seeker as he nears the end of his zodiacal journey. This could well be the reason for the enigmatic words in verse 14, 'let the reader understand'. On this reading, the Temple's destruction symbolizes the collapse of order, convention and tradition which the spiritual seeker had encountered in the Capricorn phase of his journey. Saturn, the builder of structures, has given way to Saturn the Destroyer. In purely psychological terms Saturn in destructive mode is the 'abomination that causes desolation'. Just as Saturn castrated his father Uranus, and devoured his own children, so 'Brother will betray brother to death, and a father his child; children will rebel against their parents, and have them put to death' (Mark 13:12). Now is the time when the Christ-like individual, the one who has attained spiritual illumination, who has received the kingdom of God, offers his gifts to the community. They will not be received gladly. He can expect to encounter those who would try to deceive him with false claims about their own enlightenment (Mark 13:5-6), and he can expect to be treated with contempt by religious and civil authorities, and even by his own family (Mark 13:9-13). But, as he must constantly be aware, the spiritual life is God-ordained, and God's power will sustain him in the face of every adversity (Mark 13:11, 20). The cosmic imagery is appropriate to a section on individual illumination because, as all the spiritual traditions remind us, the awakening of any person is a cosmic event. And when it comes, it turns our interior universe upside down; it shatters our world view; the sun, moon and stars of our interior space come tumbling from their orbits; our certainties are destroyed, our petty aims and expectations are totally transformed. The world can never be the same again.

What is called the kingdom of God in the Christian tradition, the Tibetan Buddhists call Rigpa. Of the moment when Rigpa is revealed, Dudjom Rinpoche says:

> That moment is like taking a hood off your head ... everything opens, expands, becomes crisp, clear, brimming with life, vivid with wonder and freshness. It is as if the roof of your mind were flying off ... All limitations dissolve and fall away ... as if a seal were broken open. (Dudjom Rinpoche, pages 157-8)

When the Buddha attained enlightenment (we read in the Buddhist scriptures) 'the earth itself shuddered as if drunk with bliss and no one anywhere was angry, ill or sad; no one did evil, none was proud, the world became quite quiet as though it had received full perfection' (Rinpoche, page 56). It is the consistent testimony of the world's religions that one person's transformation transforms the universe. The realization of the kingdom of God does not just affect the one who realizes it; its influences spread like the ripples on a pool.

What is the nature of this interior transformation? How will I know when it has arrived? It may come suddenly, like the blinding flash that struck Paul from his horse on the Damascus road, but more often it steals upon us gradually. However it occurs, it leaves the individual with a qualitatively different view of the universe from the one he or she previously entertained. The Hindu sage, Patanjali expresses it thus:

> ... all your thoughts break their bonds;
> Your mind transcends limitations,
> Your consciousness expands in every direction,
> And you find yourself in a new, great
> And wonderful world.
> Dormant forces, faculties and talents
> Become alive, and you discover yourself
> To be a greater person by far
> Than you ever dreamed
> Yourself to be.
>
> (Dyer, page 17)

The Aquarian themes continue into chapter 14 with two incidents concerning jars. The first is of the woman who pours out the precious ointment on to Jesus' head (Mark 14:1-9). This is an image of the Christ-like individual who offers to another the healing balm of her own transformation in an act of sympathy and love which is considered even more important than helping the poor materially. In John's version of this story (John 12:1-8) the woman, named as Mary, Lazarus's sister, anoints Jesus' *feet* with the ointment. The feet are ruled by Pisces and it could well be that, originally, this narrative contained a deliberate fusing of Aquarian and Piscean elements, to link the two final sections of the Gospel story.

The second is of the Water-Bearer himself (Mark 14:12-16), the enlightened, generous and androgynous* one, the 'individual who, aware of himself and his relations to his fellows, participates consciously in the corporate life of the race', and who pours out 'the Water of Life in the form of knowledge and revelation of truth' (Reid, page 92).

He is the one whom we must all follow into the final act of the drama.

---

* He is a man doing what was considered to be a woman's job.

Pisces (Mark 14:17–16:8)
The End and the Beginning

As long as you do not know
How to die and come to life again,
You are but a sorry traveller
On this dark earth.

(Goethe)

Pisces and Jupiter

With Pisces we come to the end of our zodiacal walk. The sun, which began its journey through the heavens at the vernal equinox, now enters its final thirty-day phase before it re-enters Aries and the whole cycle begins once more. Pisces is at the end of the cycle, and so has come to symbolize all endings; but it does not symbolize finality. As one cycle ends, another begins: the death of one is the birth of the other. Pisces and Aries are complementary aspects of the universally observed phenomenon of darkness, decay and death leading to light, growth and life. 'If Winter comes, can Spring be far behind?' sang Shelley, expressing perfectly the rhythm, both of nature and of the human spirit.

Pisces (Mark 14:17–16:8)

In referring to this sign, along with Gemini, Virgo and Sagittarius, as 'bi-corporeal', Ptolemy was, in part, describing its 'linking' character. These signs, called 'Mutable' signs in modern astrology, come at the end of each of the four energy pulses of the solar cycle, the equinoxes and solstices, and so join one cycle with the next. As the energy from one pulse diminishes, another one begins to build up. The signs themselves reflect this duality in their symbols: Gemini, the Twins; Virgo, the Maiden with the Sheaf of Wheat; Sagittarius, the Centaur; and Pisces, the Two Fish. Such duality inevitably produces a tension which all four of these signs symbolize, in one way or another. This is least in evidence in Virgo and Sagittarius, since the Earth of one and the Fire of the other give consistency and resolve, qualities wholly lacking in Airy Gemini and Watery Pisces. These latter two have much in common, as their glyphs show. Gemini (♊) has two parallel poles, separate but joined at top and bottom: Pisces (♓) has two fish, swimming in opposite directions, joined at the centre by a thin band.

In psychological terms, duality can become duplicity, and this, for Manilius, characterized the Piscean type. As we might expect, he tells us that the Piscean makes a good fisherman, whose skill enables him:

> To sweep smooth Seas with Nets, to drag the Sand
> And draw the leaping Captives to the land.
>
> (page 128)

But he immediately adds that he can also:

> Lay cheating Wires, or with unfaithful bait
> The Hook conceal, and get by the deceit.

So suspicious of Pisces is he that, he says, nobody should want it prominently placed in his horoscope:

> But could I rule, could I the Fates design,
> The rising Fishes ne'er should govern mine;
> They give a hateful, prattling, railing Tongue,
> Still full of Venom, always in the wrong;
> That blows up Jealousies, and heightens Fears,
> By muttering poys'nous Whispers in Men's Ears.
> Faithless the Births, and full of wild Desire,
> Their Faith is Treachery, and their Land is Fire.
>
> (page 137)

205

Manilius detects a weakness in Pisces which we might call spinelessness, unwillingness to confront anyone directly, deviousness, covert and cowardly acts. Allen tells us that the sign was 'considered ... a malignant influence in human affairs, – a dull, treacherous, and phlegmatic sign'. He goes on:

> The Egyptians, the instructors of the Hebrews in astrology, are said to have abstained from eating sea fish out of dread and abhorrence; and when they would express anything odious, represented a fish in their hieroglyphics. (page 340)

However, this is not the whole story. For the Hebrews, at least, Pisces had some redeeming features. It is probable that this sign represented Jacob's son Joseph,* the dreamer and visionary, who saved his people from famine, and whose cruel fate at the hands of his brothers was interpreted as a manifestation of God's special providence (Genesis 50:20). This attribution of Joseph, an exalted though flawed character, to Pisces seems apt because there is a gentleness to the sign and an ability to empathize. Water symbolizes emotion, and the Mutable Water sign is the sign of 'flowing' emotion, of reaching out to others in their distress, of concern for the suffering world. For modern writers, in fact, the faults of Pisces which so horrified Manilius are really just expressions of the sign's extreme sensitivity. Such faults

> spring from his being a victim of the world, in a sense – in being a sensitive soul lost in a world which has little respect for sensitivity ... The various gambits, by which Pisceans try to hide their sensitivity and their inability to deal with the world, at times include deceit, hypocrisy, and lying – three faults which emerge from a lack of real self confidence. (Gettings, 1972, pages 135-6)

The diffidence which the Piscean so often displays is our key to understanding the spiritual lessons of this sign. Lack of confidence in the self, or in the future, is characteristic of most of us, particularly so when one cycle of life is coming to an end. Part of us wants to stay in the security of the past, prefer-

---

* Most authorities give Joseph as the Piscean son of Jacob. As a 'dreamer of dreams' he seems to fit the characteristics of the sign better than the rest. Dobin thinks that the fact that no tribe of Israel was named after Joseph (his sons Ephraim and Manasseh gave their names to tribes in his stead) indicates the 'hidden' qualities of Pisces. In addition, the confusion over Jacob's blessing of Joseph's sons (Gen. 48) – he crosses his hands and so places his right hand on the head of Ephraim, the younger of the two – reflects the confusion often found in a strongly Piscean character (see Dobin, pages 47-8).

ring the devil we know to any merely promised angel. This is one of the Piscean fishes, swimming backwards into the safe waters. But it is at this point that we have to steel our resolve, to face the uncertainties of the future with confidence, to swim with the other fish into the open waters which beckon us to a newer and fuller life.

Pisces, however, is not Aries. It does not symbolize the new beginning, but it does anticipate it and prepare for it. In Aquarius we witnessed the breaking-down of the old structures in readiness to begin rebuilding. The past has already been cracked open: we now have to prepare to move through it. The Church, which was not always ignorant of these things, has long recognized the importance of this period of the solar year by designating it a time of preparation and anticipation. Lent is for reflecting on the past, and for opening up to the future: the Ash Wednesday anointing declares that our present suffering is cathartic, purgatorial perhaps, but not permanent: it is just the anguish of anticipated transformation.

Symbolic of the optimism and hope that should be evident at such a time is the Jupiterean rulership of Pisces. We have already explored the symbolism of this planet in relation to Sagittarius where the generosity, magnanimity, and dignity of Jupiter find their most convenient expression. The Jupiter (♃) of Pisces, however, is not so extroverted, but it is no less honourable, compassionate, or kind. Jupiterean expansiveness echoes the genuine humanitarian quality of Pisces which seeks the greatest good of the greatest number, and which is sometimes prepared to sacrifice itself in the process.

Since the discovery of Neptune (♆) in the last century, however, it has been customary among astrologers to assign this planet co-rulership of Pisces. According to Allen, Pisces was, in antiquity, 'under the care of the sea-god Neptune, and was called *Neptuni Sidus* by Manilius' (page 340), and the principles which modern astrologers have ascribed to this planet – mysticism, intuition, mediumship – seem, in one sense, more appropriate to the gentle, misunderstood Pisces than the more 'fiery' attributes of Jupiter. But this sign is 'bi-corporeal' after all, and it is fitting that it should have two rulers: Neptune, which seems to be associated with transcending barriers, and Jupiter which wants to jump over them.

The Spiritual Lessons of Pisces

The problem is that we tend to seek an easy and painless answer.
But this kind of solution does not apply to the spiritual path
... Once we commit ourselves to the spiritual path, it is very
painful and we are in for it. We have committed ourselves to the

> *pain of exposing ourselves, of taking off our clothes, our skin, our*
> *nerves, heart, brain, until we are exposed to the universe. Nothing*
> *will be left. It will be terrible, excruciating, but that is the way it is.*
>
> (Chogyam Trungpa Rinpoche)

This final section of Mark is so lengthy and so densely packed with symbolic and mythological elements that a whole book would be necessary to deal with it adequately. Fortunately, it is no part of my present purpose to provide such a comprehensive commentary. Instead, I will deal only with the specifically astrological themes of the text, pointing out where appropriate their relevance to our main contention, that Mark's Gospel, whatever else it might be, is a guide to the spiritual life.

There is also a possibility that, in addition to symbolic and mythological elements, the story contains some historical material. It is certainly possible that a holy man called Jesus was executed by the Romans with the connivance of the Jewish authorities. It is also possible that this man was the source of many of the sayings which are attributed to him in the gospel record, and that he founded a movement dedicated to the promulgation of divine wisdom. However, I do not think that Mark's Gospel has such things as its principal concern, even though it may indirectly reflect them. The presence in the text of genuine place-names, real historical characters, and verifiable customs and traditions does not guarantee history. Mark's narrative is so contrived, so replete with Old Testament and zodiacal echoes, that it cannot be mere chronicle.

We should be alerted to the text's heavily symbolic character by the stated dating of events. Mark leaves us in no doubt that the series of incidents with which his Gospel concludes took place at the time of the Jewish Passover celebrations. It is not unlikely that a wandering preacher would be present in Jerusalem at Passover time. Nor is it hard for us to envisage him antagonizing the authorities so greatly that they would wish him killed. However, that such an execution should take place on the very day of the Passover, as Mark declares, is well-nigh impossible. The city would be full of people who had come from all over the world for the solemn festivities, and for the normally prudent Roman authorities to risk antagonizing the crowds by executing anyone, prophet or pretender, defies reason. In addition, that the Jews themselves would plot an execution on one of the holiest days of the year is unthinkable. Even if they were prepared to risk defiling the holy day itself, where on earth would they have found the time for such chicanery? For the high priests and their minions, this was the busiest time of the year.

It is significant that John's Gospel, which at this point seems to reflect a slightly different tradition from Mark, dates the crucifixion differently. Mark tells us that Jesus ate a Passover meal with his disciples on the night before his death (Mark 14:12, 17). For John, however, this final meal took place on the day *before* Passover, 'the Day of Preparation' (John 13:1; 19:14). Timing differs, too. According to Mark, Jesus was on the cross from the third hour (9a.m.) to the ninth hour (3p.m.) (Mark 15:25, 34). (Since the Jewish day began at sunset, Jesus' death would therefore occur on the same day as Passover.) In John, however, it is at noon on the day before Passover that they lead Jesus away to his death (John 19:14), the precise time that the priests would be busy in the Temple killing the thousands upon thousands of Passover lambs.

It is impossible that both John and Mark can be right on this. The two accounts cannot be reconciled, and all attempts to reconcile them fail lamentably. But the discrepancy is really irrelevant. Both authors have the crucifixion occur during the Passover season, despite the historical unlikelihood of this, because it is symbolically appropriate that it should be so. John is concerned to show Jesus as the sacrificial lamb whose death was prefigured in the centuries-old practice of animal offerings, and so he makes the time of his execution correspond with the time of the ritual killing. Although we cannot readily discern such a theological motive in Mark, we can legitimately assume from the imagery in the narrative that he associates Jesus' death with the Passover for two reasons: the first is related to the fact that the Passover is a springtime festival; the second concerns the approach of the new age of Pisces, when the equinoctial point would move out of the constellation of the Ram and into the constellation of the Fish. Mark's symbolism in these three chapters is based on two cycles. The first is the ordinary yearly cycle which ends with the sun moving from Pisces to Aries at the equinox. The second is the cycle of the Great Year (see 'The Forgotten Language of the Stars'), in which the equinoctial point itself moves backwards through the constellations of the zodiac. We will examine them in turn.

The Yearly Cycle – From Pisces to Aries

The Passover was celebrated at 'the beginning of the year' (Exodus 12:2), at the time of the equinox, when winter is over and the new life of spring begins, when, symbolically, the sun has 'died' and been 'resurrected'. The original Passover story is, on one level at least, a dramatic presentation of the new life that spring brings to the earth.

Such springtime festivals, however, are not the preserve of Jews and

Christians. Throughout the ancient world, people would celebrate the returning sun with ceremonies which closely resemble Christian ones. Sir James Frazer has catalogued these and noted their common themes. They all have to do with a dying and rising god, or a dying and rising king. They are dramatic presentations of the cycle of nature itself, in which we observe the emergence of new life from death and decay. The myths of Tammuz, Adonis, Osiris, Dionysus, Demeter and Persephone are all of this type, and bear a striking resemblance to the Jesus story. Each involves going down into death and coming back to life again: the end of one cycle and the beginning of another; winter to spring; Pisces to Aries.

These stories are not to be dismissed as 'mere' myths fit only for the entertainment of children. The fact that they are so widespread points to them being expressions of the deepest hopes and aspirations of all humankind. To say that they are originally metaphors drawn from the observations of farmers is not to belittle their spiritual significance in any way. What Frazer says about the myth of Demeter and Persephone might be taken as applicable to all such stories:

> In the mind of the ordinary Greek the two goddesses were essentially personifications of the corn, and that in this germ the whole efflorescence of their religion finds implicitly its explanation. But to maintain this is not to deny that in the long course of religious evolution high moral and spiritual conceptions were grafted on this simple original stock and blossomed out into fairer flowers than the bloom of the barley and the wheat. Above all, the thought of the seed buried in the earth in order to spring up to new and higher life readily suggested a comparison with human destiny, and strengthened the hope that for man too the grave may be but the beginning of a better and happier existence in some brighter world unknown. (Frazer, page 433)

Mark's Gospel is one of these 'fairer flowers'. He has given the ancient pagan mythology a Jewish dress, but the garment is transparent and through it we can detect the limbs of Piscean death-rebirth themes which had their origin in agriculture but which have ever expressed the universal human hope that death is not the end, and that the ending of one cycle is the beginning of another. John's Gospel has the actual image of the seed's death and rebirth in Jesus' saying:

> 'I tell you the truth, unless a grain of wheat falls to the ground and dies, it remains only a single seed. But if it dies, it produces many seeds' (John 12:24).

In addition, both Matthew and Luke write of the 'sign of Jonah', clearly expressing the same Piscean death-rebirth themes:

> Then some of the Pharisees and teachers of the law said to him, 'Teacher, we want to see a miraculous sign from you.' He answered, 'A wicked and adulterous generation asks for a miraculous sign! But none will be given it except the sign of the prophet Jonah. For as Jonah was three days and three nights in the belly of a huge fish, so the Son of Man will be three days and three nights in the heart of the earth.' (Matthew 12:38-40)

The absence of these sayings from Mark is rather puzzling, but the fact that they are found in the other Gospels gives us some kind of clue to the meaning of all resurrection stories. The 'great fish' (*kêtos*) is Pisces into which Jonah, the son of man, and Everyman has to sink before emerging 'reborn' into the next cycle. The sun's emergence from Pisces to Aries at the spring equinox symbolizes the eternal longing of humanity for resurrection to new life.

The connection of these themes with the sun comes out clearly in Mark's narrative. The 'darkness' of its Piscean sojourn is imaged in the darkness which covered the land 'from the sixth hour to the ninth hour' as Jesus hung on the cross (Mark 15:33). The cockerel which marks Peter's denial of Jesus is associated with the sun, in that its crow announces the sunrise, and its coxcomb actually looks like a shining solar disc. And it is just possible that Jesus' troublesome cry of dereliction from the cross, *Eloi Eloi Lama Sabachtani*, given in Mark 15:34 in Aramaic and translated, 'My God, my God, why have you forsaken me?' was originally a cross-language pun which depends on the fact that the vocative of *helios*, the Greek word for sun, is *helie*. Matthew, in fact, has *elei* in his version (Matthew 27:46). Solar references pervade the resurrection story:

> Very early, on the first day of the week, just after sunrise they were on their way to the tomb. (Mark 16:2)

The first day of the week is Sun-day, the day of the sun which has its exaltation in Aries. This is an appropriate time for the Saviour, the new Samson ('Sun-one' – see 'The Forgotten Language of the Stars'), the one who symbolizes the solar principle, to arise. He had been killed on Friday, the day of Venus, the planet exalted in Pisces. Incidentally, the Friday to Sunday, Pisces to Aries, image which Mark wants to capture may go some way towards explaining the discrepancy between the 'three days' of the prophecy (Mark 9:31) and the actual time spent in the tomb, which was considerably less than three days however we calculate it.

211

The 'pagan' references do not end here, however. Frazer's work has shown that in the ancient world, the king had magical significance and his life and fortunes were intimately bound up with the life and fortunes of the people. In some cultures it was customary to put the king to death before his physical and mental decline would be known in society at large. This is a Piscean notion, since from the king's death comes new life and vigour to the people, and Mark preserves the potent symbol in his account of Jesus' crucifixion. Jesus is crucified as a king:*

> They put a purple robe on him, then twisted together a crown of thorns and set it on him. And they began to call out to him, 'Hail, king of the Jews!' Again and again they struck him on the head with a staff and spat on him. Falling on their knees, they paid homage to him. (Mark 15:17-19)

Pilate asks Jesus if he is King of the Jews (Mark 15:2), and above his cross was written 'The King of the Jews' (Mark 15:26). These motifs reflect the second decan of Pisces, Cepheus, about which Seiss has this to say:

> Here is the figure of a glorious king, wearing his royal robe, bearing aloft a branch or sceptre, and having on his head a crown of stars. (Seiss, page 85)

The king is both victim and redeemer, a notion which, says Liz Greene, 'is very close to the heart of Pisces'. She goes on:

> Whether the individual Piscean identifies more with the victim and becomes the one whom life has dismembered, or with the redeemer who is the saviour of suffering, there is not much to choose between them, for they are two facets of the same thing. So too is the voracious fish, the goddess, from whom the victim must be rescued; or to whom the redeemer must be sacrificed to absolve others of sin and damnation – they are part and parcel of the same mythic motif. It has speciously been said that Pisces people incarnate either to suffer or to save. As a generalisation, it is truer than most, and it is usually both, for only the

---

* There's a hint of the 'dismembered king' motif in the strange incident of the cutting off of the high priest's servant's ear, which occurs as Jesus is being arrested (Mark 14:47). Mark tells us very little, but John gives us a very telling detail: 'Then Simon Peter, who had a sword, drew it and struck the high priest's servant, cutting off his right ear. (The servant's name was Malchus.)' (John 18:10). Luke alone tells us that Jesus healed the man (Luke 22:51). 'Malchus' comes from the Hebrew word *melech*, which means 'king'. So the king, like Osiris in the Egyptian myth, is (partially) dismembered, but is made whole again by the power of the Christ.

Fig. 26 Cepheus, the King

injured has compassion. No sign is so inclined to present itself as life's victim, nor is any sign so inclined to genuine empathy for suffering. (Greene, 1985, page 260)

The idea of the 'suffering redeemer' is present also in the first decan of Pisces, Andromeda. The name means 'man ruler' ('King'? 'Queen'?), to which the Latins frequently added *Mulier Catenata*, the Woman Chained. The myth of Andromeda bears so many parallels with the story of the crucifixion and resurrection of Jesus that it is worth quoting the first part of Manilius's version at length:

There follows the constellation of Andromeda, whose golden light appears in the rightward sky when the Fishes have risen to twelve degrees. Once on a time the sin of cruel parents caused her to be given up for sacrifice, when a hostile sea in all its strength burst upon every shore, the land was shipwrecked in the flood, and what had been a king's domain was now an ocean. From those ills but one price of redemption was proposed, surrender of Andromeda to the raging main

213

for a monster to devour her tender limbs. This was her bridal; relieving the people's hurt by submitting to her own, she is amid her tears adorned as victim for the beast and dons attire prepared for no such troth as this; and the corpseless funeral of the living maiden is hurried on its way. Then as soon as the procession reaches the shore of the tumultuous sea, her soft arms are stretched out on the hard rocks; they bound her feet to crags and cast chains upon her; and there to die on her virgin cross the maiden hung (*et cruce virginea moritura puella pependit*). Even in the hour of sacrifice she yet preserves a modest mien: her very sufferings become her, for, gently inclining her snow-white neck, she seemed in full possession of her liberty. The folds of her robe slipped from her shoulders and fell from her arms and her streaming locks covered her body. (Manilius, G.P. Goold, pages 345-7)

But Perseus, returning from his destruction of Medusa, notices the chained Andromeda, falls in love with her, saves her from the dreadful sea monster, and eventually marries her. These images of dying that others might live, of a virgin cross, of the innocent victim, of defeating the monster, even the parental sin ('original sin'?) are all part of the Jesus story and have had a profound influence on later Christian theology. All of them are prefigured in mythology of the constellation Andromeda.

At the beginning of the twentieth century J.M. Robertson proposed the theory that the gospel account of the Crucifixion, Death and Resurrection of Jesus was originally scripted as a kind of play which would have been presented to initiates of the Christian mysteries at a springtime festival. The very structure of the piece and its dramatic quality – so different, really, from everything which precedes it – lends support to this point of view. We know that the various pagan mysteries were celebrated in this way, and Apuleius (second century CE) has given us a very graphic account of a springtime pageant in honour of the goddess Isis in *The Golden Ass*, which was originally called *Metamorphoses*, or Transformations. The hero, Lucius, who was changed into an ass instead of an owl by the application of the wrong magical potion, is eventually transformed back into a human being a year later by munching on roses. When he is subsequently initiated into the priesthood of Isis, in which ceremony he 'approached the very gates of death and set one foot on Proserpine's threshold, yet was permitted to return, rapt through all the elements', he emerges from the sanctuary at dawn, 'wearing twelve different stoles' (Graves, page 286). Robert Graves comments on this passage:

Fig. 27 Andromeda 'on her virgin cross the maiden hung'

The seasonal transformations of the variously-named god of the mystery-cults, the Spirit of the Year, were epitomized in the Athenian Lenaea festival and corresponding performances throughout the ancient world, including north-western Europe. The initiate identified himself with the god, and seems to have undergone twelve emblematic transformations – represented by Lucius's 'twelve stoles' – as he passed through the successive Houses of the Zodiac before undergoing his ritual death and rebirth. 'Transformations' therefore conveys the secondary sense of 'spiritual autobiography', and Lucius has spent twelve months in his ass's skin, from one rose-season to the next, constantly changing his House, until his death as an ass and rebirth as a devotee of Isis. (Graves, page 15)

215

In Apuleius, after twelve 'emblematic transformations' culminating in a symbolic 'death', an ass becomes a man. In the gospel story, which is, of course, by no means an exact parallel, the same series of transformations culminates in a 'symbolic death' on the cross, leading to a resurrected life, and to the initiates who would be watching the performance would appear as a dramatic representation of the ultimate spiritual transformation. As the old sun goes to its death in Pisces only to be reborn at the spring equinox; as the Israelites cross the Red Sea before entering the Promised Land; as Jonah spends three days in the belly of the fish only to be vomited out, transformed, on to dry land once more; so the old, carnal self is crucified and the new, redeemed person is reborn.

This is the 'secret' message of the Gospel narrative, a message which it shares with the dramas of the mystery cults of old, that a new kind of life – 'eternal life', 'resurrected life' – is available to those who are brave enough to embrace the Way of the Cross, the painful destruction of the ego and its appetites, so that the Christ-spirit may come to birth. This 'resurrected life' is not a post-mortem state; it is offered to us while we are still in the flesh. As Balzac says in his novel *Louis Lambert*, 'The resurrection is brought about by the winds of heaven which sweep the worlds. The angel born upon the blast saith not: "Ye dead, arise", he says, "Arise, ye living!"' The resurrection of Jesus, the resurrection of Jairus' daughter, are both 'awakenings' from the sleep of the unlived life which it is the aim of all spiritual systems to effect. Neither incident concerns a reanimated corpse.*

In addition to its 'pagan' themes, the final section of Mark has Piscean elements drawn from Jewish mythology. In the main, these concern Joseph, the Piscean son of Jacob. Luke's genealogy informs us that Jesus was the 'son of Joseph, son of Heli' (Luke 3:23), and *Heli* could easily be a corruption of the Greek word *helios*, which means sun. This information is not found in Mark, but what we do find are a number of incidents which echo the Joseph story as we find it in Genesis. Just as Joseph was sold into slavery by his brother, *Judah* (Genesis 37:28), so Jesus is betrayed to the authorities by *Judas* (Mark 14:10-11). Joseph is handed over to the Midianites for twenty pieces of silver (Genesis 37:28), Jesus earns his betrayer thirty pieces of silver (Matthew 26:15). When Joseph refuses the advances of Potiphar's wife he runs away naked as she pulls the garment from his body (Genesis 39:12): at the cruci-

---

* The sense of resurrection as 'freedom' might well be contained in the incident with Barabbas (Mark 15:6-15). 'Barabbas' in Hebrew/Aramaic means 'Son of the Father'; so there is the implication that the one who is released from all shackles is a true son of God. The dramatic context is not to be taken literally, and there was certainly no custom of releasing a prisoner at Passover time.

fixion of Jesus, a young man runs naked from the crowd, leaving his linen garment behind (Mark 14:51-2).* Even Pilate's wife's dream (Matthew 27:19) echoes the dreams of Joseph. By introducing Joseph into the narrative in this way, Mark is able to point us to the great lesson of Joseph's life: his misfortunes were part of God's plan; his slavery meant his people's liberation (Genesis 50:20). Out of darkness comes light.

Jesus' death 'between two thieves' (Mark 15:27) echoes the death of Samson (Judges 16: 23-31) between the two pillars of the temple of Dagon. Samson, as we have seen ('The Forgotten Language of the Stars' and 'Leo: Who Am I?'), is a personification of the sun. He is at the height of his powers when he kills the lion (Leo); his strength is reduced by Delilah (Aquarius); but he finally dies in the temple of Dagon, the Philistine *fish* god (Pisces). Crucified at Golgotha, The Place of the Skull, Jesus is Everyman and Everywoman, poised between the past and the future, the twin 'thieves' of the divine life, symbolized by the two fish of Pisces swimming in opposite directions.

Other characters in the drama play out the Piscean themes. Judas' treachery (Mark 14:10-11), and Peter's denial (Mark 14:27-31, 66-72) both illustrate the cowardice we all exhibit when faced with the prospect of any kind of suffering. The sleep of the apostles in Gethsemane (Mark 14:40), which can hardly be historical in view of the danger they were about to encounter, is itself Piscean, and contrasts with the wakeful agony of Jesus who is prepared to undergo his destined transformation regardless of personal cost (Mark 14:32-42). 'The spirit is willing, but the flesh is weak' (Mark 14:38), Jesus' words to his sleepy companions, epitomize the tensions inherent in this sign. The Gethsemane episode is, in fact, a dramatization of the Piscean lesson for the spiritual seeker: the pain which inevitably accompanies the end of any cycle has to be encountered. Evasion, denial or 'sleep' cannot lift us to the next phase of our existence. With Hamlet we have to say 'The readiness is all', and go forward to a future which 'could be different from the past because (it is) more evolved, more fulfilling' (Rudhyar, page 81).

But our post-resurrection journey, like that of Jesus to Galilee (Mark 16:7), is back to where we started from. The cycle has ended only to begin again as we continue to spiral, onwards and upwards, towards our eventual liberation.

---

* The name of the star Mirach in Andromeda means 'girdle or waist-cloth'; 'Hipparchos seems to refer to it in his *zônê*; and synonymously, some have termed it Cingulum' (Allen, page 36).

The Equinoctial Cycle – Aries to Pisces

Piscean themes are not restricted to the final chapters of this Gospel. The whole Gospel can, with some justification, be called a Piscean document. Early on we read of the apostles becoming 'fishers of men' (Mark 1:17); the multitudes are fed on bread and fish (Mark 6:38ff.; 8:7); and the Piscean virtue of self-sacrifice is constantly extolled. Other 'fishy' stories can be found elsewhere in the Gospels: Matthew has the curious story of the Coin in the Fish's Mouth (Matthew 17:24-7), and John tells of the Miraculous Catch of Fish (John 21:1-14).

Such stories point to the imminent 'new age', the age of Pisces, which was potentially a time of collective spiritual transformation. As the equinoctial point, moving backwards through the zodiac (see 'The Forgotten Language of the Stars'), 'passed over' from Aries to Pisces, the spiritual symbols of the people would be changed. Two thousand years earlier the Ram, or Lamb, of Aries had entered human consciousness as the symbol of the age of Aries. This great shift in spiritual awareness had been celebrated by the Jews in the Passover, in which the Lamb was ritually consumed.

In Mark's time a new Passover was imminent, and this would necessitate a new ritual. This time there would be no lamb, since the age of Aries was over (the 'Lamb' has been slain), but certain elements of the old ritual, their meaning transformed, would remain. In every new age there is the idea of breaking with the past, symbolized in the original ceremony by the un-leavened bread.* This would remain as part of the new celebration, but it would take on an added significance, representing Virgo, the Maiden with the Sheaf of Wheat, whose qualities complement those of its polar opposite sign, Pisces.

Thus, the bread of Virgo's harvest is linked with the Christ, 'the Vine' (see John 15). Wine, symbolic of all celebration, which gladdens our heart but takes away our will, is, like all drugs, Piscean. Mythologically it belongs to Dionysus (Bacchus in Roman mythology), god of the vine who died and was resurrected. It is this 'new wine', the wine of the new age, which Jesus will drink in the kingdom of God (Mark 14:25).

In John's Gospel, the Last Supper (John 13ff.) contains Piscean themes even though it is not said to be a Passover celebration. Jesus rises from the table, takes cloth and water, and begins to wash the feet of his disciples. The feet, as Manilius tells us, are ruled by Pisces, but the most important Piscean

---

* It was customary to leaven a batch of bread with a piece of dough from an earlier batch, so there was continuity from one batch to the next. Unleavened bread destroyed this continuity.

Fig. 28 'The Washing of the Feet', by Giotto

element of the story is in the self-abasement, humility and service that Jesus shows. These are the virtues that were to inform the Piscean age. Our collective failure to embrace them should leave us a little sceptical about the brotherhood promised by Aquarius. But one thing is certain: as we stand on the threshold of a new age, the symbols will change once more. The age of the Fish and the feet is coming to an end. A new Passover is upon us, and we can all legitimately, if a little apprehensively, ask, with Yeats,

> What rough beast, its hour come round at last,
> Slouches towards Bethlehem to be born?

Appendix 1: The Gospel of Mark
(A new translation by Bill Darlison)

Aries

Aries is the sign of the springtime and so signifies new beginnings, new life. It is associated with the element Fire. Its symbol is the Ram or Lamb. It was called 'The Lord of the Head' by the Egyptians and 'The Hired Man' by the Babylonians. Its 'decans' (nearby constellations) are Cassiopeia,(the Reclining Woman), Perseus, (the Hero or the Bridegroom), and Cetus (the Evil Sea Monster). In the constellation Perseus is the star Algol, called Rosh ha Satan (Satan's Head) by the Hebrews; it was considered the most evil star in the heavens.

Chapter 1

The beginning of the good news about Jesus Christ. As it says in the Book of Isaiah the Prophet, 'Look, I'm sending my messenger ahead; he'll build a road for you.' A voice is crying out in the desert, 'Prepare the way of the Lord; straighten out his paths.'

John the Baptist turned up in the wilderness, offering people an opportunity to change their ways and be released from their sins by means of a ritual immersion in water. Crowds of people from Jerusalem and from all over Judea were coming out to him, and as they confessed their sins he would plunge them in the water of the river Jordan. John's clothing was made from camel hair, and he had a leather belt round his waist; he ate locusts and wild honey. He was proclaiming, 'There's someone coming after me who's stronger than I; I'm not fit to lace his shoes. I drenched you in water, but he will drench you in holy spirit.'*

At that time Jesus came from Nazareth in Galilee and was immersed in the Jordan by John. As soon as he came up out of the water he saw the heavens splitting open and the spirit descending upon him in the form of a dove; a voice came from heaven: 'You are my beloved son. I'm very pleased with you.' Straight afterwards the spirit drove him out into the desert, where he

* According to both Matthew and Luke, Jesus will baptize 'with holy spirit and with fire' (Matthew 3:11; Luke 3:16). In John's Gospel, John the Baptist calls Jesus 'The lamb of God' (John 1:29).

spent forty days among the wild beasts being tempted by Satan. But the angels looked after him.

After John was arrested, Jesus went to Galilee preaching the good news about God. He was saying that the appointed time had come; the kingdom of God was close by. 'Change your mind and your ways and believe the good news.'

Going along by the Sea of Galilee he saw some fishermen, Simon and his brother Andrew, who were casting their nets into the sea. Jesus said to them, 'Come and follow me; I'll make you into fishers of men!' They left their nets without hesitation and followed him.

A little further on he saw Zebedee's sons, James and John, mending nets in the boat. He called out to them and they followed him at once, leaving their father Zebedee and the hired men in the boat.

They went to Capernaum and, wasting no time, he entered the synagogue on the Sabbath day and began to teach. The people were amazed at his teaching because he taught them like someone with authority, not like the experts in religious law. Suddenly in their synagogue there was a man with an evil spirit, who cried out, 'What business do you have with us, Jesus the Nazarene? Have you come to destroy us? I know who you are – God's holy one!' Jesus rebuked him. 'Shut up and come out from him!' he said, and come out it did, but not before letting out a terrific scream and throwing the man into a fit of convulsions. Everybody was astonished, so much so that they were asking one another, 'What's all this about? A new teaching? And he has authority to make the evil spirits obey him!' The report about him soon spread everywhere around the region of Galilee.

On leaving the synagogue they went to Simon and Andrew's house, along with James and John. Simon's mother-in-law was lying down, sick with a fever, and as soon as they told Jesus about her, he went in to her, and taking hold of her hand, he raised her up. The fever left her and she began to wait upon them.

In the evening, when the sun was setting, they were bringing him all those who were sick or who were possessed by demons. The whole town was gathered together by the door, and he healed many who were sick of various diseases. He also cast out many demons, but he wouldn't let the demons speak because they knew who he was.

Early in the morning, while it was still dark, he got up and went off to a deserted place to pray. However, Simon and his companions found out where he was and told him that everyone was looking for him. He said to them, 'Let's go somewhere else, to the villages roundabout, so that I can preach there. That's why I've come.' And off he went, preaching in synagogues and casting out demons throughout the whole of Galilee.

A leper approached him, and falling down on his knees begged him, 'If you want to, you can make me clean!' Moved with pity, he stretched out his hand, touched him, and said, 'I do want to. Be healed!' The leprosy disappeared immediately and the man was clean. Jesus sent him on his way, telling him in no uncertain terms that he wasn't to say anything to anybody, but to show himself to the priest and to make the appropriate offering for his cleansing, just as Moses had commanded. But the man went out and started to blab about everything and to spread the word everywhere, so that Jesus was no longer able to go openly into the city, and had to stay in the wilderness regions. Even so, people kept coming to him from all directions.

Chapter 2

A few days after he'd gone back to Capernaum, word of his whereabouts got around and there were so many people gathered that there was no room, not even by the door. While Jesus was speaking the word to them, four men arrived carrying a paralytic, but not being able to get near him because of the crowd, they made an opening in the roof of the house and let down the stretcher on which the paralysed man was lying. When Jesus saw their faith he said to the paralysed man, 'Child, your sins are forgiven.' But there were some legal experts sitting there who were asking themselves, 'Why is he speaking such blasphemy? Only God can forgive sins!' But Jesus quickly realized what they were thinking, and he said to them, 'What's your problem? What is easier to say to the paralysed man: "Your sins are forgiven", or "Get up, pick up your stretcher, and walk"? But in order to prove to you that the son of man has authority on earth to forgive sins,' he said to the paralysed man, 'I say to you, get up, pick up your stretcher and go home!' The man got up immediately, and picking up his stretcher went out in front of everyone, so that they were all amazed and were praising God, saying, 'We've never seen anything like this!'

Jesus went out again beside the sea and all the crowd came towards him and he taught them. Moving on he saw Levi, the son of Alphaeus, sitting in his tax collector's booth. Jesus said to him, 'Follow me!' which he immediately proceeded to do. Jesus was sitting down to a meal in Levi's house along with his disciples, but there were many tax collectors and sinners with them, because quite a number of such people were following Jesus. The scribes, who were the legal experts belonging to the Pharisees, pointed out to his disciples that he was eating with undesirables, and when Jesus heard it he said to them, 'It's the sick who need a doctor, not the healthy. I've not come to call the righteous; it's the sinners I'm after.'

Now the disciples of John and the Pharisees used to fast, and some people came and asked Jesus, 'Why do the disciples of John and the Pharisees fast, but your disciples don't fast?' To which Jesus replied, 'The friends of the bridegroom can't fast while the bridegroom is with them. While they have the bridegroom with them they can't fast. But the days are coming when the bridegroom will be taken away from them and that's when they'll fast. Nobody patches an old garment with new cloth because the new piece will pull away from the old, making the tear even worse. And no one puts new wine into old wineskins, because the wine splits the wineskins and both wine and wineskins are ruined. No: new wine goes into new wineskins.'

One Sabbath day he happened to be walking through the grain fields, and his disciples began plucking the heads of grain as they were making their way along. The Pharisees said to him, 'Hey! Why are they doing what they are not supposed to be doing on the Sabbath day?' So Jesus said to them, 'Haven't you read what David did when he and his companions were hungry and in need of food? How he went into the house of God when Abiathar was high priest and took the loaves of holy bread which only the priests were allowed to eat, and gave it to those who were with him?' He went on: 'The Sabbath came into existence for the sake of human beings; human beings didn't come into existence for the sake of the Sabbath. So, the son of man is Lord of the Sabbath.'

Chapter 3

He went into the synagogue again, where he found a man whose hand was shrivelled up. They were watching him closely to see if he would heal the man on the Sabbath day and so give them something to accuse him of. Jesus asked the man with the shrivelled hand to come up into the middle, and then he asked, 'Is it lawful to do good on the Sabbath or to do harm, to save a life or to kill?' They were silent, so looking round at them with anger, and deeply grieved at their stubborn insensitivity, he said to the man, 'Stretch out your hand.' He stretched it out and his hand was healed, but straightaway the Pharisees went out with the Herodians, plotting how they might kill him.

Jesus and his disciples went back towards the sea, followed by great crowds of people from Galilee, Judea, Jerusalem, Idumea, from the other side of the Jordan, and the area around Tyre and Sidon. People who'd heard what he was doing came to him. And he told his disciples to have a little boat ready because the crowds were pressing in upon him. He'd healed many, and the sick people were crowding round him, just so that they could touch him. Whenever the evil spirits saw him they would fall down in front of him and say, 'You are the son of God!' And often he would order them to keep quiet about him.

He went up the mountain and called those he wanted, and they came to him. He selected twelve to be with him, whom he called 'apostles' (emissaries) because these were the ones he would send out to preach. They would have authority to cast out demons. These are the twelve he chose: Simon, whom he called Peter; James, the son of Zebedee, and his brother John (he called these *Boanerges* – 'Sons of Thunder'); Andrew, Philip, Bartholomew, Matthew, Thomas, James the son of Alphaeus; Thaddaeus, Simon the Cananaean; and Judas Iscariot who was to betray him.

He went into a house but the crowds were so tightly packed once again that they couldn't even eat a meal. When his relatives heard about it they went out to grab hold of him, because they said he was out of his mind. And the legal experts who'd come down from Jerusalem were saying that he was in league with Beelzebub, and that he was casting out demons by the power of the chief demon. So Jesus called them to him and, using a few apposite metaphors, he said, 'How can Satan cast out Satan? A divided kingdom can't survive. Nor can a divided family. And if Satan rises up against himself and is divided, he can't survive but his end approaches. But no one is able to enter the house of a strong man and steal his property unless the strong man has been bound first; only then can he rob him. I'm telling you the truth: human beings will be forgiven for everything, no matter what sins they commit or what blasphemies they utter. But whoever blasphemes against the holy spirit won't ever be forgiven, because he's guilty of an eternal sin.' He said this because they were saying, 'He has an unclean spirit.'

His mother and brothers came and were standing outside, and they sent someone in to summon him. A crowd was sitting around him and they said to him, 'Your mother, your brothers and your sisters are outside; they are looking for you.' Jesus responded by saying, 'Who is my mother and my brothers?' And looking at those sitting in a circle round him, he said, 'Look! Here are my mother and my brothers. Whoever does the will of God is my brother, my sister, and my mother.'

TAURUS

Taurus is an Earth sign, and the Pleiades, a beautiful group of stars in the shoulder of the Bull, which has been called 'The Hen with her Chickens' by many cultures throughout history, was used by ancient farmers to mark their seeding time. This section of Mark uses the Greek word for 'earth' (translated here variously as earth, ground, soil, etc.) nine times, and nowhere else in the Gospel do we find such a wealth of agricultural imagery and vocabulary. In the ancient world Taurus was also associated with light, and was called The Bull of Light by the Egyptians, probably because in and around the constellation are some of the most beautiful sights in the night sky. Orion, one of the decans of Taurus, was called The Light of Heaven by the Babylonians.

Chapter 4

He began to teach again beside the sea, and so great a crowd gathered about him that he had to get into a boat and sit in it on the water, while the crowd looked on from the shore. He taught them many things in parables, and in his teaching he said to them, 'Listen! Look! The sower went out to sow, and while he was sowing some seed fell by the roadside and the birds came along and ate it. Some fell on the rocks where there wasn't much soil; it sprang up very quickly because there was no real depth of soil, but when the sun rose it was scorched and it withered because it didn't have any root. Some fell among the thorns, but the thorns came up and choked it and so it yielded no crop. But some fell on good soil where it grew and thrived, yielding an abundant crop – increasing thirtyfold, sixtyfold, and a hundredfold.' He said, 'Use your ears! Take notice of what I'm saying!'

When they were alone, those close to him, along with the twelve, began to question him about the parables, so he said to them, 'The mystery of the kingdom of God has been given to you, but to those on the outside everything is expressed in parables, so that although they may look they won't see, and although they may hear they won't understand in case they would need to turn around and forgiveness be given to them.'

He said to them, 'If you don't understand this parable, how are you going to understand all the other parables? The sower is sowing the word. The seed that falls on the roadside represents those who hear the word, but no sooner do they hear it than Satan comes along and takes it away from them. The seed that falls on the rocks are those people who hear the word and receive it with joy but they don't have any staying power, so they continue for a while but as soon as they encounter trouble or persecution on account of the word they let things slide. Then there are those represented by the seed among the thorns. They are the ones who hear the word but the cares of the time, the enticements of wealth and desires for all kinds of other things overwhelm them and choke the word so that they cease to be fruitful. But the seed that is sown on the good ground represents those who hear the word, receive it and produce fruit – thirtyfold, sixtyfold, and a hundredfold.'

He told them, 'You don't bring in a lamp and then put it under a measuring basket, or under the bed. No, you put it on a lamp-stand, don't you? So, there's nothing hidden that will not be revealed; and what's been carefully concealed will be brought into the open. Use your ears and take notice of what I'm saying.'*

He went on, 'Take notice of what you are hearing; what you receive by way of increase will be in proportion to what you give out; and to him who has it will be given, and to him who has not, what he has will be taken from him.

'The kingdom of God is like a man who scatters some seed on the ground and he sleeps by night and gets up by day and the seed sprouts and grows, but how it happens he doesn't know. Things grow by their own power; first the shoot, then the ear of grain, then the full head of corn, and when it is ready, he puts in the scythe because it's time for the harvest.

'With what can we compare the kingdom of God? What image can we use to describe it? It's like a grain of mustard seed which, at the time that it's sown in the ground, is smaller than all the seeds of the earth, but after it's sown it grows and becomes bigger than all other plants and produces branches so massive that the birds of heaven can nest in its shade.'

Using many parables like these, he told them just as much as they were able to grasp. Indeed he didn't speak to them except by means of a parable, but he explained everything privately to his disciples.

GEMINI

Gemini, the Twins, is the first of the Air signs, and concerns duality, fragmentation, communication, brothers and sisters. Its strength is versatility, its weakness duplicity. The two principal stars in the constellation are Castor and Pollux, which were considered the protectors of sailors. Its decans are Lepus (the Hare), Canis Major (the Big Dog), whose principal star is Sirius, the brightest star in the night sky, and Canis Minor (the Little Dog). In early classical days Canis Major was simply called Canis, after Laelaps the hound of Actaeon. Notice the unusual construction of the story of Jairus's Daughter and the Woman with the Blood Flow: it's the only 'double' miracle in the Gospel.

---

* Immediately after his version of the Parable of the Lamp, Luke has the following: Your eye is the lamp of your body. When your eyes are good, your whole body also is full of light. But when they are bad, your body also is full of darkness. See to it, then, that the light in you is not darkness. Therefore, if your whole body is full of light, and no part of it dark, it will be completely lighted, as when the light of a lamp shines on you. (Luke 11:34-36, NIV)

On the evening of the same day, he said to them, 'Let us cross over to the other side.' So, leaving the crowds they took him as he was in the boat, and other boats were with him. A great windstorm (Greek: *laelaps*) blew up and the waves were beating against the boat, so that it was already filling up. Jesus was sleeping in the stern with his head on a cushion, so they woke him up and said to him, 'Teacher, don't you care that we're going down?' He got up and rebuked the wind and said to the sea, 'Quiet! Be silent!' And the wind subsided and a great calm descended. He said to them, 'Why are you so timid? Are you still without faith?' And they were very scared and said to one another, 'Who is this man? Both the wind and the waves obey him!'

Chapter 5

They came to the other side of the lake into the land of the Gerasenes, and no sooner was he out of the boat than a man with an unclean spirit approached him.* This man was living among the tombs in the graveyard and he was so out of control that no one could subdue him or even chain him. In the past he'd been bound hand and foot, but he'd pulled the chains apart and smashed the shackles. Night and day among the tombs and on the mountains he was crying out and bruising himself with stones. When he saw Jesus in the distance he ran and fell on his knees, paying him homage and shouting at the top of his voice, 'What's your business with me, Jesus, son of God Most High? I beg you in God's name don't torment me!' He said this because Jesus was ordering the unclean spirit to come out of him. Jesus asked, 'What is your name?' He replied, 'My name is Legion; there's a whole gang of us.' He kept begging Jesus not to send them all out of that region.

There was a great herd of pigs feeding on the hillside, and the demons shouted out, 'Send us into the pigs! We want to go into them!' Jesus gave them permission, and the unclean spirits came out and entered the pigs, and the herd of about two thousand dashed headlong down the steep slope into the sea, where they drowned. The herdsmen ran off and told the story so that people came from town and country to see what had happened. They came to Jesus and they looked at the man who'd been possessed by the legion of demons, and when they saw that he was now dressed and sane they were terrified. Those who had witnessed it related what had happened to the possessed man and to the pigs, and they began to implore Jesus to leave their neighbourhood. When he got into the boat, the man who'd been possessed begged that he might go along with him, but Jesus wouldn't allow

* Matthew's Gospel has 'two men possessed by demons' (Matthew 8:28).

it, and said to him, 'Go home to your family and tell them what the Lord has done for you, and how he's taken pity on you.' But the man went away and began to announce in the Decapolis what Jesus had done for him, and everyone was amazed.

When Jesus had crossed over again to the other side, a large crowd thronged around him as he stood on the shore. When one of the rulers of the synagogue, a man called Jairus, saw Jesus, he threw himself at his feet. 'My little daughter is dying. Come and lay your hands on her so that she can be healed and live,' he begged. So Jesus went with him.

A great crowd pressed upon him. There was a woman who'd had a flow of blood for twelve years, and who'd undergone a lot of suffering at the hands of many doctors, but despite spending all her money on medical treatment, none of the doctors had been able to help her and her condition hadn't improved at all; in fact, it had deteriorated. She'd heard about Jesus and, coming up behind him in the crowd, she touched his clothing, because she'd told herself, 'If I can only touch his coat I'll be healed!' Straightaway the flow of blood dried up, and she felt in her body that she'd been cured of her condition. But Jesus, sensing that power had gone out of him, turned round to the crowd and said, 'Who touched my clothes?' His disciples said to him, 'You see the crowd milling around you, and you say, "Who touched me"!' But Jesus kept looking around to see who had done it. The woman, conscious of what had happened to her, and trembling with fear, fell down before him and told him the whole truth. He said to her, 'Daughter, your faith has saved you. Go in peace and be free of your sufferings.'

While he was speaking to her, some people came from the ruler of the synagogue's house and said, 'Your daughter has died; why bother the teacher any more?' Jesus overheard, and he said to the ruler of the synagogue, 'Don't be afraid. Just have faith.' He allowed no one to accompany him except Peter, James, and James' brother John. They went into the house of the synagogue ruler, and he saw a great commotion, people crying and wailing. Going inside he said to them, 'Why are you weeping and making such a racket? The little girl is not dead; she's asleep.' They laughed at him but he threw them all out, and taking the child's mother and father along with his companions he went in to the child's room. Holding her hand, he said to her, '*Talitha koum*,' which means 'Little girl, I'm telling you to wake up!' The girl got up immediately and started walking around. She was twelve years old. They were overcome with astonishment, but Jesus ordered them all to keep quiet about it, and he told them to give the child something to eat.

Chapter 6

Jesus, with his disciples in train, went from there to his home town, and on the Sabbath day he began to teach in the synagogue. Many of those who were listening to him were astonished, and were saying, 'Where did he get these things from? What wisdom has been given to him? He does the most amazing things! Isn't he the carpenter, the son of Mary and the brother of James, Joses, Judas and Simon? And aren't his sisters among us?' They were offended by him, and Jesus said to them, 'The only place a prophet isn't honoured is in his home town and among his relatives and in his own house!' Apart from laying his hands upon a few sick people and curing them, he wasn't able to perform any works of power there. He was amazed at their lack of faith.

He was teaching in the villages roundabout, and he called the twelve to him and, having given them authority over the unclean spirits, he began to send them out two by two. He ordered them to take nothing on the road except a staff; no bread, no bag, no money in their belts. They were to wear sandals, but they weren't to wear two coats. He said to them, 'Where you go into a house, stay there until you leave the area. When you leave a community that hasn't welcomed you or listened to you, shake the dust from your feet as a testimony against them. I'm telling you the truth: on judgement day it will be easier for Sodom and Gomorrah than for that town!'

So they went out, preaching repentance, and they cast out many demons, and cured many sick people by anointing them with oil.

Jesus' reputation was growing and a report of his activities reached King Herod, who thought that these amazing things were happening because John the Baptist had been raised from the dead. Others thought that it was Elijah, or a prophet like one of the prophets of old. When Herod heard of it he said, 'John, the one I beheaded, has been raised from the dead.' This self-same Herod had sent for John, seized him, bound him and imprisoned him, on account of Herodias, the wife of Herod's brother Philip, whom Herod himself had married. John had told Herod that it wasn't lawful for him to take his brother's wife, and so Herodias held a grudge against him and wanted to kill him, but she wasn't able to.

Herod was in awe of John because he knew him to be an upright and holy man, and he kept him safe. He would listen to him gladly, although he was puzzled by what he said.

Herodias's opportunity came when Herod threw a party on his birthday for his court, his high-ranking military men, and the leading citizens of

Galilee. When the daughter of Herodias came in and danced, she pleased Herod and his guests so much that the king said to the girl, 'Ask me for anything you want and I'll give it to you!' He gave a solemn promise: 'Even if you ask for half my kingdom I'll give it to you!' She went out and said to her mother, 'What shall I ask for?' Her mother replied, 'The head of John the Baptist!'

She rushed straight back to the king and said, 'I want you to give me right now the head of John the Baptist on a platter!' The king was very sad, but because of his oaths and his guests there was no way he could refuse her. He dispatched an executioner with orders to bring John's head immediately. He went off and beheaded him in the prison and brought the head on a platter and gave it to the girl, who gave it to her mother. When his disciples heard of it they came and took John's body and placed it in a tomb.

CANCER

Cancer is the sign of the summer solstice, when the sun begins to reverse its direction. The symbol of Cancer is the crab, a curious, scuttling creature which has its skeleton on the outside and which carries its house on its back. Cancer symbolizes the urge to protect and to nourish, and is associated with the family, the nation, traditions, memory – 'the flag, mom, and apple pie'. Its virtue is loyalty, its vice clannishness, its motto 'Blood is thicker than water'. Along with its 'ruler' the moon, it is said to govern the stomach. The name of one of its stars, Ma'alaph, means 'assembled thousands'. Its decans are Ursa Major and Ursa Minor – The Great Bear and the Little Bear – and Argo, 'the ship that conquered the waters'. Notice the strange 'crab-like' journey Jesus makes in 7:31.

The apostles came back to Jesus and told him everything they'd done and taught. There was so much to-ing and fro-ing that they'd not had a chance to eat, so he said to them, 'Come. Go off by yourselves to a secluded place and rest for a while.' They went off in the boat by themselves to a deserted spot, but many people who'd seen and recognized them as they were setting off ran on foot from all the towns and arrived at the place before them. When Jesus disembarked he saw a huge crowd, and he was moved with pity for them because they were like sheep without a shepherd. He began to teach them many things. It was already late and his disciples came up to him and said, 'This place is off the beaten track and it's getting late. Send the crowds away so that they can go into the surrounding towns and villages to buy themselves something to eat.' Jesus replied, 'You give them something to eat.' They said, 'It would cost six months' wages to feed them all!' He said to them, 'Go and see how many loaves you have.' When they'd found out they said, 'Five, and two fish.' He told the people to sit in groups on the green grass, so they sat down in groups of fifty or a hundred, looking like so many garden plots. Taking the five loaves and the two fish and looking up to heaven, he blessed and broke the bread and gave it to his disciples to distribute. He also divided up the two fish. They all ate their fill and, after five thousand men had eaten, there was enough bread and fish left over to fill twelve baskets.

Straight afterwards, Jesus urged his disciples to get into the boat and go on ahead to Bethsaida while he was releasing the crowd. Taking his leave of them, he went into the mountain to pray. It was evening and the boat was in the middle of the sea, and he was alone on the land. At about three o'clock in the morning, seeing that they were struggling to make headway because of a contrary wind, he went towards them walking upon the sea, as if he meant to go past them. Those who saw him walking on the water took him for a ghost and screamed out, because they all saw him and were very frightened. But he began to speak to them straightaway. He said, 'Take heart! It's me! (Greek: *ego eimi*, literally "I am"). Don't be frightened!' He went up to them in the boat and the wind abated and they were all utterly astonished, because they hadn't understood about the loaves and their hearts were hard.

Crossing over, they came to the land of Gennesaret where they dropped anchor, and as they were getting out of the boat the people recognized him and they came running from the whole of that area carrying their sick about on stretchers to whatever spot they thought he might be. Wherever he was – in villages, in towns or in the countryside – they'd lay their sick in the market places, and beg Jesus to allow them to touch just the hem of his robe. Those who did touch him were cured.

Chapter 7

The Pharisees and some teachers of the Law from Jerusalem came to Jesus. They'd seen that some of his disciples were eating with defiled hands – hands that had not been washed in the prescribed ritual way. The Pharisees and all the Jews don't eat unless they wash one hand with the clenched fist of the other, in the manner laid down by their ancestral traditions. Whenever they come from the market place they don't eat unless they bathe themselves, and they have many other traditions concerning the washing of cups and jugs and cooking pots.

The Pharisees and the legal experts asked him, 'Why, in defiance of the ancestral traditions, do your disciples eat with unpurified hands?' Jesus replied, 'Isaiah was right when he prophesied about you hypocrites. He says, "These people honour me with their lips, but their hearts are far from me. They worship me in vain, teaching man-made rules as doctrines." You ignore the commandment of God while faithfully observing human tradition.' He went on, 'You have a really smart way of setting aside God's commandment so that you can keep your own tradition. Didn't Moses say, "Honour your father and your mother"? And "Whoever speaks badly of father or mother deserves to die"? You, on the other hand, say that if a man tells his mother or father that any gift they might have expected from him is Corban – already offered to God – then he no longer needs to fulfil his obligation to them! And so the customs you are observing and handing on nullify God's word. And you are doing lots of things like this.'

And calling the crowd to him again, he said to them, 'Listen all of you, and understand. There's nothing outside a man which can go inside him and make him ritually unclean; it's what comes out of a man that makes him unclean.'

When he'd gone away from the crowd and entered the house, his disciples asked him what he meant. He said to them, 'Can't you understand either? Don't you realize that there's nothing which goes into a man which can make him unclean, because it doesn't penetrate the core of his being; it just goes into his stomach and then into the lavatory?' (So, Jesus was saying that all foods were 'clean'.) He went on, 'It's what comes out of a man that defiles him; from a person's very nature come bad thoughts, unchastity, theft, murder, adultery, greed, treachery, debauchery, envy, blasphemy, arrogance, senseless behaviour. All these evils come from inside a man and defile him.'

From there Jesus went to the region of Tyre, and went into a house where he hoped to escape notice. But it wasn't possible for him to remain hidden for long, and a woman whose daughter was possessed by an evil spirit heard about him, and she came and fell down at his feet. She was a Greek – a Syro-Phoenician – and she begged him to cast the demon out of her daughter. He said to her, 'Let the children be fed first; it's not right to take the children's food and throw it to the dogs.' She replied, 'Yes, Lord, but the dogs under the table eat the children's scraps!' And he said to her, 'Because of what you've just said, go on your way. The demon has left your daughter.' When she went home she found the child lying on her bed, and the evil spirit had gone.

Leaving the region of Tyre he went through Sidon to the Sea of Galilee, up through the middle of the Decapolis. And they brought to him a deaf man with a speech impediment, and they begged Jesus to lay his hand upon him.

Taking him privately, away from the crowd, he placed his fingers in his ears, and touched his tongue with spittle. Looking up to heaven he sighed aloud as he said, 'Ephphatha!' (which means, 'Be opened!'). The man's ears were opened, his tongue was loosed, and he began to speak correctly. Jesus ordered them not to tell anyone, but the more he told them to keep quiet, the more they proclaimed it. They were completely amazed, saying, 'He's done everything well; he makes the deaf hear and the dumb speak!'

Chapter 8

In those days, when once again there was a big crowd of people with nothing to eat, he called his disciples and said to them, 'I'm concerned about the crowd because they've been with me three days, and they've not eaten. If I send them off home hungry they'll faint on the way, and some of them come from far away. His disciples replied, 'Where can anyone get enough bread to satisfy these people in this lonely place?' Jesus asked them, 'How many loaves have you got?' 'Seven,' they said. He gave orders to the crowd to sit down on the ground, and taking the seven loaves he gave thanks, broke them and gave them to the disciples, who distributed them to the crowd. They also had a few little fish, and when he'd blessed them he told them to distribute these too. They ate their fill, and they collected up seven baskets full of leftovers. There were about four thousand men. Finally he let them all go.

Immediately afterwards he got into the boat with his disciples and he came to the district of Dalmanutha. The Pharisees came to him and started asking him questions. They were looking for a sign from heaven, trying to test him. He sighed deeply and said, 'Why is this generation looking for a sign? I'm telling you the truth, no sign will be given to this generation.' Then he left them, got into the boat, and went off to the other side.

They'd forgotten to bring bread; they only had one loaf with them in the boat. 'Be alert. Look out for the leaven of the Pharisees and the leaven of Herod,' instructed Jesus. But they were discussing with one another the fact that they had no bread, and Jesus, realizing this, said to them, 'Why are you discussing the lack of bread? Don't you see and understand yet? Are you completely impervious to it all? Can't you see with your eyes, and hear with your ears? Don't you remember how many baskets of leftovers you collected after I shared the five loaves among the five thousand?' 'Twelve,' they said to him. 'And how many baskets did you fill with leftovers when I shared the seven among the four thousand?' 'Seven,' they said to him. 'And you still don't understand?' he said.

They came to Bethsaida where they brought a blind man to him, begging him to touch him. Taking the blind man by the hand, he led him outside the village. He spat into his eyes, put his hands on him and said, 'Can you see anything?' The man looked up and said, 'I can see men, but they look like walking trees!' Then Jesus put his hands on the man's eyes once more. This time his sight was restored and he could see clearly. So Jesus sent him home and told him not to enter the village.

LEO

Leo, the Fixed Fire sign, is the sign of the sunshine, and is the only sign said by the ancient astrologers to be 'ruled' by the sun. Charles Carter calls it 'the sign of divine splendour'. Its symbol is the lion, 'the king of the beasts', and it is associated with royalty, glory, creativity. Its principal star is Regulus, 'the little king', one of the four 'royal' stars of the ancient world. The second star in Leo is Al Giebha, said to mean 'the exalted, the exaltation', and Zosma in the Lion's tail means 'the shining forth, the epiphany'. Its decans are Corvus (the Raven), Crater (the Cup), and Hydra (the Fleeing Serpent). The Catholic Church celebrates the Feast of the Transfiguration on 6 August, when the sun is in Leo.

Jesus and his disciples went into the villages of Caesarea Philippi and on the way he asked his disciples, 'Who do men say that the son of man is?' They said to him, 'Some say John the Baptist; others Elijah; others, one of the prophets.' He said to them, 'But who do you say that I am?' Peter answered, 'You are the Christ!' And he ordered them to tell no one about him. He started to teach them that the son of man must suffer many things, and be rejected by the elders, and the chief priests and the legal experts, and be killed, but after three days rise again. And he was telling them plainly. Peter drew him aside and started to take him to task but Jesus turned, looked at his disciples, and reprimanded Peter. 'Get behind me, Satan!' he said. 'Your thoughts are men's thoughts, not God's thoughts!'

He called the crowd and his disciples together and said to them, 'If anyone wants to come after me, let him take up his cross and follow me. For whoever wants to save his soul will lose it; but whoever loses his soul for my sake and the sake of the good news will save it. What benefit is it for a man to gain the whole world and forfeit his soul? What would a man give in exchange for his soul? Whoever is ashamed of me and my words in this faithless and sinful generation, the son of man will be ashamed of him when he comes in the glory of his father with the holy angels.'

Chapter 9

He said to them, 'I'm telling you the truth: there are some people standing here who will not taste death until they see the kingdom of God come in its power.'

After six days Jesus took Peter, James and John by themselves up into a high mountain, where he was transfigured before them. His clothing shone with intense whiteness, a whiteness which no bleaching agent on earth could possibly match. Elijah and Moses appeared to them, and were talking with Jesus. Peter, dreadfully frightened like the others and not knowing what to say, responded with: 'Rabbi, it is wonderful for us to be here. Let us make three tents: one for you, one for Moses, and one for Elijah.' Then a voice issued from an overshadowing cloud: 'This is my son, the beloved. Listen to him!' Suddenly, looking round, they saw no one with them, only Jesus.

As they were coming down the mountain Jesus sternly charged them not to tell anyone what they had seen until the son of man should rise from the dead. They kept his words to themselves, but they discussed among themselves what this 'rising from the dead' could mean. They began to question him. 'Why do the legal experts say that Elijah must come first?' they asked. Jesus said to them, 'Elijah does come first and is putting everything straight. But why do the scriptures say that the son of man must suffer many things and be treated with contempt? I'm telling you, Elijah has indeed come, and they've done to him all that they wanted, just as it has been written of him.'

When they reached the other disciples they noticed that they were arguing with some legal experts, surrounded by a huge crowd. As soon as the crowd caught sight of Jesus they were amazed, and they ran towards him and began to greet him. He said to them, 'What are you arguing with them about?' One of the crowd answered, 'Teacher, I brought my son to you because he has a spirit of dumbness, and whenever it seizes him it throws him down and he foams at the mouth and grinds his teeth, and he's wasting away.* I asked your disciples to cast it out, but they weren't powerful enough.' He answered them, 'O faithless generation! How long must I put up with you? Bring him here!' They brought him, and when the spirit saw him it immediately threw the lad into convulsions. He fell to the ground and was rolling about, foaming at the mouth. Jesus asked his father, 'How long has this been going on?' He replied, 'Since he was a little child. Many times it has thrown him into the fire and into the water in order to destroy him. If you can do anything, have pity on us and help us.' Jesus said to him, 'If you

* Matthew says that the lad was 'moonstruck' (Matthew 17:15).

can! Everything is possible to someone who has faith!' Straightaway, the boy's father cried out, 'I do have faith! Help my lack of faith!'

When Jesus noticed that a crowd was bearing down upon them, he rebuked the unclean spirit, saying, 'Deaf and dumb spirit, I order you to come out of him, and never enter him again!' With a shriek, the spirit sent the lad into terrible convulsions, and came out. The young man looked as if he was dead, but Jesus, taking him by the hand, raised him, and he stood up. When they went into a house, the disciples asked him privately, 'Why weren't we able to cast it out?' He said to them, 'Nobody can cast out this kind except by prayer.'

From there they went on their way through Galilee, and Jesus didn't want anyone to know about it. He was teaching his disciples, 'The son of man is being delivered into the hands of men, and they will kill him, but three days afterwards he will rise up.' They didn't understand what he meant, and were afraid to ask him.

VIRGO

Virgo is Mutable Earth, and is the sign of the harvest. Its symbol is the Maiden with the Wheatsheaf. In Egypt the sign was associated with the goddess Isis, who is often depicted carrying the infant Horus, and the sign has strong connections with childhood. Its keywords are service, humility, simplicity, purity, characteristics of the Virgin Mary, whose birthday is celebrated on 8 September, when the sun is in the centre of Virgo. The decans of Virgo are Coma (the Infant), Centaurus (the Centaur), and Bootes (the Shepherd).

They came to Capernaum, and when he was inside the house he asked them, 'What were you arguing about on the road?' But they were silent, because on the road they had been arguing about who was the greatest. When he'd sat down, he called the twelve and said to them, 'If anyone wants to be first, he will be the last of all, and the servant of all.' He took a little child, and stood him in their midst. Taking him in his arms, he said to them, 'Whoever receives a child such as this in my name, receives me; and whoever receives me, is not only receiving me, he is also receiving the one who sent me.'*

---

* A few verses after Luke's account of this incident with the children, he has Jesus say, 'The harvest is plentiful, but the workers are few. Ask the Lord of the harvest, therefore, to send out workers into his harvest field' (Luke10:2, NIV). Matthew's version of the parable of the Lost Sheep occurs just after Jesus has spoken about children. 'What do you think? If a man owns a hundred sheep, and one of them wanders away, will he not leave the ninety-nine and go to look for the one that wandered off? And if he finds it, I tell you the truth, he is happier about that one sheep than about the ninety-nine that did not wander off. In the same way your Father in heaven is not willing that any of these little ones should be lost.' (Matthew 18:12-14, NIV)

John said to him, 'We saw someone casting out demons in your name, and we stopped him because he wasn't of our company.'

Jesus said, 'Don't stop him. Nobody who does a powerful work in my name will then be able to slander me. Whoever is not opposed to us is on our side. I'm telling you the truth: whoever gives you a cup of water to drink because you bear the name of Christ won't go unrewarded. But it would be better for him who puts obstacles in the way of one of these little ones who believe in me to be thrown into the sea with a huge millstone tied around his neck! If your hand causes you to fall, cut it off! It's better to enter into life maimed than with both hands to go into Gehenna, into the inextinguishable fire. And if your foot causes you to stumble, cut it off! It's better for you to enter into life lame than to be thrown with both feet into Gehenna. And if your eye causes you to fall, pluck it out! It's better for you to enter into the kingdom of God with one eye than to be thrown with both eyes into Gehenna, where the worm doesn't die, and the fire is never put out! Everyone will be salted with fire; salt is good, but if ever it loses its saltiness, what will you use to make it salty again? Have salt in yourselves, and live in peace with one another.'

LIBRA

Libra, the Balance, is the sign of the autumn equinox, when day and night are equal. It is associated with relationships and marriage, and has been called 'the sign of cosmic reciprocity'. Its ruler is Venus, the goddess of love. The Greeks called it Zugos, 'the Yoke', and in Egypt it was represented by the goddess Ma'at, who judged the dead, weighing their souls in the balance: those who passed her test were said to be 'light hearted'; those who failed were 'heavy hearted'. Its decans are the Cross, the Victim, and the Crown.

Chapter 10

From there he went into the region of Judea, and across the Jordan. Once again a crowd gathered round him, and once again he taught them. And Pharisees were asking him if it was lawful for a man to divorce his wife; they were testing him. He replied, 'What command did Moses give you?' They said, 'Moses allowed divorce by the writing of a divorce certificate.' Jesus said to them, 'It was because of your spiritual immaturity that he wrote you this commandment. From the beginning of creation God made them male and female. Because of this, a man will leave his father and his mother and cleave to his wife, and the two will become one flesh, so that they are no longer two, but one flesh. So, what God has yoked together, let no man divide.'

And inside the house once again the disciples asked him about this. He said to them, 'Whoever divorces his wife and marries another woman commits adultery against her. And if a woman divorces her husband and marries another man, she commits adultery.'

They brought children to him so that he might touch them, but his disciples warned them off. But noticing this Jesus was annoyed, and he said to them, 'Let the children come to me, and don't prevent them, because the kingdom of God belongs to such as these. I'm telling you the truth, whoever does not accept the kingdom of God like a little child won't enter it.' And taking them in his arms, he blessed them.

When he'd gone back on to the road, a man came running towards him. He fell on his knees before him and said, 'Good teacher, what should I do in order to inherit eternal life?' Jesus said to him, 'Why do you call me good? No one is good except God alone. You know the commandments: don't murder, don't commit adultery, don't steal, don't tell lies, don't defraud, honour your father and your mother.' He replied, 'Teacher, I've kept all these from my youth.' Jesus, gazing at him, warmed towards him, and said, 'There's only one thing you need. Sell what you have and give it to the poor, and you will have treasure in heaven. And come, follow me!'

But the young man was upset by what Jesus said, and he went away sorrowfully because he was a man of great wealth. Looking round, Jesus said to his disciples, 'How difficult it is for a very wealthy person to enter the kingdom of God!' His disciples were astonished at his words, but Jesus told them again, 'Children, how difficult it is to go into the kingdom of God! It's easier for a camel to go through the eye of a needle than for a rich man to enter into the kingdom of God.' They were extremely shocked, and said to one another, 'Who can be saved then?' Looking intently at them, Jesus said, 'With men it's impossible, but not with God. Everything is possible with God.' Peter began to say to him, 'Look. We left everything and have followed you.' Jesus said, 'I'm telling you the truth, there's no one who has left a house or brothers or sisters or mother or father or children or fields for my sake and the sake of the good news who won't now receive a hundred times more houses, brothers, sisters, mothers and children and fields (with persecution), and in the coming age, eternal life! Many who are first will be last, and the last first.'

They were going up the road to Jerusalem, Jesus leading the way, and those following were amazed and fearful. Taking the twelve aside, he once again began to tell them what must happen:

'Look,' he said, 'We are going to Jerusalem, and the son of man will be handed over to the chief priests and the legal experts, and they will condemn him to death and hand him over to the Gentiles and they will make fun of him, and spit on him, and scourge him and kill him, and after three days he will rise up.'

SCORPIO

The sign of hidden power, death, regeneration, expiation, purgation, sexuality, and spiritual initiation into the deep mysteries of life. It concerns the hidden connections between living and dead. Hallowe'en is celebrated on 31 October, when the sun is in Scorpio. Its decans are Serpens (the Serpent), Ophiuchus (the Serpent Holder), and Hercules. A passage from what appears to have been a longer version of Mark is appropriately placed here, as is part of what is called 'the longer ending'. At this point in the narrative Jesus and the apostles are approaching Jericho, the lowest point on the earth's surface; this is appropriate for the 'descent into the depths' which Scorpio symbolizes.

*James and John, the sons of Zebedee, approached him saying, 'Teacher, we want you to do for us whatever we ask.' Jesus said to them, 'What do you want me to do for you?' They said to him, 'Allow one of us to sit on your right hand and one on your left hand in your glory.' Jesus said to them, 'You don't know what you are asking! Are you able to drink the cup which I shall drink, or to be baptized with the baptism with which I shall be baptized?' They said to him, 'We are able!' Jesus said to them, 'The cup I shall drink you shall drink, and the baptism I shall undergo, you shall undergo, but to sit on my right or on my left is not in my gift; it's for those for whom it has been prepared.' When they heard this, the other ten began to be annoyed at James and John and, calling them together, Jesus said to them, 'You know that those who consider themselves leaders among the Gentiles lord it over them, and the greatest among them exercise dominance. Well, that's not the way it is among you. No. Whoever wants to become great among you will be your servant, and whoever wants to be first among you will be a slave of all.

---

* The passage from the 'secret' Gospel of Mark occurs at this point: *And they come into Bethany. And a certain woman whose brother had died was there. And, coming, she prostrated herself before Jesus and [says] to him, 'Son of David, have mercy on me.' But the disciples rebuked her. And Jesus, being angered, went off with her into the garden where the tomb was, and straightway a great cry was heard from the tomb. And going near Jesus rolled away the stone from the door of the tomb. And straightway, going in where the youth was, he stretched forth his hand and raised him, seizing his hand. But the youth, looking upon him, loved him and began to beseech him that he might be with him.* (Barnstone, page 342)

Because the son of man hasn't come to be served but to serve, and to give his life in order to purchase the freedom of many.'*

And they came to Jericho, and when he, his disciples and a large crowd left Jericho, Bartimaeus, the son of Timaeus, a blind beggar, was sitting by the roadside. Hearing that it was Jesus the Nazarene, he began to cry out and say, 'Son of David, have mercy on me!' Many people told him to keep quiet, but he cried out all the more, 'Son of David, have mercy on me!' Jesus stopped and said, 'Call him.' They called the blind man, saying, 'Cheer up and get up. He's calling you.' Throwing off his coat, he jumped up and went to Jesus. Jesus said in response, 'What do you want me to do for you?' The blind man said to him, 'Rabbi, let me see again!' And Jesus said to him, 'Go. Your faith has saved you.' And at once he could see, and he followed Jesus on the road.

SAGITTARIUS

Sagittarius is the Archer or the Centaur, and is the third of the Fire signs. It is associated with zeal, foreigners, travel, horses and religion. Notice how Mark says that Jesus rides into Jerusalem on a young unbroken horse, before zealously venting his spleen on the hypocritical religious activity of the Temple. Two of its decans – Lyra (the Eagle or Lyre) and Draco (the Dragon) – do not appear to be significant, but there is a clear allusion to the third, Ara (the Altar, in Latin; the Curse, in Greek).

Chapter 11

When they drew near to Jerusalem, to Bethphage and Bethany towards the Mount of Olives, he sent out two of his disciples. He said to them, 'Go into the village opposite, and as soon as you enter it you will find a tethered colt on which no one has ever sat. Untie it and bring it. If anyone asks you what you are up to, tell them that your master needs it, and he will send it straight back.' They went off and found the young horse tied up by the door outside, where two roads meet, and they untied it. Some of those standing there said to them, 'Why are you untying the horse?' They replied as Jesus had instructed them and they were allowed to go. They took the colt to Jesus and placed their coats on it. Jesus mounted it. And many people spread

---

* In the so-called 'Longer Ending' of Mark, which was added later, we find the following passage which reflects the constellation Ophiuchus, The Serpent Holder, one of the decans of Scorpio: *And these signs will accompany those who believe. In my name they will drive out demons, they will speak in new tongues, they will pick up snakes with their hands, and when they drink deadly poison it will not hurt them at all; they will place their hands on sick people, and they will get well* (Mark 16: 17-18, NIV).

their coats on the road; others cut down branches from the fields. Those going on ahead, and those who were following, were shouting: 'Hosanna! Blessed is the one who is coming in the name of the Lord! Blessed is the coming kingdom of our father David! Hosanna in the highest!'

He went into Jerusalem, to the Temple, and when he'd looked round at everything he went off to Bethany with the twelve because it was already late. The next day, as they were leaving Bethany, he was hungry, and seeing a distant fig tree in leaf he went to see if he could find anything on it. But he found nothing but leaves, because it wasn't the fig season. He said to it, 'May no one eat fruit from you ever again!' and his disciples heard him.

They came to Jerusalem and, going into the Temple area, he began to throw out those who were buying and selling in the Temple, and he overturned the tables of the money changers and the seats of those who sold pigeons. And he wouldn't allow anyone to carry their goods through the Temple. He taught them: 'Isn't it written, "My house will be called a house of prayer for all the nations?" You have turned it into a den of thieves!' The chief priests and the lawyers heard of it, and they looked for a way to kill him; but they were scared because the crowd were amazed by his teaching. And when evening came, they went out of the city. Early the next day, as they were passing along, they saw the fig tree withered to its roots. Peter remembered, and said to him: 'Rabbi, look. The fig tree which you cursed has withered!'

In reply, Jesus said to them, 'Have faith in God. I'm telling you the truth. Whoever says to this mountain "Be lifted up and thrown into the sea!" and who has no doubt in his mind but believes that what he says will happen, it will be done for him! Because of this I say to you whatever you ask for in prayer, believe that it is yours and it will be! And whenever you are praying, if you are holding a grudge against somebody, forgive him, so that your father in heaven may forgive you your failings.'

CAPRICORN

The sign of the winter solstice, when the sun changes direction once more. It is the Cardinal Earth sign, ruled by the planet Saturn and connected with political and social structures, convention, propriety, authority, and the father. It was the moon sign of the Emperor Augustus, and the image of Capricorn appeared on a denarius during his reign. In this section of Mark, Jesus is shown in dispute with all the authority figures in Israel, and in the corresponding passage in Matthew he says, 'Call no man on earth your father.' The three decans are Sagitta (the Arrow), Aquila (the Eagle), and Delphinus (the Dolphin), but they don't seem to be alluded to.

They came to Jerusalem again and as he walked around in the Temple precincts some of the chief priests, lawyers and elders came up to him. They were asking him, 'Where do you get your authority to do what you do? Who gave it to you?' Jesus replied, 'I'll ask you a question. Answer me and I'll tell you in what kind of authority I do all these things. Was John's baptism from heaven or from men? Answer me!' They discussed the matter with one another. 'If we say that it was from heaven, he'll ask us why we didn't believe him. But we can't really say that it was from men either ...' (They were frightened of the crowd because everybody considered John to be a prophet.) So they said in reply, 'We don't know.' Jesus said to them, 'Nor am I going to tell you by what authority I do what I do.'

Chapter 12

He began to speak to them in parables. 'A man planted a vineyard and he fenced it, and dug a wine trough and built a tower. He let it out to vine-dressers and went on his travels. At the appropriate time he sent a slave to collect some of the fruits of his vineyard from his tenants. But they took him and beat him and sent him off empty-handed. He sent them another slave, but they struck him on the head and maltreated him. He sent another and they killed him; and many others still, but they beat and killed them. He still had a beloved son, whom he sent to them finally, saying, "They will respect my son." The tenants said to one another, "This is the heir. Come on, let's kill him and the inheritance will be ours!" They took him and killed him and threw him out of the vineyard. So, what will the owner of the vineyard do? He will come and destroy those tenants and give the vineyard to others. Didn't you ever read this scripture: "The stone which the builders rejected has become the cornerstone. This comes from the Lord and is marvellous in our eyes"?' They were seeking to seize him, but they were afraid of the crowd because they knew that he'd spoken this parable against them. So they left him and went on their way.

But they sent some Pharisees and supporters of Herod to him, so that they could entrap him in his speech. They came and said to him, 'Teacher, we know that you are sincere and that you don't bother what other people think of you. You don't judge on appearances, but you teach the way of God truthfully. Is it lawful to pay the poll tax to Caesar? Should we pay it or not?' Fully aware of their hypocrisy, he said to them, 'Why are you trying to test me? Bring me a denarius. Let's look at it.' They brought one and he said to them, 'Whose is this image and inscription?' They said, 'Caesar's.' Jesus said to them, 'Give to Caesar what belongs to Caesar, and to God what belongs to God.' They were amazed at him.

Some Sadducees, who say there is no resurrection, came to him and asked him, 'Teacher, Moses gave us the rule that if anyone's brother dies and leaves a childless wife, the man should take the woman as his own wife and raise up offspring on behalf of his brother. There were seven brothers and the first took a wife and then died without producing any children. So the second took her and then he died childless, and so did the third. All seven in fact died childless. Finally the woman herself died. In the resurrection, whose wife will she be? All seven were married to her.' Jesus said to them, 'Isn't this where you make a mistake? You know neither the scriptures nor the power of God! When they rise from the dead they won't be married; they will be like angels in heaven. About the dead being raised: haven't you read in the book of Moses, in the passage about the bush, how God said to him, "I am the God of Abraham, and the God of Isaac, and the God of Jacob." He is not the God of the dead but of the living. You are greatly mistaken.'

One of the Jewish legal experts, who had heard the disputes and who thought that Jesus had given sound answers, asked him, 'Which commandment is the most important?' Jesus answered, 'The most important one is "Hear, O Israel, the Lord our God is one Lord and you shall love the Lord your God with all your heart and all your soul and all your mind and all your strength." The second is this: "You shall love your neighbour as you love yourself." There's no greater commandment.' The lawyer said, 'Teacher, you spoke the truth. He is one and there is no other. And to love him with all the heart and with all your mind and with all your strength, and to love your neighbour as yourself – this is greater than all burnt offerings and sacrifices.' Jesus saw that he answered sensibly and said to him, 'You aren't far from the kingdom of God.' Nobody dared to question him any more.

As Jesus was teaching in the Temple precincts, he said: 'Why do the legal experts say that the Christ is the son of David? David himself, inspired by the holy spirit, said, "The Lord said to my lord, Sit on my right hand till I put your enemies under your feet." David himself calls him "Lord", so how is he his son?' A large crowd heard him with pleasure. And in his teaching he said, 'Look out for the legal experts, who want to walk around in long robes, and who want greetings in the market places and the most important seats in the synagogues, and places of honour at meals They gobble up the houses of widows but offer long prayers to hide their iniquity. They will receive the greater condemnation.'*

* At this point Matthew adds, But you are not to be called 'Rabbi', for you have only one Master, and you are all brothers. And do not call anyone on earth 'father' for you have one Father, and he is in heaven. Nor are you to be called 'teacher', for you have one Teacher, the Christ (Matthew 23:8-10, NIV).

And sitting down opposite the Temple treasury, he saw how the crowd threw coppers into the offertory box. Many rich people were throwing in large sums, but a poor widow came and threw two small copper coins, which together make about a penny. Calling his disciples to him, he said to them, 'I'm telling you the truth. This poor widow has put more than all the others into the offertory box. They all gave from their surplus; but she, despite her need, gave all she had to live on.'

AQUARIUS

The Water Bearer. Aquarius is The Fixed Air sign and, like Capricorn, it is ruled by Saturn, but is more concerned with toppling structures than with building them up, hence its association with anarchy, political and social upheaval, drastic and radical change. The whole of chapter 13 is devoted to these themes, and the image of the man carrying a jar of water (14:13) is the clearest zodiacal indicator of all. The decans are Piscis Australis (the Southern Fish), Cygnus (the Swan), and Pegasus (the Winged Horse). Both Cygnus and Pegasus are associated with the idea of going away and returning.

Chapter 13

As he was leaving the Temple one of his disciples said to him, 'Look teacher! Such stones and such buildings!' And Jesus said to him, 'You see these great buildings? There won't be one stone left upon another. There's none that won't be demolished!'

Sitting on the Mount of Olives opposite the Temple, Peter, James, John and Andrew asked him privately, 'Tell us, when will these things happen? What will be the sign that all these things are about to take place?' And Jesus began to tell them. 'Be careful that no one misleads you. Many will come in my name saying "I'm the one", and many will go astray. Whenever you hear of wars and reports of wars, don't be alarmed. These things must take place, but the end is not yet. Nation will rise against nation, and kingdom against kingdom; there will be earthquakes in various places; there will be famines. These signal the beginning of the birth pangs. Look to yourselves. They will hand you over to the courts, you will be beaten in synagogues, and you will stand before governors and kings, witnessing to them for my sake. But first the good news must be preached in all the nations. And whenever they arrest you, don't bother about what to say, but say whatever is given to you at the time, because it won't be you speaking but the holy spirit. Brother will hand over brother to death, and a father will hand over his child. Children will rebel against their parents and kill them. You will be hated by everyone because of my name, but whoever holds out to the end will be saved. When you see the abomination of desolation standing where it ought not to be (let the reader understand), then let those in Judea flee to the mountains. Let the man on the housetop not come down; neither let him go into the house to take anything out. And let the man in the field not turn back to fetch his coat. Pity those who are pregnant or who are suckling babies in those days! Pray that it doesn't happen in winter, because in those days there will be distress the like of which has not occurred from the time of the creation right up until now. Nor will it happen again. And if the Lord hadn't shortened the days no human being would be saved, but because of those whom he has chosen he has shortened the days. If at that time someone says to you, "Look, the Christ is here" or "There he is", don't believe it, because false Christs and false prophets will rise up and give such convincing demonstrations of their power that, if it were possible, even the elect would be fooled! Keep watch, then! I've warned you about everything. But after the distress of those days, the sun will be darkened and the moon will not shine. The stars will fall from the sky, and the powers of the heavens will be shaken, and then they will see the son of man coming in clouds with great power and glory.* And then he will send out the angels and gather together his chosen ones from the four corners of the earth, from the farthest bounds of earth to the farthest bounds of heaven. Learn a lesson from the fig tree: when its branch becomes tender and the leaves appear, you know that summer is near. So when you see these things taking place you will know that the end is near, at the door almost. I'm telling you the truth: this generation will not disappear until all these things have occurred; heaven and earth will pass away, but my words will not pass away. But as far as timing is concerned, no one knows, neither the angels in heaven nor the son; only the Father knows. Watch! Be alert! For you don't know when the time is. It's like a man travelling abroad; he leaves his house in the care of his servants, giving each of them a particular task; he tells the doorkeeper to keep watch. So, you keep watch, because you don't know when the lord of the household is coming – whether late in the evening, at midnight, or at cock-crow, or in the morning! You don't want him to come suddenly and find you sleeping! What I am saying to you I am saying to everyone: "Watch!"'

Chapter 14

The Passover and the feast of Unleavened Bread were two days away, and the chief priests and the experts in Jewish law were looking for a way to

* Matthew says that *the sign of the son of man will appear in the sky* ... (Matthew 24:31).

arrest Jesus secretly and kill him, but they didn't want to do it during the festival in case there was a riot among the people.

While Jesus was in Bethany, eating a meal at the house of Simon the leper, a woman came in carrying an alabaster jar full of very expensive perfumed oil, pure nard. Breaking open the jar, she poured the oil on his head, to the great annoyance of some of those present. 'Why this waste of the perfumed oil? It's worth a year's wages. It could have been sold and the money given to the poor.' They were very indignant.

But Jesus said, 'Leave her alone. Why are you bothering her? She's done a lovely thing for me. The poor are always with you, and you can always do good to them whenever you want to, but you won't always have me around. She has done what she could. She has anointed my body in anticipation of my burial. I'm telling you the truth, wherever the good news is preached throughout the world, what this woman has done will be spoken of. She will be remembered for it.'

Judas Iscariot, one of the twelve, went to the chief priests in order to betray Jesus to them. They were delighted, and promised to pay him, so he began looking for a suitable time to hand him over.

On the first day of Unleavened Bread, when the Passover lamb was customarily slaughtered, his disciples said to him, 'Where do you want us to go to prepare the Passover meal for you to eat?' He sent off two of his disciples, saying, 'Go into the city, where a man carrying a jar of water will meet you. Follow him, and say to the master of whichever house he enters, "Where is my guest room, where I might eat the Passover with my disciples?" He'll show you a large upper room, equipped and ready. Prepare for us there.' The disciples left for the city and found everything just as Jesus had said; and they prepared the Passover.

PISCES

The Two Fish. Pisces is Mutable Water and is the sign in which the sun 'dies' before being 'born anew' at the spring equinox when it enters Aries once again. Ruled by Jupiter, it is a sign of extreme sensitivity and benevolence, but it was also associated in the ancient world with secret enemies, betrayal, cowardice, diffidence, sleep, dreams, all of which appear in this final, lengthy section of the Gospel. The three decans are The Band, Cepheus (the King), and Andromeda (the Chained Woman). Both Cepheus and Andromeda are clearly referred to in the story of the crucifixion.

In the evening he came with the twelve, and as they were sitting eating at the table, Jesus said, 'I'll be honest with you. One of you who is eating with me, will betray me.' They were greatly saddened by this, and said to him, one after another, 'It's not me, is it?' Jesus said to them, 'It is one of the twelve, one who is dipping into the same dish with me. The son of man is going away, just as it is written about him, but woe to that man by whom the son of man is betrayed! It would be better for that man if he hadn't been born!'

As they were eating, he took a loaf, blessed it, broke it, and gave it to them. He said, 'Take this. It is my body.' And he took the cup, offered thanks, and gave it to them. They all drank from it. He said to them, 'This is my blood of the covenant which is shed for many. I'm telling you the truth: I shall not drink the fruit of the vine again until I drink it new in the kingdom of God.' When they had sung a hymn they went out to the Mount of Olives.

Jesus said to them, 'You will all desert me, because it is written, "I shall strike the shepherd and the sheep will be scattered." But when I have been raised up I shall go ahead of you into Galilee.' Peter said to him, 'Even if all the others desert you, I won't!' Jesus said to him, 'I'm telling you this: today, this very night, before a cock crows twice, you will disown me three times.' But Peter protested vehemently, 'Even if I have to die with you, I won't deny you!' And the rest said the same.

They went to a place called Gethsemane and he said to his disciples, 'Sit down here while I pray.' He took Peter, James and John with him, and he began to be distressed and troubled. He said to them, 'My soul is overwhelmed with deadly grief. Stay here, and stay awake.' He walked on a little before falling to the ground, praying that, if possible, the hour might pass from him. He said, 'Abba, father! All things are possible to you. Take this cup from me; but not what I want, what you want.' He came and found them sleeping, and he said to Peter, 'Simon, are you asleep? Didn't you have the strength to stay awake for one hour? Stay awake and pray that you won't be tempted. The spirit is willing, but the flesh is weak.'

He went off again and prayed as before, and when he returned once more he found them sleeping, because their eyes were heavy. They didn't know what to say to him. He came back a third time and said to them, 'You are asleep, and taking your rest. But that's enough. It's time. Look, the son of man is being handed over to sinners. Get up and let's be going. See, my betrayer has approached.'

While he was still speaking, Judas, one of the twelve, came straight up to him. He was accompanied by a crowd from the chief priests, scribes and elders, and they were carrying swords and clubs. His betrayer had given them an agreed signal: 'The one I kiss is the one (you want). Grab him and take him off under guard.' Coming up to him he said, 'Rabbi!' and he kissed him. So they grabbed hold of him. However, one of those standing by drew his sword and struck the high priest's slave, cutting off his ear. Jesus said to them, 'Have you come to arrest me with swords and clubs as you would arrest a robber? Day after day I was with you in the Temple and you didn't arrest me. But let it be, so that the scriptures may be fulfilled.' And they all abandoned him and fled, but a young man wearing just a linen sheet over his naked body followed him. They grabbed at him, but he left his linen sheet behind and ran off naked.

They led Jesus to the high priest, and all the chief priests, legal experts and elders were assembled. Peter followed him at a distance as far as the courtyard of the high priest, where he was sitting with the servants warming himself by the fire. The chief priests and the whole council were looking for evidence against Jesus so that they could execute him, but they couldn't find any. Many people were telling lies about him, but their evidence was conflicting. Some stood up and lied that they had heard him say, 'I shall destroy this temple made with hands and after three days build one not made with hands.' But their testimonies did not agree even about this.

The high priest stood up the middle of them all and questioned Jesus. 'Have you nothing to say in reply? What is it that these people are saying against you?' Jesus was silent; he didn't reply at all. So the high priest asked him, 'Are you the Christ, the son of the Blessed One?' Jesus said, 'I am, and you will see the son of man sitting at the right hand of power, coming with the clouds of heaven.' The high priest tore his own garments and said, 'We don't need any more witnesses. You heard the blasphemy! What's your verdict?' They all judged him deserving of death. Some started to spit at him, to cover up his face, and to strike him, all the while saying, 'Prophesy!' Slapping his face, the attendants took him away.

One of the high priest's servant girls saw Peter as he was warming himself. She looked closely at him and said, 'You were with the Nazarene, with Jesus!' But Peter denied it. 'I don't know what you're talking about,' he said. He went outside into the porch and the cock crowed. The servant girl spotted him and began to say to those standing around, 'This is one of them!' Peter denied it again. A little later the bystanders said to Peter, 'Yes, you are one of them. You're from Galilee!' Peter started to curse and swear. 'I don't know the man you're talking about!' he said. Immediately the cock crowed a second time, and Peter remembered that Jesus had told him, 'Before the cock crows twice, you will deny me three times.' And throwing his cloak around his head he broke down and wept.

Chapter 15

Very early in the morning, the chief priests, the elders and the legal experts – the whole Sanhedrin, in fact – held a meeting. They bound Jesus and took him off and handed him over to Pilate, who asked him, 'Are you the king of the Jews?' Jesus replied, 'Those are your words.' But the chief priests were accusing him of many things, so Pilate questioned him again. 'Have you nothing to say for yourself? See how many things they are accusing you of.' But Jesus said nothing, and Pilate was amazed.

It was the custom for Pilate to release to the people a prisoner of their own choosing. There was a man called Barabbas, imprisoned with his fellow revolutionaries, who had committed murder in the rebellion. The crowd came up and began to petition Pilate to carry out the customary procedure, and he replied by saying, 'Do you want me to release the king of the Jews to you?' He realized that the chief priests had handed him over out of spite. But the chief priests stirred up the crowd to ask for Barabbas instead. Once again, Pilate answered them, 'So, what shall I do with the one you call the king of the Jews?' Again they cried out, 'Crucify him!' Pilate said to them, 'Why? What has he done wrong?' They shouted out all the more, 'Crucify him!' Pilate, wishing to please the crowd, released Barabbas to them. He had Jesus whipped, and then handed him over to be crucified.

The soldiers took him into the courtyard inside the palace, the Praetorium, and they called the entire detachment of soldiers together. They dressed him in purple, plaited some thorns into a crown, and placed it on his head. They started to salute him: 'Greetings, king of the Jews!' they said, and they were cuffing him round his head with a reed and spitting on him. Kneeling before him, they paid him homage. When they'd finished making fun of him, they stripped the purple robe from him and dressed him in his own clothes. Then they led him out to crucify him. They forced a passer-by to carry his cross. It was Simon of Cyrene (the father of Alexander and Rufus), who was coming in from the field.

They took him to Golgotha, which means 'The Place of the Skull', and they offered him wine drugged with myrrh, but he wouldn't take it. They crucified him, and they shared out his clothing, casting lots to see who would take what. It was nine o'clock in the morning when they crucified him. The inscribed charge against him read, 'The king of the Jews.' And they crucified two thieves with him, one on his right, and one on his left. Those who passed by hurled abuse at him, shaking their heads and saying, 'Aha! You were going to tear down the Temple and build it up again in three days, were you? Well, save yourself by getting down off the cross!' Similarly, the chief priests and the lawyers were joining in the fun, saying, 'He saved others, but he can't save himself! Let's see the Christ, the king of Israel come down from the cross now! We'd believe him then!' Even those who were being crucified with him were jeering at him.

At about noon, darkness fell on the whole earth and lasted until three o'clock in the afternoon, at which time Jesus cried aloud, 'Eloi, eloi, lama sabakhthani', which means, 'My God, my God, why have you forsaken me?' Some of those standing by heard it and said, 'Look! He's calling Elijah!' Someone put a sponge with sour wine on a reed and gave it to him to drink, saying, 'Let's see if Elijah will come to take him down.' But, with a loud cry, Jesus died, and the Temple curtain split in two, top to bottom. A centurion standing opposite him as he died said, 'This man was certainly a son of God!'

Some women were looking on from a distance. Among them was Mary Magdalene, and Mary, the mother of the younger James, Joses and Salome. These had been with him, and had taken care of him, when he was in Galilee; and there were many others who had come up to Jerusalem with him.

It was already evening, and since it was the day of preparation, that is the day before the Sabbath, Joseph of Arimathea, a respected council member, who was himself waiting for the kingdom of God, plucked up the courage to go to Pilate and ask for the body of Jesus. Pilate was amazed that Jesus could be dead so soon, so he called the centurion and asked him whether Jesus was, in fact, dead. Assured that this was the case, he granted the body to Joseph, who took it down, and wrapped it in a linen cloth which he had bought. He placed him in a tomb which had been hewn out of rock, and he rolled a stone against the door of the tomb. Mary Magdalene and Mary the mother of Joses saw where he had been put.

Chapter 16

When the Sabbath was over, Mary Magdalene and Mary the mother of James and Salome bought spices with which to anoint him. Very early in the morning on the first day of the week they came to the tomb. The sun had risen. They were saying to each other, 'Who will roll away the stone from the door of the tomb for us?' But when they looked up they saw that the stone had already been rolled away, even though it was very large. Going inside the tomb they saw a young man dressed in white sitting on the right hand side. They were astonished. He said to them, 'Don't be so shocked! You are looking for Jesus the Nazarene, the one who was crucified; but he has been raised up. He's not here. See the place where they laid him. Go and tell his disciples and Peter that he is going on ahead to Galilee. You will see him there, just as he told you.'

When they came out they ran away from the tomb because they were trembling with astonishment. And they said nothing to anyone because they were afraid.

(The Gospel ends at this point. Alternative endings appear in most Bibles but these are much later additions. It is possible, however, that at least one verse from these belonged to the original text. See the Scorpio section above.)

Appendix 2

a The Signs of the Zodiac and their Planetary Rulers

Sign	Symbol	Planet	Symbol
Aries	♈	Mars	♂
Taurus	♉	Venus	♀
Gemini	♊	Mercury	☿
Cancer	♋	Moon	☽
Leo	♌	Sun	☉
Virgo	♍	Mercury	☿
Libra	♎	Venus	♀
Scorpio	♏	Mars	♂
Sagittarius	♐	Jupiter	♃
Capricorn	♑	Saturn	♄
Aquarius	♒	Saturn	♄
Pisces	♓	Jupiter	♃

Notes

i. Each planet rules two signs, with the exception of the sun and moon which each rule one.

ii. Only seven planets (including the sun and moon) were known to the ancients. In modern astrology, Scorpio is ruled by Pluto, Aquarius by Uranus, and Pisces by Neptune.

b. Planetary Exaltations

Planet	Exalted in
Sun	Aries
Moon	Taurus
Mercury	Virgo
Venus	Pisces
Mars	Capricorn
Jupiter	Cancer
Saturn	Libra

c. The Signs of the Zodiac and Parts of the Body

Manilius's attributions are the traditional ones:

> For as in Man, the Work of Hands Divine,
> Each member lies allotted to a Sign;
> And as the Body is the common Care
> Of all the Signs, each Limb enjoys a Share:
> The Ram defends the Head, the Neck the Bull,
> The Arms bright Twins are subject to your Rule;
> I'th' Shoulders Leo, and the Crab's obey'd
> I'th Breast, and in the Guts the modest Maid;
> I'th Buttocks, Libra, Scorpio warms Desires
> I'th secret Parts, and spreads unruly Fires;
> The Thighs, the Centaur, and the Goat commands
> The Knees, and binds them up with double Bands.
> The parted Legs, in cold Aquarius meet,
> And Pisces gives protection to the Feet.
>
> (Manilius, *The Five Books*, page 141)

d. The Constellations of the Sky and their Decans

These are taken directly from Seiss's work *The Gospel in the Stars* (pages 17-20). The decans are the constellations which are around the zodiacal constellations and rise with them. Seiss bases his attribution of decans to zodiacal constellation on the work of the Arab astronomer, Albumazer, who lived about a thousand years ago. Manilius attributes them differently (*The Five Books*, pages 157-176). I have generally followed Seiss.

Aries, the Ram: by some nations called the Lamb: the figure of a strong sheep with powerful, curved horns, lying down in easy composure, and looking out in conscious strength over the field around it.

The Decans of Aries
1. Cassiopeia, the woman enthroned;
2. Cetus, the Sea Monster, closely and strongly bound by the Lamb;
3. Perseus, an armed and mighty man with winged feet, who is carrying away in triumph the cut-off head of a monster full of writhing serpents, and holding aloft a great sword in his right hand.

Taurus, the Bull: the figure of the shoulders, neck, head, horns, and front feet of a powerful bull, in the attitude of rushing and pushing forward with great energy.

The Decans of Taurus

1. Orion, a glorious Prince, with a sword girded on his side, and his foot on the head of the Hare or Serpent;
2. Eridanus, the tortuous River, accounted as belonging to Orion;
3. Auriga, the Wagoner, rather the Shepherd, carrying a she-goat and two little goats on his left arm, and holding cords or bands in his right hand.

Gemini, the Twins: or a man and a woman sometimes called Adam and Eve: usually two human figures closely united, and seated together in endeared affection. In some of the older representations the figure of this constellation consists of two goats, or kids.

The Decans of Gemini

1. Lepus, the Hare, in some nations a serpent, the mad enemy under Orion's feet;
2. Canis Major, Sirius, the Great Dog, the Prince Coming;
3. Canis Minor, Procyon, the Second Dog, following after Sirius and Orion.

Cancer, the Crab: the figure of a crab, in the act of taking and holding on with its strong pincer claws. In Egyptian astronomy the scarabaeus beetle, grasping and holding on to the ball in which its eggs are deposited, takes the place of the crab.

The Decans of Cancer

1. Ursa Minor, anciently the Lesser Sheepfold, close to and including the Pole;
2. Ursa Major, anciently the Greater Sheepfold, in connection with Arcturus, the guardian and keeper of the flock;
3. Argo, the Ship, the company of travellers under the bright Canopus, their Prince, the Argonauts returned with the Golden Fleece.

Leo, the Lion: the figure of a great rampant lion, leaping forth to rend, with his feet over the writhing body of Hydra, the Serpent, which is in the act of fleeing.

The Decans of Leo

1. Hydra, the fleeing Serpent, trodden under foot by the Crab and Lion;
2. Crater, the Cup or Bowl of Wrath on the Serpent;
3. Corvus, the Raven or Crow, the bird of doom, tearing the Serpent.

Virgo, the Virgin: the figure of a young woman lying prostrate, with an ear of wheat in one hand and a branch in the other.

The Decans of Virgo

1. Coma, the Infant, the Branch, the Desired one;
2. Centaurus, a centaur, with dart piercing a victim;
3. Bootes, or Arcturus, the great Shepherd and harvester holding a rod and sickle, and walking forth before his flocks.

Libra, the Scales: the figure of a pair of balances, with one end of the beam up and the other down, as in the act of weighing. In some of the old planispheres a hand, or a woman, appears holding the scales.

The Decans of Libra

1. The Cross, over which Centaur is advancing, called the Southern Cross;
2. Victim of Centaur, slain, pierced to death;
3. The Crown, which the Serpent aims to take, called the Northern Crown.

Scorpio, the Scorpion: the figure of a gigantic, noxious, and deadly insect, with its tail and sting uplifted in anger, as if striking.

The Decans of Scorpio

1. The Serpent, struggling with Ophiuchus;
2. Ophiuchus, wrestling with the Serpent, stung in one heel by the Scorpion, and crushing it with the other;
3. Hercules, wounded in his heel, the other foot over the Dragon's head, holding in one hand the Golden Apples and the three-headed Dog of hell, and in the other the uplifted club.

Sagittarius, the Bowman: the figure of a horse with the body, arms, and head of a man – a centaur – with a drawn bow and arrow pointed at the Scorpion.

The Decans of Sagittarius

1. Lyra, an Eagle holding the Lyre, as in triumphant gladness;
2. Ara, the Altar, with consuming fires, burning downward;
3. Draco, the Dragon, the old Serpent, winding himself about the Pole in horrid links and contortions.

Capricornus, the Goat: the figure of a goat sinking down as in death, with the hinder part of its body terminating in the vigorous tail of a fish.

The Decans of Capricornus

1. Sagitta, the Arrow, or killing dart sent forth, the naked shaft of death;
2. Aquila, the Eagle, pierced and falling;
3. Delphinus, the Dolphin, springing up, raised out of the sea.

Appendix 2

Aquarius, the Waterman: the figure of a man with a large urn, the contents of which he is in the act of pouring out in a great stream from the sky.

The Decans of Aquarius

1. The Southern Fish, drinking in the stream;
2. Pegasus, a white horse, winged and speeding, as with good tidings;
3. Cygnus, the Swan on the wing, going and returning, bearing the sign of the cross.

Pisces, the Fishes: the figures of two large fishes in the act of swimming, one to the northward, the other with the ecliptic.

The Decans of Pisces

1. The Band, holding up the Fishes, and held by the Lamb, its doubled end fast to the neck of Cetus, the Sea Monster;
2. Cepheus, a crowned king, holding a band and sceptre, with his foot planted on the polestar as the great Victor and Lord;
3. Andromeda, a woman in chains, and threatened by the serpents of Medusa's head.

Bibliography

Abbot-Smith, G. (1986), *A Manual Greek Lexicon of the New Testament*. T. and T. Clark, Edinburgh.

Allen, R.H (1899), *Star Names: Their Lore and Meaning*. Dover, New York.

Ankerberg, J. and Weldon, J. (1988), *The Facts on Astrology*. Harvest House, Eugene, Oregon.

Ankerberg, J. and Weldon, J. (1989), *Astrology: Do the Heavens Rule Our Destiny?* Harvest House, Eugene, Oregon.

Apuleius (1954),*The Golden Ass*, translated by Robert Graves. Penguin, London.

Arnold, E. (1993), *The Bhagavad Gita*. Dover Thrift Editions, New York.

Ashe, G. (1977), *The Ancient Wisdom*. Abacus, London.

Bailey, A. (1934), *From Bethlehem to Calvary*. Lucis Publishing Company, New York. (1999 edition)

Bailey, A. (1951), *Esoteric Astrology*. Lucis Publishing Company, New York. (1971 edition)

Bailey, A. (1974), *The Labours of Hercules: An Astrological Interpretation*. Lucis Publishing Company, New York.

Ballou, R.O. (1959), *The Pocket World Bible*. Readers Union, Routledge and Kegan Paul, London.

Barnstone, W. (ed.) (1984), *The Other Bible*, Harper and Row, San Francisco.

Barclay, W. (1966), *The Gospels and Acts, Vol. 1: The First Three Gospels*. SCM Press, London.

Barclay, W. (no date), *The Daily Study Bible: The Gospel of Mark*. The Saint Andrew Press, Edinburgh.

Barclay, W. (1975), *The Gospel of Matthew, Vol. 1*. The Westminster Press, Philadelphia.

Barnett, P. (1986), *Is the New Testament History?* Hodder and Stoughton, London.

Beatty, L. (1939), *The Garden of the Golden Flower: The Journey to Spiritual Fulfilment*. Random House, London. (1996 edition)

Besant, A. (1901), *Esoteric Christianity*. The Theosophical Publishing House, Adyar, Madras. (1975 edition)

Bielecki, T.(1996), *Teresa of Avila: Ecstasy and Common Sense*. Shambhala, Boston and London.

Blavatsky, H. (1877), *Isis Unveiled*. Sphere Books, London. (1974 edition)

Blavatsky, H. (1888), *The Secret Doctrine*.The Theosophical Publishing House, Pasadena, California. (1963 edition)

Bobrick, B. (2005), *The Fated Sky*. Simon and Schuster, New York.

Brady, B. (1998), *Brady's Book of Fixed Stars*. Samuel Weiser, York Beach, Maine.

Bucke, M. (1993), *Cosmic Consciousness*. Citadel Press, New York. (First published c.1900)

Bultmann, R. (1963), tr. John Marsh, *History of the Synoptic Tradition*. Harper and Row, New York.

Campbell, J. (1964), *Occidental Mythology*. Penguin, London.

Campbell, J. (1968), *Creative Mythology*. Penguin, London.

Campbell, J. (1972), *Myths to Live By*. Paladin, London.

Campbell, J. (1986), *The Inner Reaches of Outer Space*. Harper and Row, New York.

Campbell, J. (1988), *The Power of Myth*. Doubleday, New York.

Campion, N. (2006), 'Culture and Cosmos: a Journal of the History of Astrology and Cultural Astronomy', Volume 9, No 1, Spring/Summer 2005.

Carpenter, E. (1920), *The Origin of Pagan and Christian Beliefs*. Random House, London.

Carter, C. (1925), *The Principles of Astrology*. Theosophical Publishing House. Wheaton, Illinois (1963 edition)

Carter, C. (1965), *Essays on the Foundations of Astrology*. Fowler, London.

Carter, C. (1968), *The Zodiac and the Soul*. Theosophical Publishing House, London.

Carrington, P. (1952), *The Primitive Christian Calendar: A Study in the Making of the Marcan Gospel. Vol. 1: Introduction and Text*. CUP, Cambridge, England.

Chadwick, H. (1967), *The Early Church. The Pelican History of the Church, Vol. 1*. Penguin Books, London.

Cooke, D. (1996), *Persecuting Zeal: A Portrait of Ian Paisley*. Brandon Books, Ireland.

Collins, R.F. (1987), *Introduction to the New Testament*, Image, Doubleday, New York.

Cornelius, G. (1997), *The Starlore Handbook*, Duncan Baird, London.

Davies, J. (1968), *Biblical Numerology*. Baker Book House, Grand Rapids.

Davies, S. (2003), *The Gospel of Thomas, Annotated and Explained*. Darton, Longman and Todd, London.

Dean, M. (1980), *The Astrology Game*. Beaufort Books, New York.

Dobin, J. (1977), *The Astrological Secrets of The Hebrew Sages*. Inner Traditions International Ltd, Rochester, Vermont.

Dudjom Rinpoche, S. (1992), *The Tibetan Book of Living and Dying* Harper-Collins, San Francisco.

Dyer, W. (1998), *Wisdom of the Ages*. Thorsons, London.

Elwell, D. (1987), *Cosmic Loom*. Unwin Hyman, London.

Emerson, R.W. (1982), *Selected Essays*, Penguin, London.

Fagan, C. (1951), *Zodiacs Old and New*. Anscombe, London.

Fleming, K. (1981), *God's Voice in the Stars: Zodiac Signs and Bible Truth*. Loizeaux Brothers, Neptune, New Jersey.

France, R.T. (2002), *The Gospel of Mark: A Commentary on the Greek Text*. Eerdmans, Grand Rapids, Michigan.

Frankl, V. (1946), *Man's Search for Meaning*. Washington Square Press, New York.

Frazer, Sir J. (1890), *The New Golden Bough*. Version abridged by Theodor H. Gaster (1959). Mentor, New York.

Freke, T. and Gandy, P. (1999), *The Jesus Mysteries*. Thorsons, London.

Freke, T. and Gandy, P.(2001), *Jesus and the Goddess*. Thorsons, London.

Friedman, R. (1987). *Who Wrote the Bible?* Harper and Row, New York.

Fromm, E. (1942), *The Fear of Freedom*. Routledge, London and New York. (1984 edition)

George, L. (1989), *The New A-Z Horoscope Maker and Delineator*. Llewellyn Publications, St Paul, Minnesota.

Gettings, F. (1972), *The Book of the Zodiac – A Historical Anthology of Astrology*. Hamlyn, London.

Gettings, F. (1987), *The Secret Zodiac: The Hidden Mediaeval Astrology*. Arkana, Penguin, London.

Goldstein, J. (1983), *The Experience of Insight*. Shambhala, Boston.

Graham, L. (1975), *Deceptions and Myths of the Bible*. Citadel, New York.

Green, L.K. (1975), *The Astrologer's Manual*. Arco, New York.

Greene, L. (1983), *The Outer Planets and their Cycles: The Astrology of the Collective*. CRCS Publishers, Reno, Nevada.

Greene, L. (1985), *The Astrology of Fate*. George Allen & Unwin, London.

Haddon, C. (2003), *One Hundred Lamps for the Soul*. Hodder and Stoughton, London.

Hall, Manly P. (1928), *The Secret Teachings of all Ages*. Tarcher/Penguin, New York. (2003 edition)

Hamilton, E. (1940), *Mythology*. Mentor, New York.

Hay, D. (1982), *Exploring Inner Space*. Penguin, London.

Heline, C. (1971), *The Bible and the Stars*. New Age Press, Los Angeles.

Helms, R. (1988), *Gospel Fictions*. Prometheus Books, Buffalo, New York.

Hesse, H. (1951), *Siddhartha*. Bantam, New York.

Hickey, T.J. (1990), *Free Catholicism and the God Within*. Free Catholic Press, Hartford, Connecticut.

Hickey, T.J. (1991), *Monastery Without Walls*, Esoterica Press, Richland, Iowa.

Hodson, G. (1967), *The Hidden Wisdom in the Holy Bible*. Theosophical Publishing House, Illinois.

Howell, A.O. (1988), *Jungian Symbols in Astrology*. Quest Books, Theosophical Publishing House, Wheaton, Illinois.

Howell, A.O. (1990), *Jungian Synchronicity in Astrological Signs and Ages*. Quest Books, Theosophical Publishing House, Wheaton, IL.

Huxley, A. (1994), *The Perennial Philosophy*. Flamingo, London.

Irenaeus, (1868), *The Writings of Irenaeus*, translated by Alexander Roberts and W.H. Rambaut. The Ante-Nicene Library, Vol. 1. T&T Clark, Edinburgh.

Jefferson, T. (1904), *The Jefferson Bible: The Life and Morals of Jesus of Nazareth*. Beacon Press, Boston. (1989 edition)

Jones, M.E. (1977), *How to Learn Astrology*. Shambhala, Boulder, Colorado.

Josephus (1998), *The Complete Works,* translated by William Whiston. Thomas Nelson, Nashville, USA.

Jung, C.G. (1933), *Modern Man in Search of a Soul*. Harvest/HBJ, New York.

Keller, H. (1927), *My Religion*. Hodder and Stoughton, London.

Krishnamurti (1964), *Think on these Things*. Harper and Row, New York.

Kummel, W.G. (1973), *Introduction to the New Testament*, translated by Clark Kee. Abingdon Press, Nashville, USA.

Lawrence, T. (1990), *The Secret Message of the Zodiac*. Here's Life Publishers, San Bernardino, USA.

Lemesurier, P. (1977), *Gospel of the Stars*. Compton Press, Tisbury, England.

Lewi, H. (ed.) (1946), *Philo: Philosophical Writings*. Phaidon Press, Oxford.

MacDonald, D.R. (2000),*The Homeric Epics and the Gospel of Mark*. Yale University Press, USA.

MacNeice, L. (1964), *Astrology*. Doubleday, New York.

Manilius, M. (no date), *The Five Books*. American Federation Of Astrologers, Washington. (1697 translation, 1953 edition)

Manilius, M. (1992), *Astronomica*, translated by G.P. Goold. Harvard University Press, USA.

Bibliography

Mayo, J. (1964), *Astrology*. Hodder and Stoughton, London.

Mayo, J. (1972), *The Planets and Human Behaviour*. Fowler, London.

Mckenzie, J.L. (1999), *Dictionary of the Bible*, Simon & Schuster, London.

Mullan, D. (2003), *The Little Book of Blessed Mother Teresa*. The Columba Press, Dublin.

Nineham, D.E. (1969) *St. Mark*. Pelican Gospel Commentary, Penguin Books, London.

Origen (1869), *The Works of Origen*, translated and edited by Alexander Roberts and James Donaldson. The Ante-Nicene Library, Vol. 10. T&T Clark, Edinburgh.

Pagan, I. (1911), *From Pioneer to Poet*. Theosophical Publishing House, London. (3rd edition, 1930)

Pagels, E. (1979), *The Gnostic Gospels*. Vintage Books, New York.

Plunket, E. (1903), *Calendars and Constellations of the Ancient World*. Senate, Random House, London. (Reprinted 1997)

Philo: *The Works of Philo* (1993), translated by C. D. Yonge, foreword by David M. Scholer. Hendrickson Publishers, Peabody, Massachusetts.

Pliny, *Letters, Volume 2* (1915), translated by William Melmoth. Loeb Classical Library. Heinemann, London.

Powell, R. (1985), *The Zodiac: A Historical Survey*. ACS Publications, San Diego.

Prabhavananda, Swami (1948), *The Upanishads*. Mentor, New York.

Prophet, E.C. (2000), *Fallen Angels and the Origins of Evil*. Summit University Press, Corwin Springs, Montana.

Ptolemy, C. (no date), *The Tetrabiblos*, translated by F.E. Robins. Heinemann, London. (1940 edition)

Reid, V. (1944), *Towards Aquarius*. Rider, London.

Rhoads, D. and Michie, D. (1982), *Mark as Story*. Fortress Press, Philadelphia.

Robertson, J.M. (1903), *Pagan Christs*, Barnes and Noble Books, New York (1993 edition).

Robinson, E. (1977), *The Original Vision*. Religious Experience Unit, Oxford.

Robinson, J. (1957), *The Problem of History in Mark*. SCM Press, London.

Robson V.E. (1923), *The Fixed Stars and Constellations in Astrology*. Ascella Publications, Mansfield, England. (Modern reprint, no date)

Rolleston, F. (1865), *Mazzaroth*. Weiser Books, Maine. (2001 edition)

Rossner, J. (1989), *In Search of the Primordial Tradition and the Cosmic Christ*. Llewellyn, St Paul, Minnesota.

Rudhyar, D. (1979), *Astrological Insights into the Spiritual Life*. Aurora Press, New York.

Sandars, N.K. (ed.) (1960), *The Epic of Gilgamesh*. Penguin, London.

Sayce, A.H. (1981), *Astronomy and Astrology of the Babylonians*. Wizards Bookshelf, San Diego.

Schopenhauer, A. (1970), *Essays and Aphorisms*, edited by R.J. Hollingdale. Penguin, London.

Seiss, J.A. (1882), *The Gospel in the Stars*. Kregel Publications, Grand Rapids. (1972 edition)

Sepharial (no date), *Hebrew Astrology*. Foulsham, London.

Smith, M. (1973), *The Secret Gospel*. The Dawn Press, Clearlake, California.

Steiner, R. (1988), *The New Spirituality and the Christ Experience of the Twentieth Century*. Anthroposophic Press, Hudson, New York.

Strachan, G. (1985), *Christ and the Cosmos.* Labarum Publications, Dunbar.
Teilhard de Chardin, P. (1968), *The Divine Milieu.* Harper and Row, New York.
Tester, J. (1987), *A History of Western Astrology.* Ballantine Books, New York.
Thoreau, H.D. (1854), *Walden and Other Writings.* Bantam, New York. (1989 Edition)
Van Linden, P. A. (1982), *The Gospel of St Mark.* The Liturgical Press, Collegeville.
Wemyss, M. (no date), *The Wheel of Life or Scientific Astrology, Volume 111.*
    International Publishing, Edinburgh.
Womack, D. (1978), *12 Signs, 12 Sons.* Harper and Row, San Francisco.
Wood, F. and K, (1999), *Homer's Secret Iliad.* John Murray, London.
Wright, P. (1987), *The Literary Zodiac.* Anodyne Publishing, Edinburgh.
Zolar (1972), *The History of Astrology.* Arco, New York.

General Index

Aben Ragel, 79
Abib, 56
Abraham, 10, 40, 47, 56, 58, 61, 70, 118,
 185, 197
abridgement, 24
Acts (of the Apostles), 26, 35, 87, 88
Adams, 160
Addison, 154
Adonis, 210
Adoptionism, 26
aemulatio, 17
Aeolus, 16
Aesculapius, 166, 168
Age of Aquarius, 40, 189,190, 192, 199
Agni, 80
agriculture, 74, 78, 210
aion, 198
Air (signs), 86, 90, 102, 106, 191
Akiba, Rabbi, 148
Akkadia, 78, 127
Al Giebha, 126
Albertus Magnus, 132
Albumaser, 55, 110
alchemy, 174
Alcmena, 35
Aldebaran, 79, 81, 127
Alexandria, 11, 18, 19, 23, 26, 27, 74, 76,
 83, 164
Alexandrine, 29
Algol, 67
Alkaid, 107
All Saints' Day, 158
All Souls' Day, 158
allegorical, 7, 19, 20, 27, 164, 165
allegories, 27, 84
Allen, Richard Hinckley, 49, 67, 74, 79,
 80, 89, 107, 110, 116, 122, 126, 127,
 147, 154, 155, 171, 175, 199, 200, 206,
 207, 217
Alma Mater, 104
Alphaeus, 58
Alpherkadain, 107
Altar, 175
ambiguity, 2, 57, 163

ambition, 116, 157, 162, 163
amnos, 60
Amphitryon, 35
anarchy, 180, 189, 193, 199
Andrew, 57, 58, 68, 69
Andromeda, 67, 68, 69, 213, 214, 217
Angelou, Maya, 63
Antares, 127
Anthroposophy, 18
Antichrist, 56
Aphrodite, 141, 146
apocalyptic, 36, 61, 82, 123, 195, 196,
 198, 200
Apollo, 166
apologetic, 6, 10, 11, 12, 18
apologist(s), 11, 12
Apostle(s), 14, 17, 19, 38, 59,63, 64, 69,
 75, 83, 94, 98, 105, 109, 112, 136, 151,
 154, 155, 162, 163, 164,173, 217, 218
Apuleius, 89, 214, 216
Aquarian, 21, 191, 193, 196, 198, 199,
 200, 201, 202
Aquarius, 21, 35, 36, 37, 40, 43, 127, 145,
 189-203, 217, 219
Aquinas, 71, 72
Ara, 175
Arabs, 155
Aramaic, 69, 94, 112, 123, 163, 211, 216
Aratos, 49, 67, 69, 101
arcane, 24
Archaeologists, 35
archetypal, 45, 70, 72
Arcturus, 142, 143
Argo, 107
Aries, 7, 23, 30, 33, 40, 42, 44, 53-70, 72,
 83, 97, 101, 102, 120, 131, 144, 145,
 146, 160, 167, 181, 197, 198, 200, 204,
 207, 209, 210, 211, 218
Arish, 33
Aristophanes, 149
Aristotle, 29, 71
Armageddon, 195
Arnum, 55
arrow, 59, 168, 171, 188

57, 58, 59, 60, 62, 63, 64, 67, 69, 74,
83, 84, 86, 87, 90, 94, 95, 98, 100, 101,
102, 105, 106, 109, 112, 113, 115, 117,
118, 119, 120, 121, 123, 126, 128, 129,
130, 131, 132, 135, 136, 137, 138, 144,
149, 153, 154, 155, 158, 161, 162, 163,
164, 165, 166, 182, 186, 190, 195, 196,
199, 200, 201, 203, 208, 209, 210, 211,
216, 218
Gospel of John, 6, 54
Gospel of Thomas, 8, 62, 115, 119, 144,
149
Goya, 194
Gradgrind, Mr., 29
Graves, Robert, 214, 215
Great Pyramid, 44
Great Year, 40, 44, 209
Greater Benefic, 146, 170
Greek, 7, 11, 17, 18, 33, 35, 41, 42, 44, 49,
62, 64, 81, 85, 87, 89, 95, 102, 110,
112, 116, 117, 120, 121, 123, 124, 127,
140, 142, 143, 146, 154, 155, 156, 163,
171, 172, 175, 180, 193, 198, 200, 210,
211, 216
Greene, Liz., 192, 212, 213
Greer, Germaine, 191
Grewgious, Mr., 28
Guardian, The, 92
Gulliver's Travels, 176
habit, 104, 129, 139, 164, 170
hair, 69, 141, 143
Hair, (musical), 189
Hamer, Dean, 128
Hamlet, 65, 217
harmony, 33, 36, 38, 47, 71, 93, 145, 146,
150, 153, 177, 189
Harney Point, 39
harvest, 74, 76, 82, 130, 132, 218
heart, 8, 9, 17, 31, 44, 75, 78, 95, 116, 153,
171, 174, 186, 208, 211, 212, 218
hearth, 179
heavens, 7, 17, 20, 28, 29, 32, 33, 34, 36,
37, 38, 49, 62, 67, 79, 127, 154, 168,
192, 204
Hebrew(s), 3, 11, 15, 16, 19, 32, 33, 34,
35, 40, 41, 55, 67, 72, 79, 82, 102, 107,
116, 117, 123, 131, 143, 158, 171, 174,
190, 206, 212, 216
Hector, 16, 17
helios, 120, 124, 126, 211, 216
Helms, Randolph, 18
Hen with her Chickens, 79

Hercules, 35, 46, 116, 121
heresy 7, 26
Herod, 9, 98, 108, 109, 117
Herodians, 183
Herodias, 98
Herschel, 193
Hesiod, 115
Hestia, 179
Hickey, Thomas, 119
Hicks, Bill, 176
Hierapolis, 25
high priests, 10, 11, 208
Hillel, 148
Hinayana, 8
Hindu(s), 44, 59, 80, 93, 119, 126, 153,
202
Hippotes, 169
Hipparchus, 44, 145, 217
Hippocrates, 74
Hired Man, The, 55
hired men, 57, 58
historical, 2, 5, 8, 9, 10, 11, 12, 13, 14, 18,
46, 70, 98, 109, 113, 118, 119, 163,
196, 208, 209, 217
historicizing, 8, 11, 25
history, 2, 7, 8, 9, 13, 18, 19, 20, 27, 36,
40, 45, 47, 72, 79, 119, 124, 140, 151,
196, 198, 199, 201, 208
Holy of Holies, 39
Holy Souls, 158
Holy Spirit, 19, 60, 185
Holy Week, 155, 156
Homer, 14, 15, 16, 80, 88, 101, 172
homophones, 120
honey, 16, 61, 116
Hood, Robin, 14
Hopkins, Gerard Manley, 78, 79, 117
horoscope, 29, 76, 87, 97, 103, 120, 181,
184, 205
horse, 91, 168, 169, 171, 172, 173, 200,
202
Horus, 131
Hosanna, 171
Hosea, Book of, 148
Houlding, Deborah, 138
house of bread, 130
Howell, 44, 110
Hua Hu Ching, 150
Huckleberry Finn, 14, 70
Hudibras, 176
Hughes, Ted, 29
humanoids, 113

Joshua, 2, 11, 19, 41, 58, 102, 107
jovial, 29
Joyce, James, 193
Judah, 64, 116, 117, 124, 216
Judas, 16, 64, 216, 217
Judea, 11, 12
Judges, Book of, 32, 35, 116, 190, 217
Jung, Carl, 29, 45, 122
Jupiter, 55, 146, 167, 170, 189, 204, 207
justice, 102, 113, 145, 146, 153, 155, 166, 192
Kafka, Franz, 103
Kali Yuga, 44
Kant, Immanuel, 71, 72
karma, 162
Katha Upanishad, 87
Keats, John, 80
Keller, Helen, 114
kenosis, 136
Kepler, 29
King, 98, 126, 127, 199, 212, 213
kingdom, 62, 63, 64, 67, 82, 83, 84, 98, 99,
    102, 116, 120, 122, 123, 130, 137, 138,
    140, 141, 143, 145, 149, 152, 158, 163,
    164, 166, 171, 186, 195, 199, 201, 202,
    218
Kirk, Eleanor, 169
Kith and Kin, 97
Koester, Professor Helmut, 8
Koran, 186
Krishna, 8, 126
Krishnamurti, 84
Laelaps, 89
lamb, 40, 47, 56, 209, 218
Lampadias, 79, 81
Last Supper, 10, 106, 155, 218
Law 102, 124, 145, 181, 183,
Lazarus, 164, 203
leaven, 218
Legion 85, 91, 93
Leibnitz, 103
Lemesurier, P., 199
Lenaea, 215
Lennon, John, 4
Lent, 207
Leo, 31, 36, 37, 40, 43, 64, 71, 115-129,
    130, 132, 134, 136, 145, 156, 160, 162,
    167, 179, 190, 199, 201, 217
leprosy, 65
Lepus, 93
Levi, 58, 72
levirate, 184
Levites, 58

Leviticus, Book of, 31, 38, 91
liberal, 5, 9, 13, 18, 47, 102, 170, 186, 195
Libra, 31, 35, 42, 71, 102, 138, 144-156,
    158, 162, 181
Light, 77, 78, 79
lightning, 198, 199, 200
lion, 36, 37, 38, 116, 121, 124, 125, 126,
    199, 217
Literalism, 13, 196
loaves, 9, 31, 105, 106, 109
Lobster, 100
Locke, John, 3
Louis Lambert, 216
Lu Hunga, 55
Lucifer, 79
Luke, 4, 5, 9, 10, 13, 21, 23, 25, 38, 40, 47,
    54, 55, 60, 61, 62, 64, 79, 80, 81, 96,
    100, 102, 113, 117, 120, 130, 131, 132,
    163, 172, 176, 195, 211, 212, 216
lunatic, 29
lupeo, 155
lupomenos, 155
Lupus, 154, 155, 156
lutron, 162
Lystra, 87
Ma'alaph, 46, 107
Maat, 145, 155
Macaulay, 89
Macbeth, 65, 157
MacDonald, D. R., 16, 17
MacNeice, Louis, 184
macrocosm, 45, 117
Madonna, 131
Mahayana, 8
Malachi, Book of, 124, 148
Malchus, 212
Manasseh, Tribe of, 72, 206
Manger, 101, 107
Manilius, 49, 56, 73, 100, 103, 107, 110,
    116, 127, 132, 134, 145, 154, 159, 166,
    169, 171, 175, 176, 191, 192, 205, 206,
    207, 213, 214, 218
Manly Hall, 124
manna, 61, 106
Mark
    and Alexandria, 27
    and Peter, 4, 25, 26
    Augustine's opinion of, 4
    author of Gospel of, 26
    profound significance of Mark's Gospel,
    47-8
    represented by the Lion, 37

Index to Appendix 1